INVISIBLE CONVERSATIONS

Studies in Christianity and Literature 3

EDITORIAL BOARD

INVISIBLE CONVERSATIONS

Religion in the Literature of America

Roger Lundin, Editor

BAYLOR UNIVERSITY PRESS

Scripture quotations are from the *New Revised Standard Version Bible*, copyright 1989, Division of Christian Education of the National Council of the Churches of Christ in the United States of America. Used by permission. All rights reserved.

Cover Design by Sue Lundin

Library of Congress Cataloging-in-Publication Data

Invisible conversations : religion in the literature of America / Roger Lundin, editor.
     p. cm. — (Studies in Christianity and literature ; 3)
   Includes bibliographical references and index.
   ISBN 978-1-60258-147-0 (alk. paper)
   1. American literature—History and criticism. 2. Religion in literature.
   3. Religion and literature—United States—History. 4. Christianity and literature—United States—History. I. Lundin, Roger.

   PS166 .I58
   810.9'382—dc22   2008029713

Printed in the United States of America on acid-free paper with a minimum of 30% pcw recycled content.

CONTENTS

CONTRIBUTORS

Katherine Clay Bassard, Associate Professor of English, Virginia Commonwealth University

Lawrence Buell, Powell M. Cabot Professor of American Literature, Harvard University

Andrew Delbanco, Julian Clarence Levi Professor in the Humanities, Columbia University

Denis Donoghue, Henry James Professor of English and American Letters, New York University

Stanley Hauerwas, Gilbert T. Rowe Professor of Theological Ethics, Duke University

Roger Lundin, Blanchard Professor of English, Wheaton College

Elisa New, Professor of English and American Literature and Language, Harvard University

Mark A. Noll, Francis A. McAnaney Professor of History, University of Notre Dame

Barbara Packer, Professor of English, UCLA

Albert J. Raboteau, Henry W. Putnam Professor of Religion, Princeton University

John Stauffer, Chair, History of American Civilization and Professor of English and African and African American Studies, Harvard University

Alan Wolfe, Professor of Political Science, Boston College

Ralph C. Wood, University Professor of Theology and Literature, Baylor University

INTRODUCTION

Roger Lundin

Invisible Conversations adapts its title from works by two American writers, one of them being the greatest theologian this culture has produced and the other an excellent scholar whose untimely death cut short a promising career.

The first of these two is Jonathan Edwards, and the passage in question is to be found in his "Apostrophe to Sarah Pierpont," the young woman who eventually became his wife. After a lengthy tribute to the "strange sweetness" of Sarah's love of "almighty Being," Edwards concludes with a winsome tribute to her love of nature and nature's hidden God: "She loves to be alone, and to wander in the fields and on the mountains, and seems to have someone invisible always conversing with her."[1]

From the first exploration of this continent to the present day, countless men and women of all types and inclinations have carried on their "conversations with the invisible." This has been true for Jews and Protestants, Catholics and Hindus, Muslims and Eastern Orthodox believers alike, just as it has also proved to be the case for many who doubt whether Sarah Pierpont's "almighty Being" even exists. In Chapter 10 of this book, Andrew Delbanco reminds us of the pogrom survivor in Saul Bellow's *The Adventures of Augie March*: "After the things he had seen, this character admonishes his friends and family not to dare to 'talk to me about God.' And yet, as Bellow remarks, 'it was he who talked about God, all the time.'"

For understanding those conversations *to* and *about* that "invisible God," the literature of the United States offers exceptional resources. From their discussions of Emily Dickinson and Andre Dubus to their analyses of Frederick Douglass and Flannery O'Connor, the chapters in this volume move over a broad historical and cultural landscape that has become, over the history of this culture, packed with private meditations and public reflections on the existence of God, the nature of religious experience, and the place of faith in public life. Often lively, sometimes divisive, and invariably illuminating, these conversations have been central to American culture for centuries, and they will be at the center of attention throughout this book.

There is, however, another sense of "invisibility" that *Invisible Conversations* seeks to address. It has to do with what the late Jenny Franchot once described as the "invisible domain" of religion in American literary studies. Writing more than a decade ago, Franchot observed that, even though "America has been and continues to be manifestly religious in complex and intriguing ways," a thorough "lack of interest in religion . . . has produced a singularly biased scholarship" in the academic study of the literature of the United States. In recent decades, this bias has manifested itself most frequently as a stubborn refusal to engage religious questions on anything like their own terms. "Religious questions are always bound up with the invisible," she wrote, and they "are therefore peculiarly subject to silencing—whether through an outright refusal to inquire" or through the rush to translate "the invisible" into what are for the contemporary intellectual the more visible (and obvious) "vocabularies of sexuality, race, or class." In using these vocabularies to avoid "America's engagement with 'invisibles,'" Franchot concludes, "we have allowed ourselves to become ignorant."[2]

Invisible Conversations is an effort to dispel such ignorance. This book grew out of the fruitful collaboration of one group of scholars that was made possible by the visionary determination of another group. The visionaries happened to work together for a decade at the University of Notre Dame, where one of them, Nathan Hatch, led the Evangelical Scholarship Initiative, and another, James Turner, served as the founding director of the Erasmus Institute. (These two are also professors of history, and at the time, Hatch was serving as Notre Dame's provost.) The initiatives led by Hatch and Turner supported numerous scholarly projects that explored the interplay of religion and the major academic disciplines. As one of those projects, the American Literature and Religion Seminar had a straightforward goal, which was to assemble a team of scholars from various religious backgrounds to study the intersection of religion and literature in the United States from Ralph Waldo Emerson to the present.

At a time when acrimony and suspicion have often marked the academic discussion of religion and American studies, the work of the seminar unfolded in a spirit of civil and vigorous dialogue. Seminar members held sharply divergent views on the nature of religious experience and the significance of religious truth-claims. Yet despite their differences, the participants all took religion to be a substantial subject in its own right and not merely an epiphenomenon of a primary economic, political, or material reality. Similarly, as the chapters in this book demonstrate, the participants in the seminar assumed significantly different stances vis-à-vis the question of American exceptionalism.[3]

In the seminar, our work was tacitly guided by principles of interpretive pluralism of the kind promoted by Mikhail Bakhtin, Paul Ricoeur, and Kenneth Burke, among others, in recent decades. In *The Philosophy of Literary Form*, Burke reminds us "that every document bequeathed us by history must be treated as a *strategy for encompassing a situation*." History is a "'dramatic' process, involving dialectical oppositions," and no work from the past can be considered "in isolation, but as the *answer* or *rejoinder* to assertions current in the situation in which it arose."[4] *New Historicism – See Klassen's dialectic*

Yet the obvious question here is, where does the drama get its materials? Burke's answer: "From the 'unending conversation' that is going on at the point in history when we are born." He asks us to imagine ourselves entering a room where a "heated discussion" is already underway and the participants are too passionately engaged to explain to us the nature of the debate or the background to the points being made. "In fact, the discussion had already begun long before any of them got there," so that no one presently talking is able to retrace the countless steps that led to this point.[5] *rhetoric distinct.* *isn't this Nabokov?*

"You listen for a while," Burke continues, "until you decide that you have caught the tenor of the argument," and then you "put in your oar." Someone challenges what you say and you respond; someone else comes to your defense and either embarrasses you with his poor reasoning or wows the crowd with an astute observation. But the conversation proves to be "interminable," and eventually you must take leave of the conversation, even as we all must take leave of life. "And you do depart, with the discussion still vigorously in progress."[6] *Me*

To balance the idealism of the conversational model, Burke notes that, although the "unending conversation" supplies the materials for the human drama, "this verbal action" is not "all there is to it." For our language and our stories are grounded in "contexts of situation," and among those contexts are "the kind of factors considered by Bentham, Marx, and Veblen, the material interests (of private or class structure) that you symbolically defend or symbolically appropriate" when you are making "assertions." Such "interests do not 'cause' your discussion," for its real source is "man himself as *homo loquax.*" Nevertheless, "they greatly affect the *idiom* in which you speak, and so the idiom by which you think."[7]

In saying that "every document bequeathed us by history must be treated as a *strategy for encompassing a situation*," Burke provides a counterweight to one of Walter Benjamin's famous "Theses on the Philosophy of History." The historical materialist, writes Benjamin, must view "cultural treasures . . . with cautious detachment," for they "have an origin which he cannot contemplate without horror." Given the oppression and suffering hidden within the unwritten history of cultural production, we can only conclude that "there is no document of civilization which is not at the same time a document of barbarism."[8]

In practical terms, what does a Burkean view of the conversational and dramatic nature of historical understanding mean for the study of American literature? To begin, one consequence involves the central place given to Christianity and Judaism in the cultural history of the United States. From the colonial period to the end of the nineteenth century, Protestant and Catholic voices dominated the conversations of American religion, and Judaism played an increasingly powerful role in the twentieth century. And while the influence of these traditions, particularly that of New England Puritanism, may not have been as overwhelming as twentieth-century scholarship often claimed, they undeniably provided enduring "strategies for encompassing the situation" of American religious life.

Near the end of his essay in this book, Andrew Delbanco speaks of the need for every academic institution to have within its ranks "a strong contingent of religion scholars." In making his case, he quotes Alexis de Tocqueville's observation that "incredulity is an accident; faith is the only permanent state of mankind." Given that this judgment "seems today" to have been right, Delbanco argues, "we can only hope that he was also right in believing that the American experiment in toleration will not prove finally incompatible with the very essence of religious passion."

The American Literature and Religion Seminar was an experiment seeking to prove the compatibility of tolerance and passion, and that *Invisible Conversations*—the book that you hold in your hands—is a product of that experiment. The authors of the following essays were given a wide-ranging charge—that is, to write on a series of topics having to do with the interplay of literature and religion in the American experience. Each main chapter is followed by a response, and in the case of literature and the African American experience, there are three chapters plus a response.

We begin with a series of studies of fiction and poetry, each of which starts out on the landscape of New England only to range widely beyond that ground. But where Elisa New and Barbara Packer are in substantial agreement about the nature and value of New England's influence, Denis Donoghue and Lawrence Buell open the conversation in this book by taking serious issue with that influence. They do so, however, for markedly different reasons.

For Donoghue, the opposition to Emerson and his associates is fundamentally theological, and he highlights his differences with them in a proposition that he admits is "so stark that I must try to mellow it at once." His thesis is "that modern American literature is a substitute for religion, but a substitute in which the original has been absorbed." His is a study of the expunging of explicit religious concerns in the poetry and fiction of the United States. A faintly religious scent may still waft through the pages of the national literature, but of the substance of religious belief and practice there is little or none. According to Donoghue, the process of supplanting religion started in the nineteenth century with Emerson, who "began as a religion but ended as literature"—Donoghue is quoting Alfred Kazin on this point—and the absorption continued with Nathaniel Hawthorne, who "replaced God with nature and community." The novelist also turned sin into an offense against the community, and he celebrated the power of the self to transgress those limits and thereby claim its identity. In the history that Donoghue describes, the process Emerson and Hawthorne initiated was to be sustained and furthered by Herman Melville, Henry Adams, F. Scott Fitzgerald, and Harold Bloom, among others.

Bloom holds the key to the views (and practices) to which Donoghue takes strong exception. For several decades, he has argued that American religion is a strange mixture of distorted Christianity and ancient Gnosticism, with the Gnosticism predominant. For Americans, at least as Bloom assesses the situation, religion is a matter of feeling and private experience sans liturgy, sans ritual, sans church. The freedom promised by American religion is not some hard-won liberty but "a solitude in which the inner loneliness is at home in an outer loneliness." Bloom asks why the United States has produced so little literature of substance—"Devotional poetry or narrative or drama, of any aesthetic eminence, or of any profound spirituality, hardly exists among us"—but Donoghue complains that Bloom "does not stay for an answer."

To move beyond the isolating loneliness of the Emerson-to-Bloom impasse, Donoghue returns to his discussion of Andre Dubus's "The Father's Story," a short story that frames his argument in the essay. Near the end of it a character is in the midst one of his frequent conversations with God. How does he know, Donoghue asks, "that he is not merely talking to himself?" The critic then answers for the character: "What enables it [the conversation with God] . . . is his membership of the Church, the sacraments, the rituals, the Mass, Confession, and Communion." These give him a means of participating in a story "of sacrifice and meaning that he enters by himself but not entirely by himself: there are the others. He is not looking for 'a God within the self.'"

We might say that in his reading of religion in the American experience, Donoghue seeks to reinstate the distinction between metaphor, per se, and religious belief and practice, while New and Packer will appear willing, with some reservations, to accept the Emersonian conflation of the two. To Lawrence Buell, both the granting of centrality to the New England religious experience and the lamentation of its decline into secularity are questionable. He opens his spirited response by pointing out that Donoghue focuses exclusively on the United States, which is but a "portion of 'America'" as it is now understood in literary studies. As a sign of the divide that separates the old discipline of *American* studies and the new problematics of cultural history in the *United States*, Buell repeatedly uses *U. S.* to speak of the literature of this land. He notes that a reader of Donoghue's essay "could never tell" from it that we are now in the third decade of a "canon war in U.S. literary studies," nor would that reader know that Emerson has been deposed as the *ur*-father of the "U.S. literary emergence."

Buell reads Donoghue's argument as a forceful restatement of a long-standing narrative of Romantic secularization and decline. He takes exception to Donoghue's leveling of the distinctions between Emerson and Hawthorne, for the novelist's "conception of sin is . . . more charged with the sense of radical evil" than the critic acknowledges. But the larger problem, Buell avers, is the failure of Donoghue and the critical tradition on which he draws to recognize that "American literature is and has for centuries been imbued with spiritual striving." Literature has often been willful and idiosyncratic in its explorations, but it has also persistently held "up a mirror to the dominant culture's stolid complacencies." And Buell believes it ought to receive credit, even thanks, for having done so and for continuing to do so.

In the end, Buell's differences with Donoghue, and with Stanley Hauerwas and Ralph Wood, are rooted in a fundamental disagreement over the nature of religious belief and practice. Donoghue lists Church, sacraments, and rituals as the essence of religion, while Buell counters with a question that reads like a plea: "Why should not the religious be identified mainly . . . with the arenas of moral or spiritual inquiry and practice?" He objects to the effort to tie the category of religion to "theologic belief or church affiliation" and suggests the alternative of "leaving religion to each individual's considered private judgment." This would guard against both the "imperial zealotry" of the state and the "policing" of religious experience by the church. Buell asks, "If that was good enough for George Washington, Benjamin Franklin, John Adams, and Thomas Jefferson, why not for us?" He suggests that when the literature of the United States is viewed in this way, as a series of spiritual quests that may or may or may not be tied to "sect or creed," then it seems likely that the work of Emerson, Hawthorne, and James will continue to resonate, regardless of future canonical judgments or new theoretical concerns.

In their discussion of American poetry, Elisa New and Barbara Packer stake out a critical position that situates them somewhere between Donoghue's religious critique of American literary history and Buell's call for a vastly expanded understanding of U.S. literary studies. Through a sophisticated updating of the American studies tradition of F. O. Matthiessen and Perry Miller, New and Packer examine the intricate interplay between metaphorical exploration and religious expression in the history of American poetry. New's chapter centers upon the nineteenth century, and Emily Dickinson in particular, but it also reaches back to the prose of the Puritans (John Cotton and Jonathan Edwards) as well as forward to the poetry of the Modernists (Robert Frost and Hart Crane).

Metaphor, New writes, is the most delicate instrument we possess for catching the "pulse" of meaning and thereby registering "the inmost character of things." She is interested specifically in metaphor as the key to "a linguistic realm where phenomena discover and catch their truest likenesses by entertaining unlikenesses." According to New, the subversion of identity that takes place through this discovery of "unlikeness" proves to be "key to that identity's truer self-transcendent revelation as mixed structure." Dickinson understood and employed this power of metaphor perhaps more fully than anyone else in the nineteenth century, yet her view of it has "a very long American foreground."

Standing squarely in that foreground is the seventeenth-century Puritan John Cotton, whose "favorite metaphors for the state of grace prefigure Dickinson's own." What links Cotton in the seventeenth century to Crane in the twentieth are the rich possibilities that Puritan plain style created for metaphor as a religious vehicle. New says Cotton's "extravagant understanding" of plainness "gave scope and quite serviceable latitude" to later American writers who believed passionately in "beauty's revelatory power." For New, the secret of this power is to be found in the paradoxical yoking together of plainness and metaphorical extravagance that is the hallmark of both Puritan preaching and poetics in the tradition of Emerson and Dickinson. The capacity of beauty to ring "changes on sameness" and to summon "variety out of monotony" has remained throughout the culture's history "an article of both aesthetic and Christian faith for practitioners of a distinctive American poetics."

In New's formulation, by revealing "change" within "sameness" and by relieving the "monotony" of singularity with the "variety" of difference, metaphor does for a largely secular culture the work that Trinitarian belief has performed throughout Christian history. With its lively play of opposites, metaphor mediates the relationship between sameness and difference that is at the heart of religious experience, cultural identity, and poetic discovery: "Grace and metaphor, committed to mutual recognizance, will, in John Cotton's words, 'poise one another.' In Cotton's homiletics, as in later American poetics, the test of grace is not unity but the variety that gives life to religious, as to aesthetic, experience."

In her response to New, Barbara Packer offers a historical context for the experiments in metaphor that became crucial to the lives as well as the works of such writers as Dickinson, Emerson, and Thoreau. She quotes from the preface that New had provided to her essay; in that passage, which is not part of the chapter in this book, New says that Dickinson's understanding of poetic meaning teaches us "patience before obscurity," and it "reminds revelation that its origin is mystery." This insight strikes Packer as being "profoundly true," and she observes that "in flight from" the "shallowness" of Enlightenment literature and religion, Emerson, Dickinson, and others set out to "recover the richness" of earlier religious expression without sacrificing their own "hospitality to universal religion or to progressive thought." To judge the authenticity and gauge the authority of religious claims to truth, they proposed the "litmus test" of studying "a writer's metaphors." Trite metaphors point to a "mind that is either unoriginal or servile," while "arresting" ones reveal an imagination attuned to "the analogies inscribed by the First Cause on nature."

Near the close of her response, Packer correctly notes Emerson's fear of "metaphor's petrifying powers." He took religious traditions to be calcified metaphors, and "he traced the bloody history of Christian theology" to a "fatal literal-mindedness that always seems to dog a prophet's inspired tropes." These Emersonian fears are in stark contrast, however, to the state of affairs that Mark Noll describes in the opening paragraph of the next chapter, the first of four that deal specifically with literature, religion, and the

African American experience. Noll refers to a "fixation on the Bible" that remained central to African American literature for more than two centuries. This intense focus upon the scriptures led to the Bible's power as a source of comfort and inspiration in the African American "struggle for redemption from slavery." It also contributed to that community's efforts to "redeem" the Scriptures and release them from their bondage to the slavery-condoning interpretations the majority population gave to them.

Noll explains that, from the early eighteenth century on, there had been a "steady stream" of writings on the Bible and slavery that justified the latter by finding sanctions for it in the former. But this stream "became from the early 1830s onwards a great flood of works" that took slavery for granted as a reality of history and as a practice of the present. What Noll calls "the simple point" of his chapter is to describe how black Americans produced a literature of "an unusual depth" and "an unusual breadth" of forms to challenge "proslavery interpretations of the Bible" between the Revolutionary War and the Civil War.

The genres that Noll treats include memoirs, treatises, sermons, manifestoes, and dialogues. Yet despite their having employed an astonishingly diverse array of rhetorical strategies, "African American interpretations of Scripture never exerted broad influence in antebellum society." What they did accomplish, however, was to testify "to the power that the Scriptures were exerting" in the lives of African Americans, even as they "also were testifying to the sanctified power of their own prose in redeeming the Scriptures." Here, at least, the "petrifying" potential of metaphor in the scriptural tradition became a liberating power.

Albert Raboteau's chapter begins with a searing personal account that reminds us of the other, divisive side of the religious equation. It has to do with a painful separation and an act of exclusion at the core of Christian experience, in this case at the Communion rail. From his own experience and the accounts of others, Raboteau concludes that we in American culture "suffer a form of partial amnesia" because of our collective failure to remember and mourn the suffering of our past: "Our nation has need of tears, tears for all those lynched, maimed, whipped, shamed, and debased by our history of race hatred."

It is to African American autobiography that Raboteau turns in his search for a "method of healing the wounds" inflicted by the history of racial hatred in the United States. The first autobiographical account he treats is that of Olaudah Equiano, and in it he discovers rhetorical strategies that were to become commonplace in black autobiographies. Like Noll, Raboteau sees African Americans simultaneously using the Bible to inform their quest for freedom and employing their unique experience to "redeem" the Scriptures. Equiano, for example, casts the drama of African humanity against the background of the Bible, uses the theme of chosenness to convict Anglo-Europeans of their sin, and discerns in the experience of African slaves "a providential and universal message of reconciliation."

For Raboteau, what these works offer may be best summarized by a comment one of his students made at the end of a recent course on African American autobiography. She said, "we have been breaking apart the bread of the texts and offering each other communion." Raboteau believes her language was intentionally "Eucharistic," because it spoke of "calling to mind" the sacrifice of Christ and pointed to the liturgical offering of his body and blood in the Communion experience. As Raboteau's student spoke, "a murmur of recognition and approval emerged from the class and, when she had finished, a burst of applause. She enabled all of us to glimpse a more profound vision of the transformative power of memory and mourning."

In a thought-provoking essay, Katherine Clay Bassard pulls together a number of the strands of argument found in Noll and Raboteau and weaves them into a complex account of "race, faith, theory." She focuses specifically upon the sign of the cross, the central symbol of the Christian faith, and traces its journey through more than 150 years of the African American experience.

As Raboteau does, Bassard opens with a personal incident. In this case, it has to do with a large crucifix a parishioner had brought back from Mexico to the Baptist church of her youth. Bassard reports that her own feeling was almost one "of offense at the grotesque figure described by someone as 'bleeding from every pore.'" She recounts the discussions that swirled around that crucifix and all the injunctions her Protestant church had against the bodily representation of Christ's suffering. To her Baptist friends and family, the empty cross represented the presence of Christ rather than his absence. "The central evidence upon which Christianity rests," after all, "is an *empty* tomb, an *absent* body, as the sign" of God's redemptive power.

Bassard raises a number of questions about this heritage of disembodiment, and her discussion ranges widely from the period of antebellum slavery to Toni Morrison's *Paradise* (1997) and the experience of what she terms "black postmodernity." Bassard uncovers in this history "a shift in the figuration of the cross from a more orthodox African American Protestantism to a displacement of its meanings out onto the African American (women's) community itself." This transfer of spiritual authority becomes total in *Paradise*, where a black Christ "has no takers and yields no deliverance or hope for justice." In the ironic ending to her chapter, Bassard wonders openly about the price to be paid for the massive shift of moral authority and spiritual responsibility from the cross to the community. She closes by quoting Eugene McCarraher's recent prediction that theology may fill the space vacated by cultural theory. "Revolution is indissoluble from resurrection," he claims. To which Bassard replies: "The question is, what Body do we imagine rising from the grave?"

John Stauffer's response to these three accounts of the African American experience is remarkable for the degree of sympathy he has for their central assertions. There is no questioning here of fundamental assumptions, as there was in Lawrence Buell's critique of Denis Donoghue, no challenge to any theoretical paradigms or theological claims. Instead, what Stauffer provides is an amplified discussion of the historical and literary context for each chapter, and in each case, he offers nuanced suggestions for further reflection or consideration. While praising Noll's thematic comprehensiveness, Stauffer observes that "what Noll gives up by organizing his chapter around genre is a clear sense of change over time in black resistance to slavery and proslavery theological arguments." Further, he suggests the need to place greater weight on the importance of black protest and the influence that African American interpretations of scripture had on white abolitionists and the larger culture alike.

Stauffer's reservations about Raboteau's chapter also have to do with a missing account of historical change. He praises the use of autobiography and the emphasis upon memory but at the same time asks for a more extensive discussion of how "the transformative power of memory and mourning changed" dramatically over time. And in response to Bassard, Stauffer says historical change has also led to changes in the questions we pose to the African American experience and the works that have issued from it. To Bassard's question—"What Body do we imagine rising from the grave?"—Stauffer responds with one of his own: "To this I would add another question, with which Noll, Raboteau, and Bassard all implicitly grapple. It concerns the location of God's kingdom and thus the relation between religious faith and social justice: 'What kind of Spirit do we imagine inhabiting our bodies?' What does it look like and what forms does it take?"

With Alan Wolfe's chapter on the role of religion in modern nonfiction, we move from the wide-ranging and geographically dispersed experience of African Americans to a setting decidedly more time and place specific—that is, New York City in the first three decades after the World War II. Yet at this time and from this place, a relatively small group of writers, most of whom were Jewish, managed to exercise an influence completely out of proportion to their numbers. In the words of Andrew Delbanco, they "made twentieth-century New York the intellectual capital of the United States," and they did so despite the fact that the "upper-crust Protestants" excluded them from most centers of power and learning.

As Delbanco observes, Wolfe places little explicit emphasis on the question of Jewishness, but it does serve as the backdrop to his account of the treatment religion received in a series of remarkable books dealing with the American character and its postwar prospects. To introduce his subject, Wolfe discusses the curious career of C. Wright Mills, a Catholic, who wrote with great insight about the power elites who ruled mid-twentieth-century America. Mills seemed to cover every subject and perspective imaginable, save that of religion. In his rendering of the national culture, Americans struggle with poor schools, difficult industrial and corporate environments, and inadequate political leaders, but they seem to do so "without ever attending church, confessing their sins, or asking God for meaning."

Using a template established by his reading of Mills, Wolfe proceeds to examine the sociological analyses of David Riesman and Betty Friedan, as well as the historical treatments offered by Arthur Schlesinger, Jr., and Richard Hofstadter. He calls "inexcusable" the failure of Mills, Riesman, and Friedan—"first-rate writers, all of them"—to treat religion seriously, and although his judgment of the historians (Schlesinger, Hofstadter) is more favorable, they too are called out for having come up short: "Yet while they did treat religion more explicitly than their colleagues in the social sciences, they essentially 'secularized' religion, modifying it to be part of a larger story that had no particular religious meaning." Admittedly mystified by the failure of these writers to understand the role of religion in American life, Wolfe concludes it may be that they exemplify the limits of his own discipline of sociology. Perhaps that discipline cannot account for religion, because religion is a psychological phenomenon rather than a sociological one. "Americans do not believe in order to belong; they believe in order to be," he observes. "If religion means organization and doctrine, Americans are not all that religious. If it means purity of heart and sincerity of spirit, they are religious beyond recognition."

In response to Wolfe's use of the word "inexcusable" to describe the indifference of postwar intellectuals toward religion, Delbanco seeks to offer "some contexts, if not excuses, for that indifference." One key element here, he says, has to do with the history of anti-Semitism in American culture. Mixing cultural history with personal anecdotes, Delbanco concludes that to this day "tensions [have] persisted between Jews and Christians even in America's leading institutions." As a result, he writes, "there was a certain wariness, shall we say, on the part of America's minority intellectuals toward America's majority religion."

Yet even more important may have been the fact that "New York Jews were not necessarily committed in any deep sense to their own religious heritage." To them, politics in its neo-Marxist garb was more important as a religion "than the Christian idea of a merciful redeemer," and this proved to be even more the case after Auschwitz, when the very idea of Christianity seemed "an unbearable affront" to the victims of the Holocaust. That left politics as the acceptable religion for the contemporary American intellectual, whether he or she is based in New York or somewhere else well beyond the Hudson. For members of the intellectual elite, many of whom reside in university departments of English, "religion is an embarrassment at best and a menace at worst."

Delbanco regrets this turn of affairs and closes with a query. If in the early twentieth century Freud said that guilt was the greatest problem of modern civilization, might it not be the case that our greatest problem today "is finding a way to satisfy the human craving for belief while containing the proselytizing and purifying passion of true believers. Riesman and Hofstadter and the rest can be excused, I think, for failing to see that problem as clearly as we are compelled to see it today."

In his analysis of Wolfe's themes, Delbanco astutely cites the authors of our final chapter, Ralph Wood and Stanley Hauerwas, as examples of intellectuals in whom "suspicion runs deep toward religion," when it is used to justify "the kind of transcendental nationalism" that has marked American civil religion. It may seem counterintuitive to claim that these two preachers—Baptist and Methodist, respectively—are somehow hostile to religion. But Delbanco's point makes theological sense and is borne out by the interpretation of American literature that Wood and Hauerwas offer, for these two share toward American exceptionalism an antipathy rooted in the theology of Karl Barth and the ethical thought of the Anabaptist tradition.

To Wood and Hauerwas, the most important question to ask about the literature of the United States does not have to do with its religious background or its Emersonian legacy. Instead, the question for them is why "a nation with the soul of a church" has "produced so few writers who are Christian in any substantive sense of the word." Their answer to this question may seem surprising, for they place the blame not at the feet of the writers but at the heart of the churches. These institutions, they write, have so fully identified themselves "with the American project that our artists have had little cause to heed any unique and distinctively Christian witness in the churches." They claim that a "Constantinian shift" took place early in the national experience of the United States, as the church and state became effectively yoked together. This linkage permitted Protestant Christianity to enjoy "a cultural establishment that, for being so subtle, may be far more pernicious than the old-style conflation of realms." As an alternative, they search for works of American literature that show "the church as the one transformative community" through whose offices "the triune God is fashioning an alternative history for all people."

Given the scope of what they seek, it is not surprising that the only examples Wood and Hauerwas discover come from our novelists rather than our poets. In Flannery O'Connor's fiction, they come upon convincing evidence of divine grace freely given and convincingly rendered. Yet even O'Connor remained incapable of depicting the "faithful community" of the church as a place where "divine grace might be socially embodied and ethically sustained." For the depiction of this ideal, they turn to a single novel: Willa Cather's *Death Comes for the Archbishop*. Here the church, which is "nearly everywhere else occluded from our imaginative vision, clearly and redemptively emerges."

My response to Hauerwas and Wood highlights the fruitful tensions that ran through the American Literature and Religion Seminar and that animate most serious studies of the role of religious belief in the history of American culture. Although I share a number of Hauerwas's and Wood's deepest theological convictions, I question the tightness of their argument concerning the "Constantinian" captivity of American Christianity. Their clarion call to overcome the triumphalist allure and to resist the coercions of state and culture alike seems to run counter to the fact that, through the mystery of grace, triumphalism and coercion often work together toward redemptive ends, both in the rich fiction these two admire and in the deeply intertwined lives we all lead. "The lion lies in wait for the antelope at the ford," observes a character in one of Isak Dinesen's extraordinary *Seven Gothic Tales*, "and the antelope is sanctified by the lion, as is the lion by the antelope, for the play of the Lord is divine." There is nothing, this character tells his conversational partner, that sanctifies or is sanctified, except by this "play of the Lord, which is alone divine." It will not do, he says, to declare that only some notes on the musical scale—"say, *do*, *re* and *mi*"—are sacred, while the others are profane, for "no one of the notes is sacred in itself, and it is the music, which can be made out of them, which is alone divine." As the essays in this volume brilliantly attest, such polyphonic play has long marked the religious and cultural life of the United States, just as it continues to animate the conversations our literature carries on in the presence of the Invisible or in the shadows cast by its absence.

Part 1

RELIGION AND AMERICAN FICTION

1

FINDING A PROSE FOR GOD

Religion and American Fiction

Denis Donoghue

For the purposes of this chapter (and for some purposes beyond it), I take religion to be Christianity, the expedient—as Nietzsche called it in *The Genealogy of Morals*—"that paradoxical and awful expedient, through which a tortured humanity has found a temporary alleviation, that stroke of genius called *Christianity*—God personally immolating himself for the debt of man, God paying himself personally out of a pound of his own flesh."[1] It follows that I do not allude to other religions or to the sinister possibility of "religion without religion" to which Derrida refers in *The Gift of Death* as "this immense and thorny question."[2] Whether Christianity is an achieved entity or a *mysterium tremendum* always yet to be fulfilled is a question I do not address. I begin with some general considerations that do not bear peculiarly on American fiction. They are perhaps mere five-finger exercises in the vicinity of the topic, but I hope by this means to make a space for some that do.

Ministry of Fiction, Ministry of Form

I assume that literature is language subject to the double ministry of fiction and form. It is life as a writer imagines it within the constraints of the language in which it is written. The factor common to religion and literature is language. But that apparently simple notion does not report a harmonious relation between the two values. Geoffrey Hill, brooding over the twenty volumes of the *Oxford English Dictionary* in its second edition, was persuaded that "sematology is a theological dimension: the use of language is inseparable from that 'terrible aboriginal calamity' in which, according to Newman, the human race is implicated."[3] In a lighthearted world a language would be comprehensive. There would be words and sentences in it fully expressive of whatever perceptions, judgments, feelings, sentiments, and desires are humanly possible. But that does not appear to be the case, as Wittgenstein held when he maintained that whereof one may not speak, thereof one must be silent. In *The Things They Carried*, Tim O'Brien's narrator records that Rat Kiley shot a baby buffalo several times for no clear reason. All he can say is this: "We had witnessed something essential, something brand-new and profound, a piece of the world so startling there was not yet a name for it."[4] Maybe there was a name for it that O'Brien could not find. It is still a matter of debate whether or not there are feelings that never transpire in language. There is always silence, the silence into which the words, after speech, reach, according to the "Burnt Norton" of T. S. Eliot. Or John Cage's silence, which is presumably different from mine or anyone else's. Heather McHugh has a poem ("What He Thought") about the burning of Giordano Bruno and how his captors put an iron mask on his face to prevent him from speaking. The poem ends: "poetry is what / he thought, but did not say."[5] Nonetheless, language seems to be more enabling than one could anticipate. D. W. Harding has argued in *Experience Into Words* that writers are distinguished from other people by bringing language to bear upon their thinking at an unusually early stage of the transaction. They do not conceive thoughts independently of language and then search about for the best means of expressing them; it is as if the words pressed themselves forward and the thoughts came, a split second later, to complete the action. But words often seem to be not the right ones, and in that character they offer a show of truculence that they have no apparent right to offer. In *Style and Faith*, Hill quotes Benjamin Whichcote as saying that "by wickedness [a man] passes into a *Nature* contrary to his own," and comments that "when you write at any serious pitch of obligation you enter into the nature of grammar and etymology, which is a nature contrary to your own." You cannot "extricate yourself from this 'contrary nature' by some kind of philosophical fiat or gesture of spiritual withdrawal."[6] Language in that character is enemy country. This makes a problem for religion, which the churches resolve as best they can by allowing an aura to suffuse their rituals and prayers.

There is another difficulty. Kenneth Burke noted that there is no special vocabulary for the supernatural. Indeed, the words "supernatural" and "preternatural" are merely inflections of "natural." The ineffable has to go without saying because the only sayings are defeated substitutes for it. That is one reason why, as Pater maintained, "all art constantly aspires toward the condition of music," form and content in that medium being one and the same.[7] There are a few words that seem to be applicable to religious experience, such as (in the Christian calendar) God, divine, spirit, sacrifice, prayer, sacrament, Word—as in Word of God—grace, Father, Son, and Holy Ghost. But these words—with the possible exception of "God"—issue from natural or social experience and then are applied figuratively and rather desperately to one's religious occasions. "And the Word was made flesh and dwelt amongst us" is clear enough if faith clarifies it; otherwise not. Ralph Waldo Emerson anticipated Burke in his sense of the limitations of language, but he was not dismayed by them. In his first book, *Nature*, he observed that "words are signs of natural facts. . . . Every word which is used to express a moral or intellectual fact, if traced to its root, is found to be borrowed from some material appearance."[8] In *Paradise Lost*, God has to speak English and, worse still, has to use ordinary English words. When he speaks to his son in book 3, his speech is that of any devoted father to any dutiful son. He cannot transcend the diction and syntax of seventeenth-century English:

Man shall not be quite lost, but saved who will,
Yet not of will in him, but grace in me
Freely voutsafed

When he explains to his son the faculty of free will and the conditions under which man lives with it, the words "will"—first a verb, then a noun—and "grace" get their meaning from social life, even if theologians and moral philosophers treat both as technical terms. In book 4, Raphael tells Adam that man's speech is discursive while that of angels is intuitive (lines 487–89). To explain to Adam "what surmounts the reach / Of human sense,"

I shall delineate so,
By lik'ning spiritual to corporal forms,
As may express them best

Dr. Johnson was troubled by this and thought "the confusion of spirit and matter" caused "incongruity" in the whole narrative. Raphael himself was not at ease with the device. He immediately wondered,

though what if earth
Be but the shadow of heav'n, and things therein
Each to the other like, more than on earth is thought?[9]

He seems to mean that the analogy between spiritual and corporal forms is doubtful, because things in heaven do not differ, one from another, as much as their counterparts on earth appear to do. Still, he retains the analogy, if only because no other way of explaining spiritual forms is conceivable.

A nuance of this situation arises again in *Nature* where Emerson sets the analogy stirring freely, things in nature are signs of spiritual correlatives:

> Sensible objects conform to the premonitions of Reason and reflect the conscience. All things are moral; and in their boundless changes have an unceasing reference to spiritual nature. Therefore is nature glorious with form, color, and motion, that every globe in the remotest heaven; every chemical change from the rudest crystal up to the laws of life; every change of vegetation from the first principle of growth in the eye of a leaf, to the tropical forest and antediluvian coal-mine; every animal function from the sponge up to Hercules, shall hint or thunder to man the laws of right and wrong, and echo the Ten Commandments. Therefore is nature ever the ally of Religion: lends all her pomp and riches to the religious sentiment.[10]

Near the end of this passage, Emerson drives the analogy from sweet to sour—we hear of religion through the laws of right and wrong and the Ten Commandments, but in the last sentence he reverts to easy alliances and sentiments. The whole passage depends on the assertion, which is not self-evident, that "all things are moral."

The history of Romanticism shows that many writers acted on Emerson's congenial assumptions: the more they delighted in landscapes, the more they thought of themselves as somehow, however informally, acknowledging God and expressing everything "upon the bosom of a Nature perceived as holy," as Cynthia Ozick describes it.[11] There were moments, especially in Wordsworth and Coleridge, when the hoped-for revelation between the world and one's presence in it went blank, and these moments constituted a crisis. The question was: whose fault was the blank—the human mind looking wrongly, impiously or sullenly, at the world or God arbitrarily withholding his good will? Hopkins is the most extreme example of this in English poetry. He had his blank moments and usually blamed himself but sometimes blamed God. But he had many moments of fulfilled presence in a landscape he deemed the work of God. He also believed in God—with the certitude that adds two to three and gets five—independent of the landscapes he took pleasure in. It was harder to retain this sentiment when the landscapes gave way to cities, heavy industry, noise, and traffic, but the Romantic conviction remained in place and still does, for particular writers, despite I. A. Richards's insistence in *Science and Poetry* on the "neutralization of nature." Richards thought it a mark of modern writers that they had given up thinking of nature and God as kin, and he regarded as anachronistic the writers who held on to such a belief. Richards's position is a blunt version of the "secularization of inherited theological ideas and ways of thinking" that M. H. Abrams has elucidated in *Natural Supernaturalism*.[12] Richard Rorty has carried the secularizing process further by asserting that "the world does not speak. Only we do."[13] The trouble with that quip is that it does not help us decide whether what we say is true or false.

The consideration that there is no diction specific to experience of the supernatural leads to another issue. Burke has again clarified it. I quote from *The Rhetoric of Religion*:

> Insofar as man is the "typically symbol-using animal," it should not be surprising that men's thoughts on the nature of the Divine embody the principles of verbalization. And insofar as "God" is a *formal* principle, any thorough statements about "God" should be expected to reveal the formality underlying their genius as statements. The Biblical avowal that *man* is made in *God's image* has made us wary of the reversed anthropomorphic tendency to conceive of *God* in *man's image*. But the present inquiry stands midway between those two positions, contending merely that, insofar as religious doctrine is verbal, it will necessarily exemplify its nature as verbalization; and insofar as religious doctrine is thorough, its ways of exemplifying verbal principles should be correspondingly thorough.[14]

But many modern writers have not been wary of the anthropomorphic tendency to conceive of God in man's image, and that is precisely what they have done, especially in the act of exalting man beyond any reasonable conception of Him. When Wallace Stevens writes in "Final Soliloquy of the Interior Paramour," "God and the imagination are one," it is as if he reported that the only meaning we are willing to ascribe to the word "God" is the word "imagination" and then claimed that the human imagination is somehow divine or as close as one can imagine to divinity.[15]

"The Poetry in Which We Believe"

Stevens's sayings (and much else) prompt me toward a proposition so stark that I must try to mellow it at once. The proposition is that modern American literature is a substitute for religion, but a substitute in which the original has been absorbed. What could that mean? It could mean that while the "cultural unconscious" in America may be religious, the culture so far as it is conscious is secular. It may observe its Sabbath for an hour or two once a week, but the rest of the week is dedicated to worldly pursuits. It could mean that its "political concepts are secularized theologico-political concepts."[16] Or that the distinctive merits of American literature are regularly sought in default of the credences of religion. Or that some writers who do not hold any religious beliefs regard that state as a predicament and do the best they can with it, as Stevens wrote his poems without Christian convictions, despite the plaintive yearning for such that he ascribed to the woman in "Sunday Morning." The proposition could also mean (to acknowledge that these sentiments are not confined to American writers) what Matthew Arnold said in "The Study of Poetry" and Santayana virtually repeated in *Interpretations of Poetry and Religion*, that is, the strongest part of our religion is its unconscious poetry. "Our religion is the poetry in which we believe," Santayana claimed. He looked upon religion "as on a kind of poetry . . . that expresses moral values and reacts beneficently upon life."[17]

The proposition does not say that modern literature is a valid or effective substitute for religion, or even that it is a poor substitute, of necessity. Nor does it say that literature is the only substitute that has been tried. Allen Tate maintained in "Religion and the Old South" that because the South "never created a fitting religion, the social structure of the South began grievously to break down two generations after the Civil War. For the social structure depends on the economic structure, and economic conviction is still, in spite of the beliefs of economists from Adam Smith to Marx, the secular image of religion." In the same essay, Tate said that Southerners inherited Thomas Jefferson's belief that the ends of man are sufficiently contained in his political destiny and "may be fully achieved by political means."[18] This is now a common sentiment, especially among philosophers in the pragmatist tradition who want to turn philosophy into politics and who regard truth as nothing but an axiom of intersubjectivity, in force for the time being only. But in another context, W. B. Yeats, coming upon Thomas Mann's assertion that "the destiny of man presents its meaning in political terms," wrote a poem called "Politics" to say, in effect, that you could make the same claim for any comprehensive term, such as sex.[19]

So we have religion, politics, economics, and sex as ambitious values. It is to be expected that one of these will be in the cultural ascendant at a particular moment. But if, with Schelling and Coleridge, a writer chooses religion as supreme in principle if rarely in practice, it is because, as Northrop Frye maintained, "the transcendental and apocalyptic perspective of religion comes as a tremendous emancipation of the imaginative mind."[20] Or because the ultimate term appears to be religious and analogous to the divine act of creation. As Coleridge says, again following Schelling, in the *Biographia Literaria*, willing to see religious belief absorbed in worldly or humanist terminologies: "The IMAGINATION then I consider either as primary, or secondary. The primary IMAGINATION I hold to be the living Power and prime Agent of all human Perception, and as a repetition in the finite mind of the eternal act of creation in the infinite I AM. The secondary I consider as an echo of the former, co-existing with the conscious will, yet still as identical with the primary in the *kind* of its agency, and differing only in *degree*, and in the *mode* of its operation."[21] It is a pity that Coleridge called the two forms of imagination primary and secondary. The one he calls primary can hardly be primary if it repeats in the finite mind the eternal act of creation in the infinite I AM. The eternal act must be primary, first in principle, so the later kinds should respectively be secondary and tertiary. But the analogy with the divine power is still deemed to hold, and it guarantees the human imagination a trace of religious affiliation, even in the line I quoted from Stevens. The other ambitious terms, by comparison, are merely social instruments, however preponderant they may be in social practice.

The Idiom of God

Modern American fiction is hardly the place one would visit to find these issues taken seriously. Why they are taken lightly, on the whole, is a question for Emerson. But I begin with a story in which religion in the forms of doctrine, ritual, and sacramental practice is taken very seriously indeed. Andre Dubus's "A Father's Story" is told in the first person by Luke Ripley, a man in his middle years who lives in northeastern Massachusetts. In his worldly life he owns a stable of thirty horses. He has young people who teach riding and he boards horses, too. He seems to make a fairly comfortable living, but he lives by himself. His wife Gloria left him some years ago and took the children with her to Florida—three sons and a daughter, Jennifer, who is now twenty and comes every summer to Massachusetts to visit her father for six weeks. Meanwhile Ripley lives his life as a Roman Catholic. He goes to Mass and receives Communion every day. He goes to Confession once a month. Every morning while making the bed and boiling water for coffee, he talks to God:

> I offer Him my day, every act of my body and spirit, my thoughts and moods, as a prayer of thanksgiving, and for Gloria and my children and my friends and two women I made love with after Gloria left. This morning offertory is a habit from my boyhood in a Catholic school; or then it was a habit, but as I kept it and grew older it became a ritual. Then I say the Lord's Prayer, trying not to recite it, and one morning it occurred to me

that a prayer, whether recited or said with concentration, is always an act of faith.

Ripley's best friend is the local priest, Father Paul LeBoeuf, an older French-Canadian man. One night they talk about faith, and Father Paul says, "belief is believing in God; faith is believing that God believes in you." Luke accepts this and takes it to heart.

When Jennifer comes on her summer visit, she gathers up her friends, young women like herself and at her stage of womanly bloom. This does not trouble Ripley much, but he is susceptible to its intimations: "It was womanhood they were entering, the deep forest of it, and no matter how many women and men too are saying these days that there is little difference between us, the truth is that men find their way into that forest only on clearly marked trails, while women move about in it like birds. So hearing Jennifer and her friends talking so quietly, yet intensely, I wanted very much to have a wife." One evening, Jennifer goes to meet a few friends and drinks more beer than she should. Driving back to Ripley's house, she hits something on the road. She tells her father about the accident. He goes to the scene and finds a young man dying, not dead. However, Ripley does nothing about it:

> I stood. Then I knelt again and prayed for his soul to join in peace and joy all the dead and living; and, doing so, confronted my first sin against him, not stopping for Father Paul, who could have given him the last rites, and immediately then my second one, or I saw then, my first, not calling an ambulance to meet me there, and I stood and turned into the wind, slid down the ditch and crawled out of it, and went up the hill and down it, across the road to the street of houses whose people I had left behind forever, so that I moved with stealth in the shadows to my truck.

Later, Ripley takes Jennifer's car and, to conceal the damaged front of it, crashes it into an old pine tree beside Father Paul's church. He cannot confess what he has done, but he receives Communion. The story ends:

> I do not feel the peace I once did: not with God, nor the earth, or anyone on it. I have begun to prefer this state, to remember with fondness the other one as a period of peace I neither earned nor deserved. Now in the mornings while I watch purple finches driving larger titmice from the feeder, I say to Him: I would do it again. For when she knocked on my door, then called me, she woke what had flowed dormant in my blood since her birth, so that what rose from the bed was not a stable owner or a Catholic or any other Luke Ripley I had lived with for a long time, but the father of a girl.
>
> And He says: I am a Father too.

Yes, I say, as you are a Son Whom this morning I will receive; unless You kill me on the way to church, then I trust You will receive me. And as a Son You made Your plea.

Yes, He says, but I would not lift the cup.

True, and I don't want You to lift it from me either. And if one of my sons had come to me that night, I would have phoned the police and told them to meet us with an ambulance at the top of the hill.

Why? Do you love them less?

I tell Him no, it is not that I love them less, but that I could bear the pain of watching and knowing my sons' pain, could bear it with pride as they took the whip and nails. But You never had a daughter and, if You had, You could not have borne her passion.

So, He says, you love her more than you love Me.

I love her more than I love truth.

Then you love in weakness, He says.

As You love me, I say, and I go with an apple or carrot out to the barn.[22]

"A Father's Story" has been much discussed. The only aspect of it I need to remark for the moment is its saturation in the vocabulary of religion, its appeal—doomed as that may be—to the idiom of God and sin and sacrament, confession and Eucharist, and the rival idiom of father and daughter. Whatever the moral of Luke Ripley's story may be, the moral of Dubus's telling it is that one is not compelled to capitulate to the humanist *Zeitgeist*. Or to settle for silence. One cultural practice does not veto another, though the rhetorics of sequentiality and progress try to persuade us that it does. Even after the accident, Luke Ripley keeps on talking to God; he may not have adequate words, but he speaks the words he has.

I leave aside the question of whether or not the emphasis on faith, observance, grace, and sin, which we find in Dubus's story and J. F. Powers's "The Presence of Grace," is now to be found only in Roman Catholic writers, as in Flannery O'Connor, who said that "the Catholic novelist believes that you destroy your freedom by sin; the modern reader believes, I think, that you gain it that way."[23] There are other narrative traditions. I think of the Yiddish story—if it is a story rather than a memoir—by Chaim Grade, called "My Quarrel with Hersh Rasseyner," which takes issues of belief and observance with appropriate seriousness.

Finding a Prose for God: Literature as Social Force

I have implied in my remark about the *Zeitgeist* that I do not regard the "spirit of the age" as having decisive or inescapable force; nor do I believe in the veridical status of sequence, except locally. So I doubt myself when I say that Nathaniel Hawthorne takes up where Emerson left off. They are evidently very different writers; Emerson buoyant in casting aside his Christian ministry and urging his audience at the Harvard Divinity School to take on themselves the responsibility of Christ. No wonder Alfred Kazin could say of him that "he began as a religion but ended as literature."[24] Although reluctantly and mostly with contempt, Hawthorne obsessively returned to the Puritan images that haunted his imagination.

But Emerson and Hawthorne are alike in one respect: each of them tried to find "the prose for God." I take this phrase from an episode in Harley Granville-Barker's play *Waste* where two politicians, Henry Trebell and Sir Charles Cantelupe, discuss religion. "Now shall we finish the conversation in prose," Trebell proposes. "What is the prose for God?" Sir Charles counters. "That's what we irreligious people are giving our lives to discover," Trebell says.[25] Emerson, irreligious to this extent, tried the experiment of replacing God with nature and deemed the soul to be indistinguishable from the autonomous self, psychologically understood. He had behind him—if far behind him—the Puritan sermon, the essay according to Montaigne, and the periodical essay according to Addison and Steele. Hawthorne was a novelist, or at least a romancer, and he had behind him the lost epic, in keeping with Lukács's observation that "the novel is the epic of a world that has been abandoned by God."[26] It is my contention that Hawthorne replaced God with nature and community—nature as an Emersonian substitute for God in his notionally benign aspects, community as a substitute for Him in his stringency, promulgator of the Ten Commandments. Hawthorne then reduced sin to a social offense, a transgression against the community, but a transgression that had to be committed if a self were determined to claim its independence. In "The May-Pole of Merry Mount," the festivities and mummeries of the forest "pour sunshine over New England's rugged hills" until Governor Endicott and his Puritan legion arrive to put a stop to the merriment.[27] In the chapter of *The Scarlet Letter* called "A Flood of Sunshine," when Dimmesdale has agreed with Hester that they will take Pearl and set out for a new or resuscitated life together in Europe, Hester throws away the scarlet letter and lets her hair fall over her shoulders: "See! With this symbol, I undo it all, and make it as if it had never been!" Immediately, the sun comes out to rejoice that the lovers are together again. The narrator comments, "Such was the sympathy of Nature—that wild, heathen Nature of the forest, never subjugated by human law, nor illumined by higher truth—with the bliss of these two spirits! Love, whether newly born, or aroused from a deathlike slumber, must always create a sunshine, filling the heart so full of radiance, that it over-flows upon the outward world."[28]

Human law and higher truth would be equally repellent in such a forest: inevitably, Dimmesdale goes back to the community, and the pastoral idyll is destroyed. But the only sin he recognizes is that of keeping one's actions secret: that alone is the offense against one's community. It is Ethan Brand's unpardonable sin, as well as Parson Hooper's in "The Minister's Black Veil." But the offense of secrecy is, in Hawthorne's terms, horrific: it is the only cor-relative he can imagine to a mortal sin.

This is quite different from Melville's sense of sin in *Pierre*, who says "yes" to sin only if it is grand enough—like Satan's: "And as the more immense the Virtue, so should be the more immense our approbation; likewise the more immense the Sin, the more infinite our pity. In some sort, Sin hath its sacred-ness, not less than holiness. And great Sin calls forth more magnanimity than small Virtue. What man, who is a man, does not feel livelier and more gen-erous emotions toward the great god of Sin—Satan,—than toward yonder haberdasher, who only is a sinner in the small and entirely honorable way of trade?"[29] But Hester's sin is commonplace; it calls forth from Hawthorne nothing like Blake's or Melville's thrilled assent to Satan's.

Henry James's explanation of Hawthorne's religious sense, or the expla-nation he arrived at after much talk of sin and gloom, is that Hawthorne took images lightly in the end by taking them aesthetically. His relation to his Puritan inheritance "was only, as one may say, intellectual; it was not moral and theological." He was not haunted by it, having found himself capable of being light and airy despite its oppression. James seems to mean that even when Hawthorne disposes his images and themes such that a comprehen-sive imagining of them would entail entering metaphysical or moral dark-ness, he resorted in the end to an aesthetic sense of them and held off from their importunity. James says of "Young Goodman Brown" that "it evidently means nothing as regards Hawthorne's own state of mind, his conviction of human depravity and his consequent melancholy; for the simple reason that if it meant anything, it would mean too much."[30] In "Hawthorne and his Mosses," Melville maintained that "in spite of all the Indian-summer sunlight on the hither side of Hawthorne's soul, the other side—like the dark half of the physical sphere—is shrouded in a blackness, ten times black." Whether Hawthorne "has simply availed himself of this mystical blackness as a means to the wondrous effects he makes it to produce in his lights and shades; or whether there really lurks in him, perhaps unknown to himself, a touch of Puritanic gloom," Melville said, "this, I cannot altogether tell."[31] Melville was determined a few months before the publication of *Moby-Dick* to make Hawthorne seem blood-brother to himself, both writers with an immense power of blackness. But the case is still disputed. Lionel Trilling has given us reasons for thinking it a limitation in Hawthorne's genius that he did not take the risk of having his fictions mean too much, if they were to mean at all. Trilling's comparison of Hawthorne with Franz Kafka carries this critical judgment. He says of them, "they stood in equivalent relations to religion: unbelievers both, their imaginations were captivated by the faiths to which they were connected by family tradition, and from these unavowed faiths they derived the license for the mythic genre which constitutes so much of their appeal, for the representation of agencies of human destiny which are not of the actual world." But finally, as Trilling says in the spirit of James's monograph: "Hawthorne always consented to the power of his imagination being controlled by the power of the world."[32]

This is persuasive, but there is, I think, a further explanation. Hawthorne's replacement of the hidden God by the dual values of nature and community was so tactically reductive that neither of those values could compel the full stretch of his imagination. Nature meant mostly the forest, the place of pastoral freedom and guiltlessness, though it could have entailed more dangerous forces if "Young Goodman Brown" had been imagined as fully as it might have been. It could have entailed redemptive forces, too, as Ike's imagining of the wilderness does in Faulkner's "Delta Autumn," a conception of nature that "amounts to the sacramental," as Cleanth Brooks says.[33] Community to Hawthorne meant mostly law and its observances. Only in "My Cousin Major Molineux" and "Young Goodman Brown"—and then ambiguously— did he imagine that a community could easily turn into an orgiastic crowd, a mob, as Elias Canetti shows in *Crowds and Power*. Before Canetti, Durkheim remarked on the force of enthusiasm to which a society is susceptible: "The aptitude of society for setting itself up as a god or for creating gods was never more apparent than during the first years of the French Revolution. At that time, in fact, under the influence of the general enthusiasm, things purely laical by nature were transformed by public opinion into sacred things: these were the Fatherland, Liberty, Reason."[34]

Such a transformation, as Roberto Calasso explains in *Literature and the Gods*, became most appalling when it sounded most natural: it expressed itself in tautology and self-advertising. What was once the preserve of religion became the power of society, taken for granted; "being anti-social would become the equivalent of sinning against the Holy Ghost."[35] In a more recent book, *K*, Calasso refines this perception in terms of social absorption:

Certainly it's not the case, as some continue to maintain, that the religious or the sacred or the divine has been shattered, dissolved, obviated, by some outside agent, by the light of the Enlightenment. That would have resulted in a world made of secular funerals, in all their awful bleakness. What happened instead is that such things as the religious or the sacred or the divine, by an obscure process of osmosis, were absorbed and hidden in something alien, which no longer has need of such names because it is self-sufficient and is content to be described as *society*: All the rest is, at best, its object of study, its guinea pig—even all of nature.[36]

Hawthorne's tactical reduction of God to nature and community was not a device that engaged Melville's interest: his imagination refused to be satisfied with available terms. If he had attempted any such reduction, he would have treated the attempt with disgust. In *Moby-Dick*, he hands over the devices of commonsense to Ishmael, thereby indicating how genially mundane he judges them to be. Sometimes he lets Ishmael play games with nouns and adjectives, but always on the understanding—I mean the reader's understanding—that the deep truth of things is beyond or beneath Ishmael's syntax. Beneath, as in the truth of the primitive; beyond, as in that of the sublime. Sometimes, Melville has Ishmael report the ordinary truths, and the report is convincing so far as it goes. The short chapter "The Prairie" has this gorgeous piece of nonsense, but it is not entirely nonsense:

> And this reminds me that had the great Sperm Whale been known to the young Orient World, he would have been deified by their child-magian thoughts. They deified the crocodile of the Nile, because the crocodile is tongueless; and the Sperm Whale has no tongue, or at least it is so exceedingly small, as to be incapable of protrusion. If hereafter any highly cultured, poetical nation shall lure back to their birth-right, the merry May-day gods of old; and livingly enthrone them again in the now egotistical sky; in the now unhaunted hill; then be sure, exalted to Jove's high seat, the great Sperm Whale shall lord it.[37]

This is an example of Melville's middle style, discursive and equable. It is the style of intelligent conversation. It is capable of making a point worth making, that "in the now egotistical sky" and "in the now unhaunted hill" are parallel phrases because they are companionable perceptions. The hill is unhaunted because the gods have been dispelled, and the new god is the ego, not Emerson's invention but his reiterated motto. Melville can write in this style because he can write in every style, but his handing over of this particular style to Ishmael shows that he does not take its deliverances with much gravity. They are true enough but not the truth. The character who transcends the limi-

tations of the middle style most comprehensively while remaining committed
to its legal force is Captain Vere in "Billy Budd," who is not only loving but
also love itself. In *Moby-Dick* the style Melville cares about is Ahab's, and that
is the style of blasphemy for the most part, or any of the other high or sublime
utterances including Father Mapple's. Melville appropriated other versions of
the sublime—the King James Bible, Shakespeare, Sir Thomas Browne, Bur-
ton, and Milton among them—not to participate in the shared *copia* of the
English language but to overwhelm it, to make it submit to his violence.

Moby-Dick is not a book about Ahab, Ishmael, Queequeg, Father Mapple,
and other people; it is centrally about Ahab and the White Whale, though
there are readers who want to read it otherwise. The whale is not a figure of
evil in the world but rather a figure of the world itself, of Being, which Ahab
hates as much as he hates the God of Calvin he holds accountable for it. They
make the double object of his blasphemy, the only mode in which Melville's
imagination is religious. David Reynolds has noted that Calvinism in American fiction in the late eighteenth and early nineteenth centuries was gradually
replaced by the doctrine of good works, but it had a remarkable growth again
in the years up to 1840. Melville may have had pressing reason to be appalled
by it during those years, though by the 1850s the question of one's religious
denomination, if religious fiction is evidence, became "inconsequential for
the Protestant novelist."[38] Many years ago, Lawrance Thompson argued in
Melville's Quarrel with God that Melville's pervasive attitude to Christian
dogma and the Christian concept of God was one of "taunting ridicule," most
clearly seen in *The Confidence-Man* and *Pierre*.[39] I find that hard to refute.

Between Devotion and Irreligion: The Sacramental Space

But there are other possibilities of experience between irreligion and devotion. Allen Tate has argued, in an essay on Emily Dickinson that was taken
up and developed by R. P. Blackmur, that Dickinson came at a time that
may have been arduous for her soul but was enabling to her poems, a time
when the theocracy of New England had nearly collapsed but was still felt
as sufficiently in force to be interrogated and challenged, mocked as often
as respected. While it lasted, the theocracy had "an immense, incalculable
value for literature: it dramatized the human soul." It gave meaning, or least
the possibility of meaning, to life: "the life of pious and impious, of learned
and vulgar alike." Puritanism "could not be to Dickinson what it had been
to the generation of Cotton Mather—a body of absolute truths; it was an
unconcious discipline timed to the pulse of her life." Blackmur veers from

Tate at this point. He does not believe that Puritanism was for Dickinson an uncompromising discipline or that the timing was right for her pulse: "Faith was sophisticated, freed, and terrified—but still lived; imagination had suddenly to do all the work of embodying faith formerly done by habit, and to embody it with the old machinery so far as it could be used." In such conditions, faith, in the hands of the individual and while the institutions of faith are crumbling, "becomes an imaginative experiment of which all the elements are open to new and even blasphemeous combinations, and which is subject to the addition of new insights." Puritanism was no longer much good as doctrine or received wisdom, but it was good enough to be teased and provoked. The theocracy was still there as machinery, though feeble for more personal purposes. As a result, Dickinson could have only an experimental relation to it, but that was what she needed, her sensibility being what it was. She came at the most fortunate moment for the poetry she had it in her to write: "the poetry of sophisticated, eccentric vision," as Blackmur calls it. It had to be eccentric and probably willful, because it did not issue from a living tradition of faith and observance. It had to be sophisticated, because it could not be simple, sensuous, and passionate all at once. That explains why her poems, like the Bible, can be quoted in favor of nearly every cause, for she is never doctrinal. Blackmur claims that "the great advantage for a poet to come at a time of disintegrating culture is [that] the actuality of what we are and what we believe is suddenly seen to be nearly meaningless as habit, and must, to be adequately known, be translated to the terms and modes of imagination."[40]

Emerson, according to this emphasis in Tate and Blackmur, hardly knew what he was doing, but he ended up removing any tragic possibilities from the culture he addressed. The effect of Emerson's doctrine of individualism, according to Tate, is that "there is no drama in human character because there is no tragic fault."[41] There is no sin, no action for which anyone would think of seeking forgiveness. One of the most shocking passages in Emerson's "Experience" is this flourish of exoneration:

> We believe in ourselves, as we do not believe in others. We permit all things to ourselves, and that which we call sin in others is experiment for us. . . . Saints are sad, because they behold sin (even when they speculate), from the point of view of the conscience, and not of the intellect; a confusion of thought. Sin, seen from the thought, is a diminution or *less*; seen from the conscience or will, it is pravity or *bad*. The intellect names it shade, absence of light, and no essence. The conscience must feel it as essence, essential evil. This it is not; it has an objective existence, but no subjective.[42]

I wonder what Emmanuel Levinas, who regarded as the primary act the acknowledgment of another person and the acknowledgment of one's self as secondary and derivative, would think of that.

Tate thought that Hawthorne "kept pure, in the primitive terms, the primitive vision; he brings the puritan tragedy to its climax." Man, "measured by a great idea outside himself, is found wanting."[43] I doubt this and think that Blackmur had the better case when he asserted, "some say Hawthorne was a great student of evil; I think rather that he studied how to avoid and ignore it by interposing the frames of his tales between evil and the experience of it."[44] Perhaps this is to say that Hawthorne saw evil as omnivorous but diffuse, and that his imagination was not willing to identify evil with its local manifestations. There had to be more evil at large than he could specify. But if he rejected the world, he did not do it blithely. Tate says,

> Mastery of the world by rejecting the world was the doctrine, even if it was not always the practice, of Jonathan Edwards and Cotton Mather. It is the meaning of fate in Hawthorne: his people are fated to withdraw from the world and to be destroyed. And it is one of the great themes of Henry James.

But the theme was much diminished by the time James took it up:

> Between Hawthorne and James lies an epoch. The temptation to sin, in Hawthorne, is, in James, transformed into the temptation not to do the "decent thing." A whole world-scheme, a complete cosmic background, has shrunk to the dimensions of the individual conscience.[45]

Tate does not say what this reduction of scale entails. Presumably he means what Dickinson meant: "The abdication of Belief / Makes the Behavior small."[46]

But in James there is more to it than the temptation not to do the "right thing." The problem for James was to imply a context of grave reference within which his little fable would work out its life. In a different culture and a different social class, such a context would be religious, but James could not give himself to that resource. His sense of religion was inert. Trilling remarks in "Art and Fortune" that what theologians call "faith" is what James, in the preface to *The American*, calls "romance":

> The real represents to my perception the things we cannot possibly *not* know, sooner or later, in one way or another; it being but one of the accidents of our hampered state, and one of the incidents of their quantity and number, that particular instances have not yet come our way. The romantic stands, on the other hand, for the things that, with all the facilities in the world, all

the wealth and all the courage and all the wit and all the adventure, we never *can* directly know; the things that can reach us only through the beautiful circuit and subterfuge of our thought and desire.[47]

Sometimes the subterfuge gives itself away. Though there is much talk of wings and doves in *The Wings of the Dove*, none of the characters, including Milly, could be expected to recall the Psalm from which James culled his title, which is Psalm 55: "Fearfulness and trembling are come upon me, and horror hath overwhelmed me. And I said: Oh that I had wings like a dove! For then I would fly away, and be at rest." And Psalm 68: "Though ye have lain among the pots, yet shall ye be as the wings of a dove covered with silver, and her feathers with yellow gold." James is remembering for his characters, trying to give them something of his own affluence of sensitivity. His religious sense being lethargic, he had to find other ways of making stories seem weighted, even if the weight was entirely a matter of social acquisition and taste. The story of *The Wings of the Dove* is so odious that only the succession of high-toned reflections and conversations deflects us from seeing how odious it is. References to the Bible are consistent with a cultural period in which it was becoming common to read the Bible as literature, the first of the Great Books, to be read without incurring the obligation of believing a word of it.

In Henry Adams, the conclusion to every question of religion is foregone. He had no faith, only the need of it because only a great faith would have seized his energy and given it form. He wrote the *Education* to show cause—pathetic, indeed—why none of the interests he took up was worth his sustained attention. His account of religion in Boston in the years from 1848 to 1852 is predictably and appropriately dismissive. Even in *Mont-Saint-Michel and Chartres*, where he expended every nuance of appreciation and tenderness for the Virgin, he could not let her go until he had presented her "looking down from a deserted heaven, into an empty church, on a dead faith."[48] Nothing appeased his desire but failure. In *Esther*, his novel of religion, Adams makes his heroine Esther Dudley an agnostic. She could be drawn, in frail theory, to the minister Rev. Stephen Hazard, who loves her. But in the end she is more taken with the Niagara Falls than with anything Stephen Hazard finds to say to her. The penury of her imagination is made clear when she says to Stephen, "Is it not enough to know myself? . . . Some people are made with faith. I am made without it."[49] A bolder man than Stephen would have answered: "No, it is not enough to know yourself, especially if you don't know that your talk of 'some people' who are made with faith and 'I' without it is specious. Have you no part in your own making?"

A subterfuge similar to James's in its enhancing reach is resorted to in *The Great Gatsby* when Nick meditates on Gatsby: "The truth was that Jay Gatsby, of West Egg, Long Island, sprang from his Platonic conception of himself. He was a son of God—a phrase which, if it means anything, means just that— and he must be about His Father's Business, the service of a vast, vulgar and meretricious beauty."[50] Nick is endowing Gatsby with mythic justification, and for that purpose he needs to give him a second self-independent of his first. The allusion is impudent. There is no proper analogy between the young Jesus teaching his peers in the temple and Jay Gatsby inventing himself to make money and achieve a style. The analogy, specious as it is, is Nick's way of accepting that Gatsby is at worst a minor god, even if the cause he serves is meretricious. Nick has become one of those millions of Protestant Americans who, as Northrop Frye observed, "have drifted, and are continuing to drift, away from their earlier religious moorings, not always through indifference, but very often because they feel that a secular life is the most mature, civilized, and serious form of the kind of Christian liberty offered them by Protestant- ism."[51] William James's *Varieties of Religious Experience* and Robert Bellah's *Habits of the Heart* might be quoted to make Frye's point. I think Frye means middle-class American Protestants. Working-class Protestants resort to God and the Bible at least in moments of crisis, as Mrs. Griffith does in *An Ameri- can Tragedy* when her son Clyde is found guilty and awaits execution: "Clyde must pray for her and for himself. Read Isaiah. Read the psalms—the 23rd and the 51st and the 91st daily. Also Habbakuk. "Are there walls against the Hand of the Lord?"[52] These are not the prayers of Northrop Frye's American Protestants. For the same reason, Henry Adams thought that all Americans were naturally Conservative Christian Anarchists. To Adams, as Blackmur explained, "what kept American society together and plastic was the fact that deep in its unconscious feeling for the human ideal it had never committed itself to any single version of the good as supreme."[53] One little god is as good as another.

The reason for this may be that the American religion is not what it thinks it is. Harold Bloom has put forward the claim arguing that the Ameri- can religion is a bewildered mixture of Christianity and Gnosticism, Christi- anity other than it knows itself, Gnosticism as it doesn't know itself at all. The religious experience is apart from clergy or church. "No American pragmati- cally feels free if she is not alone," Bloom says, "and no American ultimately concedes that she is part of nature." That seems to make her post-Emerson and post-Stevens, a point insisted on later when Bloom says that "the freedom assured by the American religion is not what Protestants once called Christian Liberty but is a solitude in which the inner loneliness is at home in an outer loneliness." That seems to make it at once post-Stevens and post-Frost, a redaction of Stevens's "Snow Man" and Robert Frost's "An Old Man's Winter Night." Much later in *The American Religion*, Bloom asks a question that seems odd until we reflect that any American religion he posits must submit to poetic and aesthetic criteria. The question he asks is, Why is it that we have produced so few masterpieces of overtly religious literature?, "we" meaning Americans: "devotional poetry or narrative or drama, of any aesthetic eminence, or of any profound spirituality, hardly exists among us." Bloom does not stay for an answer. He merely suggests more Emerson: "the issue is not self-worship; it is acquaintance with a God within the self." American ecstasy, Bloom says, is solitary, "even when it requires the presence of others as audience for the self's glory."[54] I thought we already had that with "Self Reliance" and "Song of Myself." It appears that there is no fiction, no poetry, commensurate with Bloom's sense of the American religion: only "a full-scale return to the wars of religion" is foreseen.

After that impasse on Bloom's part, it is time to return to Dubus's "A Father's Story." In that conversation with God at the end, how does Luke Ripley know that he is not merely talking to himself? He has shown none of the misgiving that would hobble the discourse of one who knew that there is no special language for supernatural experience. He has not been seeking the prose for God or brooding on the differences between that prose and some sublime poetry. He has committed himself to the middle style. Yet here he is, after all that has happened, talking to God; it is a difficult conversation, but a conversation nonetheless. What enables it, and what protects him from the loneliness on which Bloom's putative citizen insists, is his membership of the Church, the sacraments, the rituals, the Mass, Confession, and Communion. It is not enough that these make a community utterly free from the vigilant and punitive mission that held the community together in *The Scarlet Letter*. The sacraments give him access to, and participation in, the modes of sacrifice and meaning that he enters by himself but not entirely by himself: there are the others. He is not looking for "a God within the self."

2

AMERICAN LITERATURE
AND/AS SPIRITUAL INQUIRY

Lawrence Buell

To generalize in short form about the relation between "American fiction" and "American religion" is a very tricky undertaking, so vast is the terrain and so variously might these rubrics be understood.

The United States—that is, the portion of "America" Denis Donoghue discusses in Chapter 1—is both the most materialistic nation on earth, measured by its disproportionate consumption of earth's resources, and the most pious, measured by comparative polling data on the percentage of citizens relative to all other modern nations who affirm that they believe in God, afterlife, hell, and so forth. The U.S. is arguably the most religiously diverse nation on earth, the country that stands *par excellence* for freedom of worship and receptivity to immigrants and the disparate faiths they bring with them, but it is also arguably one of the most religiously homogeneous (with more than 75 percent professing Christianity, Protestantism being especially influential during the first two centuries of colonial and national history but Catholicism outnumbering any single Protestant sect as early as the mid-1800s).[1]

As for American narrative, a case can be made for it being either haunted by religion or insulated from it. Which is the more culturally symptomatic document, Jonathan Edwards's "Narrative" or Benjamin Franklin's *Autobiography*? Harriet Beecher Stowe's *Uncle Tom's Cabin* or Fanny Fern's *Ruth Hall*? Mark Twain's *Huckleberry Finn* or his *The Mysterious Stranger*? William Faulkner's *Flags in the Dust* or his *Go Down, Moses*—not to mention *A Fable*? The fiction of Flannery O'Connor or the fiction of Carson McCullers? Toni Morrison's *The Bluest Eye* or her *Paradise*? Marilynne Robinson's *Housekeeping* or her *Gilead*?

Faced with such paradoxes, one has no choice but to narrow down the field of investigation in order to make it manageable. Denis Donoghue does this in some long-familiar, indeed old-fashioned, ways. He defines classic "American fiction" in terms of the traditional high canon through Henry James and Henry Adams and the core of "American religion" as a secularized, individualized emanation from Protestantism, with Emerson as the liberalizing pivot-point, beyond which "the religious" loses its spiritual rigor and robustness and dwindles into a solitary negotiation of ethical dilemmas. This secularized attenuation he diagnoses as a legacy of Romanticism's usurpation of the place of religion from Coleridge through Stevens. To the extent that these moves shape the chapter as a whole, it threatens to read like a thrice-told tale, derived from the great mid-twentieth-century critics Donoghue characteristically uses as his preferred reference points, among whom R. P. Blackmur and especially Allen Tate loom largest. One could never tell from this chapter, for example, that there had ever been a canon war in U.S. literary studies, that scholars of the past two decades have retold the story of U.S. literary emergence in such a way as repeatedly, although by no means conclusively, to depose Emerson from the position of gateway to U.S. literary emergence that first-wave American literary studies had assigned him.[2]

Donoghue's essay is no mere recycling project, however. It is too crafty and incisive for that. What to me particularly gives it pith, bite, and originality is its sturdy but subtle counterreformationary brief against the attenuation if not the positive evaporation of the religious wrought by the postromantic Protestant imagination, American style. Three dimensions of this brief strike me as especially provocative, meaning of course that I shall want to quarrel with all of them, but I hope respectfully so.

First, and most briefly, the opening rumination that follows from the postulate that "the factor common to religion and literature is language." This is a deliciously clever trap for the unwary reader. Presumably the author is quite aware that what he states as a self-evident truth could reasonably be disputed as an arbitrary restriction. (Why "language"? Why not, say, "affect" or "invention" or "magic"?) But I take it that he counts, and counts rightly, on his target audience of literature scholars being charmed and disarmed by this seductive proposition, with its promise of containing "religion" within the familiar domain of literary discourse. Yet the argument developed from this starting point turns out to press the very opposite claim, to deny the sufficiency of language to characterize the divine. This leads directly to the ensuing contention that imagination cannot legitimately function as a stand-in for religion or a carrier of religious inspiration. Only in retrospect does one fully appreciate that "language," which immediately called attention to the epistemological problems of the representation gap, was the perfect choice of common denominator to set up an argument for humbling literature relative to religion in the author's sense of what ought to count as religion. Affect, invention, and magic could just as easily have cut the other way.

The chapter's other two arresting moves follow soon after as Donoghue launches into the main part of his argument. Constructing a set of analytical pincers from the juxtaposition of Andre Dubus's "A Father's Story" and Nathaniel Hawthorne's *The Scarlet Letter*, Donoghue weighs the noncanonical contemporary tale against one of the most notoriously religiocentric texts in all of classic American fiction and finds religious imagination in the former much more robust, the latter tendentiously secularized by comparison. "Hawthorne replaced God by nature and community," then "reduced sin to a social offense," in particular the sin of secrecy. ("The only sin [*The Scarlet Letter*'s Arthur Dimmesdale] recognizes is that of keeping one's actions secret: that alone is the offense against one's community.") Whereas the no less secretive father in Dubus's tale is "protected" against loneliness and isolation through "his membership of the Church, the sacraments, the rituals, the Mass, Confession, and Communion."

These are bracing reductionisms. In the register of the literary criticism, they enact the "daemonism" that Angus Fletcher brilliantly ascribes to fictive allegory.[3] In each case, a good thing is taken too far. The argument that Hawthorne's fiction synchronizes with Emersonianism to the extent that it takes sin to be more "a social offense" than a theological matter is right on target. It has been said before, but it bears reassertion given the seemingly ineradicable habit among Americanists of setting Hawthorne and Emerson at opposite poles. Donoghue is probably right in that Henry James's surmise that Hawthorne treated sin aesthetically rather than theologically is closer to the mark than Melville's more famous pronouncement that Hawthorne's imagination was suffused, whether he knew it or not, with a "great power of blackness" that derived "its force from its appeals to that Calvinistic sense of Innate Depravity and Original Sin, from whose visitations, in some shape or other, no deeply thinking mind is always and wholly free."[4] Yet Melville's diagnosis should not, I think, be discounted as mere wish-fulfilling projection.[5] Hawthorne's conception of sin is, at least sometimes, more charged with the sense of radical evil than Donoghue indicates in Chapter 1 when he equates the cases of Dimmesdale, Ethan Brand, and Parson Hooper in "The Minister's Black Veil." Two distinct, though related, Hawthornian ideas get conflated here. When Hawthorne muses in his *American Notebooks* about what an "unpardonable sin" might be, or when a Hawthorne character like Brand is conceived as having possibly committed one, it does has to do not only with secrecy or refusal to confess in public but also and more particularly with cold-blooded violation of or experimentation with another human soul, such as what Roger Chillingworth in *The Scarlet Letter* does to Dimmesdale.[6] Here, too, the "sin" (if indeed "sin" be the proper term—in itself a debatable point, I agree) is conceived as an interpersonal, horizontal offense rather than a vertical offense of cutting oneself off from God or disobedience of a divine commandment. But whether or not one accepts that Hawthorne's so-called unpardonable sin deserves to be dignified by that name, it remains that Hawthorne imbues this kind of offense with much more of a sense of ultimate horror than the self-corrosive social-bond-denying effect of guilty secrecy as such.

Now to turn to Donoghue's reading of "A Father's Story." Surely he is right that this tale imagines its narrator as engaged in conversation with a transcendent God, the terms of his relationship with whom are mediated by theology, church membership, and ritual practice. But the distinction between the father's conversation and, say, Dimmesdale's more hysterical attempt to communicate with the divine in *The Scarlet Letter* are not so clear cut as Donoghue wants to make it out to be. I myself read the story's ending differently, as suspended uneasily between two unappetizing alternatives. Either the father is whistling uneasily in the dark to cover up the emptiness that has overtaken him since his secret has kept him from participating in the rituals in good faith or he has availed himself of the shield of belief to fashion a self-servingly and self-deceivingly one-sided bargain with the almighty to let his conscience off the hook. I am not convinced that Dubus's fictional father is any better off, spiritually speaking, at story's end than Hawthorne's minister is simply because his brand of faith allows him to muddle on with an equipoise that Dimmesdale's faith lacks. Or that Faith with a capital "F" is any less important to Dimmesdale, even if you accept the view (which I share and suppose Donoghue does as well) set forth most eloquently by another Hawthorne critic named Denis that Dimmesdale's conviction of having been saved at the end by his public confession is narratively undercut by his rapturous self-absorption.[7]

Altogether, Donoghue's critique of canonical American literary-religious imagination strikes me as less plausibly complex than the Stanley Hauerwas and Ralph Wood characterization (later in this volume) of "nearly all our great writers" as occupying a continuum of heterodox to atheistic in opposition to what the two scholars call the "Constantinian" mainstream. A more persuasive lumping conclusion on the basis of the texts cited here would be that American literature is and has for centuries been imbued with spiritual striving, even though that striving mostly expresses itself in willfully idiosyncratic forms whose larger public office is to hold up a mirror to the dominant culture's stolid complacencies, whether that culture be religiously to the left (as in the young Emerson), to the center (as in Dubus), to the right (as in different ways for Hawthorne and Melville and Emily Dickinson), or thoroughly secularized (as in Henry James).

Earlier I characterized this chapter as a "counterreformationary" critique of canonical U.S. literary-religious imagination. That was overly simple. Its designs are more farreaching. Its ultimate target is neither lapsed Protestantism as such nor even American high canonical fiction as such but something even bigger than these: the whole legacy of the Romanticist conception of artistic creativity in whatever sense as the privileged arena of the religious, as instanced by the presumptuousness of Coleridge's theory of Primary Imagination. The apotheosis of human imagination is seen as a slippery slope to secularism and with it sooner or later the death of God and the chaos of moral relativism. That in a nutshell I take to be the grand narrative underwriting Donoghue's essay—a narrative of transhemispheric rather than merely national proportions against which figures like Emerson and Hawthorne and Melville and James are weighed and found wanting.

It is a familiar argument, of course, but no less important on that account, and forcefully reexpressed here. It also invites various lines of rebuttal. Hauerwas and Wood suggest one such: for cultures in the grip of a distorted faith, artists who pit themselves against institutionalized religion play potentially crucial roles both as critics and as indices. Another line of argument would be to contest the degree to which both Donoghue, Hauerwas, and Wood tie the category of the religious to particular institutionalized faiths or communities, Catholic, Protestant, or otherwise. Why should not the religious be identified mainly, if not exclusively, with the arenas of moral or spiritual inquiry and practice rather than with theologic belief or church affiliation? Why should not the ethos of leaving religion to each individual's considered private judgment not after all on balance be the best of possible alternatives, that is, the best of all checks, for instance, against imperial zealotry or the policing of the faithful by church authority? If that was good enough for George Washington, Benjamin Franklin, John Adams, and Thomas Jefferson, why not for us?

The more we allow ourselves to entertain such alternatives, the more we disenchant ourselves from the lure of Donoghue's astringency and begin (or begin again) to credit Hawthorne's fictive attempts to find secularized equivalents of the working out of original sin as being legitimate acts of religious imagination and the more the intricate plots of Henry James begin to look like more deeply instructive casuistic meditations than any number of formal tracts.

Yet Donoghue's astringency is not so easily dispensed with today as it might have been a generation ago, if only because it resonates with the broad decline in American literary and intellectual history during the last several decades of the perceived centrality of liberal Protestantism. Donoghue's vision of a postromantic slide into secularism by way of a postreligious artistry that kills religion off even while purporting to serve as its surrogate or successor is likely to appeal more strongly than I believe it should to the increasing number of American literature and history scholars who believe Christianity of the liberal-pluralist sort ceased to be a significant force sometime during the middle third of the twentieth century.

I myself well remember two epiphanic incidents that befell me near the end of that same period, the connection between which took me a long time to work out. One was my encounter with Sydney Ahlstrom's just-published monumental *A Religious History of the American People*, which ends by pronouncing that "a distinct quadricentennium" ended in the 1960s—the decade when the "age of the WASP" "drew to a close," when "the terms 'post-Puritan' and 'post-Protestant' [were] first popularly applied to America."[8] The other incident took place at a party given on my then-campus for visiting novelist John Barth, at which Barth prophesied with an earnestness quite atypical of his own writing (for it is hard to mistake John Barth for Karl Barth) that the next seismic shift in American culture would be a sharp turn to the right—by which he meant conservative values even more than political.

At the time, Ahlstrom's dictum left me with an elegiac but basically contented sense of the inexorable, multiculturalist rebel against old-style prep school and Ivy League monoculture that I was. Barth's, on the other hand, seemed absolutely incredible for precisely the same reason. Only years later did I grasp how both these seemingly incompatible prophecies might be fulfilled, and how I might have been living in a time warp.

Today we are in a different time warp. The revival is in full swing, and the standing of conservative Christianity—Protestant, Catholic, Mormon— is stronger in high places than ever before in national history. Never has there been a period in U.S. history to rival our postbicentennial era, during which every successful presidential candidate has at least made a show of presenting himself as a born-again Christian. The stone so long regarded with contempt by system-building scholars at leading-edge U.S. universities seems to have become the cornerstone. Faced with the seeming impotence of liberal religious pluralism in the public sphere and the striking asymmetry between it and at least the professed theocentrism of Americans at large *versus* the rest of the developed world, it is tempting to overcorrect against the myopia of late twentieth-century academe's "secularization hypothesis" by reading religious liberalism's history as nothing more than a declensionist story of a long-moribund elite, in which pragmatism (for instance) figures as nothing more than politics of culture.

If Donoghue is right, modern Anglophone postreligious imagination broadly and in particular the strongly I-centered Emersonian American wing of it truly are impotent and bankrupt things. But is he right? Even if it looks true now, how will it look a quarter century from now? I myself would rather think that sociologist of religion Robert Wuthnow is right in characterizing present-day Americans—left, center, and right—as predominantly spiritual seekers engaged in individual life pilgrimages that take on resonance, depth, and rigor to the degree that seeking and striving become robust and sustaining in proportion to their being grounded in disciplined spiritual practice, which may or may not involve close allegiance to a sect or creed.[9] If that is true, then the work of Emerson, Hawthorne, and James (both William and Henry) will likely continue to resonate spiritually and aesthetically, at least for the serious educated reader.

Part 2

Religion and American Poetry

3

Variety as Religious Experience

The Poetics of the Plain Style

Elisa New

Open Emily Dickinson's poetic daybooks of 1862–63 to virtually any page and find the same scene—the light altered, a new array of objects standing at the ready—in process. A reversal of hemispheres is under way. The poet, a student of reversal's laws, is breasting the streams and updrafts of a richly currented environment, which the poem fits her to navigate. The transformations find the speaker now liquid, now solid, now diffused in the elements, now given density by their admission. Committed to changes, she uses the poem to make passage from one state to another.

Thus, in #255, she is "The Drop, that wrestles in the Sea" and so "Forgets her own locality." Knowing herself "an incense small," she yet "sighs, if *all*, is *all*, / How *larger*—be?" A distinct drop, atomized in "an incense," occupies a space simultaneously limited and indefinite. The drop's spatial ambiguity evokes a corollary enigma of the emotional life, namely, the power of a sense of insignificance to plumb, then fill, the basin of what is large. The awe that small things feel, that wishful diffidence that releases itself in an exhalation, is uncannily expansive; smallness's sigh gives "an incense" breadth or raises a plangent tide, each individual drop agitating the swell with its turmoil. Or take another poem, "Heaven is so far of the Mind" where the speaker imagines that,

were the Mind dissolved—
The Site—of it—by Architect
Could not again be proved.[1]

The lines intimate the solidity of a Heaven undiscoverable on ordinary blueprints, but more, they also hint at this Heaven's eclectic situation in a zone far "of" the mind." This "of," grammatical cousin to the "an" of "an incense" puts Heaven somewhere between deep in mind and far off from mind: just not, it is clear, among plain ideas. Heaven is not simply a dream we sustain till empirical tests prove it moot. Nor is it a form, a Platonic template, or a realm of "intellectual beauty." Rather, Dickinson passionately surmises a reality which, while not internally confined, is yet guaranteed by internal life. Her poems' repeated conviction is that poetic experience sustains states and opens worlds, whose properties remain inexplicable to all but the delicate instruments and sensitized adepts of this same experience.

The most delicate of these instruments is metaphor, which functions for Dickinson to catch meaning's pulse, and so, by extension, to register the inmost character of things. Following Dickinson's lead, I will be using metaphor in this most general sense to describe a linguistic realm where phenomena discover and catch their truest likenesses by entertaining unlikenesses, the vehicle's contravention of identity key to that identity's truer self-transcendent revelation as mixed structure. Further, I will be proposing that Dickinson's development and advancement of metaphor has, as Emerson would say, a very long American foreground. Her resistance to institutional Christianity very much to the point, Dickinson's understanding of metaphor as just enigmatic enough to indicate the soul resembles no one's more than John Cotton's, for whom the outward signs of grace are always "mixed" or "coupled" and whose own favorite metaphors for the state of grace prefigure Dickinson's own. As it happens, Cotton (himself attracted again and again to conceits of the "drop" in suspension, that is, waterfalls, clouds, and, of course "Christ, the Fountain") found many ways to call the soul "an incense": to aerate grace's fluency, to consolidate faith's buoyancy, but more: to match the figural turns of his own homilies with grace's most ordinary motions. In these terms, Cotton's legendary recanting of a High Church baroque in favor of the so-called plain style will bear a look at close range and not only for what it reveals about Puritan rhetorical scruples but also for what it augurs of the later history of such scruples in American poetry and poetics.

By the end of this chapter, then, I shall have returned us to John Cotton, whose sometimes extravagant understanding of what plainness permitted gave scope and quite serviceable latitude to later American believers in beauty's revelatory power. "Puritan plainness in style," Kenneth Murdock succinctly warned, "did not imply tameness."[2] And if Perry Miller's argument, that plain-stylists relied on the logical method of Peter Ramus to deliver doctrinal truth without embellishment, has not worn well, yet Miller's essential observation, that Puritans suspected "harmony . . . as the lighter part of rhetoric," resisting "likeness of sounds, measures and repetitions" in favor of "similes, metaphors, illustrations and examples," has.[3] Indeed, in Harry Stout's words, Puritan preachers found in "metaphor or 'similitude' all the latent extravagances of the minister's imagination."[4] Beauty's faculty for ringing changes on sameness, for summoning variety out of monotony, will, as I shall show, remain an article of both aesthetic and Christian faith for practitioners of a distinctive American poetics.

Thus I shall work my way back to Cotton by way of two other virtuosos: Jonathan Edwards, America's premier impresario of gravity, buoyancy, and complex beauty, and Edward Taylor, American champion of the mixed metaphor. As I go, I shall be interested especially in testing Andrew Delbanco's rich assertion that for Cotton "to be a Christian is to grasp the essence of metaphor."[5] This claim has, I think, great implications for the study of American poetry and American preaching, suggesting the foreground of that poetic tradition oriented away from apparent (and therefore accessible) and toward more enigmatic (and necessarily less accessible) forms of poetic pleasure. Along the way, my interest in conspicuous forms of beauty will occasion examination of some less glorious moments in metaphor's American career: moments, specifically, when the fullness of grace, an exquisite condition, attenuates itself in more conspicuous convulsions of style. But my focus in the coming pages will be to show where the metaphoric not only describes but also sustains spiritual liveliness.

In the end, I would like to have brought out how, for those committed to it, metaphor functions (as the Puritan saw goes) to keep open that valve between life in, and of, this world. Cleared by the grateful helix of metaphor—tenor and vehicle transfusing revelatory experience back and forth through an aperture of rare situation—the self is stirred out of a stagnancy and made a place of access and movement. Thus, too, Protestant innerness is delivered from self-absorption, and the regimens of the spirit are delivered from mere occultism or priestcraft. From Martin Luther we recall that Grace, while inward, should never be reclusive. The sign of its presence is, indeed, an expressive versatility not context dependent, yet never alone where the Word goes with it: Protestant grace is, we might say, consent dependent. Thus, Cotton insists, grace is outgoing; not even its signs go alone: "but how is it coupled, for God couples every grace with another grace that they may poise one another, as Christ sent out his disciples two and two together; for all the Graces of the spirit join one another."[6]

Dwelling in Possibility: The Coupling of Poetic Graces

"How is it coupled?" is, of course, the enigma motivating Dickinson's own method. In poem after poem, she tracks meaning to its source in "internal difference," a seam of encounter that neither purely external observation nor solely inner intuition detects.[7] There, summer has a "further" as light has a "heft." The torque of the poem, rearranging vectors in the course of its action, reveals all the iridescences that either the removed or the privileged view will occlude. By the 1860s, and by such poems as "I dwell in Possibility," Dickinson simply takes for granted that any spiritual endeavor with half a chance must find its dwelling place not in "prose" but in this mixed zone of "possibility" (#466). Prose, dispatched by the poet to describe, all at once, linguistic univocality, dull perceptual wit, and religious literalism, will prove inadequate to discern the many mansions within the Father's house. Poetry, on the other hand, discovers planes, divines proportions that, while manifold, are not—and this is crucial—simply many. The poem manages a dense internal complication of the many in the one but without exiling that complication in merely mimetic or repetitive excrescency. If, as Kierkegaard showed, the common symptom of poetic superfluity and spiritual deadness is a willed and meaningless repetition, which confirms rather than relieves atrophy of structure, Dickinson develops a complexity free of repetition where, for instance, degree is an internal dynamic of structure itself rather than an anxious mimetic chafing of structure's fixed extremities. Under this degree's auspices, even the most extravagant predicates of possibility may escape hyperbole and language itself maintains that fidelity to function Puritans called plain. For instance, "numerous" and "superior" in "I dwell in Possibility" do not impound or engross merit but rather recognize, admit, and give play to its many shades. Like marvelous hinges, "numerous" and "superior" open the poem to fresh and fresher drafts, that is, to full, partial, and still invisible planes of implication. This is why in this poem we see, or think we see, all at the same time Pentateuchal tabernacle, Solomonic Temple, and City of God. This is why the mansions of possibility are not ranked as to genre. The Kingdom of Revelation by other lights, after all, is just a castle in the air. By still others, half-up, its open portals admit even homelier scents: cedar chest, sawdust, beams; the smell of changing weather. Frontier, the poem reminds, is one of our words for possibility.

Such connotative impasto might be heavy, to be sure, but for the sheerness of each element, so that an evanescence of image prevents the poem's surface from that overelaborated obscurity Moore had in mind when she reviled sophistication for its way of muddying "prismatic color." Prevents it too, from that certain decadence Crane had in mind when he made Poe, to whom I shall return, fallen prince of the Underworld, and not so much for his Gothic themes as for an actually grislier trespass for a poet—that is, love of the dead letter, love of effects. In Dickinson's poem, though, the images here lie translucent on each other or simultaneous with one another; or, they prefigure and recall one another, each the penumbral hint or echo of the other, contrapuntal ciphers of a less visible, still unrealized, but eagerly expected order of being. The temporal dimension is as crucial as the spatial dimension, since the images we see seem to depend on are an eccentric temporality of possibility that retains the affective tones and halftones of life in time—eagerness, anticipation, anticlimax, giddiness, tedium, regularity—but dispenses with its workaday divisions—past, present, future (it happened then, it is happening now, etc.). Further, as time is pressed in this poem for its elixir of feeling (not the increments of sequence but the pangs that seam or "rivet" such sequence together), tones, too, will disclose many faces, the least telling of which, the emptiest, will be the self-evident.[8] We know from other poems that monochromatics of tone belong to very dull personages, to those "somebodies" who evict the more vital nobody ("I'm Nobody! Who are you?" [#260]). The croak of self-declaration, of identity, proves beyond doubt a usurpation, a frog installed in a nobody's place to service the tone deaf.

Tones mixed in a suspension, on the other hand, indicate the happy disappearance of this doughty personage behind one whose glimmering coexistences leave her no adequate moniker. Thus, the tonal complexity of "I dwell in possibility" is compounded, alchemized, out of lesser moods, greedier selves, now relieved of assertion and mass. The final lines, in which the speaker "spread[s] wide [her] narrow hands / to Gather paradise," hint at these less subtle somebodies—the social pugilist or queenly diva of circumference who "sneered softly" at lesser transports. Or, she of nebulous outline and existential emergency, she whose terror of empty space and various "columnar selves" forestalled. These confute each other. The poem's final pose, relieving any vacancy of self, transfigures antinomian overassertion as well. This self neither incorporates nor, in Myra Jehlen's terms, incarnates.[9] It knows overrealization, literalization, for the surest way to run afoul of meaning and strand expectation, like the prince, in green warts in a "bog." Rather, by means of a certain subtle process that metaphor enables—a poise in space, of time, by mood—she who gathers wide her narrow hands is graced with openness and fullness both.

Or, and here I make my turn, perhaps this poem is not simply graced with fullness (a pleasant but honorific condition) but full of grace. What I have been pointing to in such detail are the near and further ranges of a state which Dickinson's most accomplished lyrics labor to achieve and the poetic tools she deploys in achieving it. What I want now to explicate is the rather advanced stage of development to which such tools were already brought by Dickinson's precursors, and thus the gestalt of a certain kind of religious experience, the pursuit and cultivation of which necessarily imbued Calvinist rigor with distinctly aesthetic, specifically poetic, kinds of sense.

This rigor, you will have surmised me to be contending, runs counter to certain still quite live assumptions about the Protestant subject. But the significance of an internality not equivalent to solid self-presence (or identity) cannot really be overstressed, since it is not yet generally recognized just how normative for early American Christians were stipulations to grace's ductile and even eclectic character. Our attention to purities and identities still defers notice of the more recondite discourses springing up not around selves, or even subjects, but around souls.

Unlike the self, this soul has, in place of identity, a knack for what Edwards calls consent, which is to say a gift for living doubly, contrapuntally, responsively, or, to invoke a favorite Protestant figure for this adjustment, musically. The graced soul is that gifted with talents for modulation and transposition; in place of an identity it has—and I want to use this word spatially and musically—*range*. While selves seek selves, disporting themselves in such binary choreographies that give identity center and ballast, souls, on the other hand, sing, but as they sing, they also fly, both the singing and the flying—and here is the hard part—more like the other activity than like life itself. Souls are characterized by their variety and not their self-presence. Indeed, as I shall show, music that confines itself to mere singing exiles itself in its most obvious talent, like Dickinson's frog in its bog. Music, however, that transposes chords in flight, as flight finds tempo in it, achieves diviner scale. Such music ranges in possibility.

This capacity for transposition is the salient virtue, for instance, that Jonathan Edwards finds to praise in his love letter and saint's portrait of Sarah Pierpont:

> They say there is a young lady in [New Haven] who is beloved of that almighty Being, who made and rules the world, and that there are certain seasons in which this Great Being, in some way or other invisible, comes to her and fills her mind with exceeding sweet delight, and that she hardly cares for anything, except to meditate on him—that she expects after a while to be received up where he is, to be raised up out of the world and caught up into heaven; being assured that he loves her too well to let her

remain at a distance from him always. . . . She will sometimes go about from place to place, singing sweetly; and seems to be always full of joy and pleasure; and no one knows for what. She loves to be alone, and to wander in the fields and on the mountains, and seems to have someone invisible always conversing with her.[10]

Sarah is a person whose habit of singing is here adduced to exemplify a spiritual reciprocity of inner turns and outer forms, not to be confused with mere grace of carriage nor with the admirable but finally one-dimensional accomplishments of the Proverbial woman of valor. Self-possessed but in constant converse; living in sacred space while among local hills; eager for, but not impatient of God's visitations; expressive but impressed, open and mysterious, Sarah Pierpont's excellency recalls that of the traditional Eshet Chayil (woman of valor) but with this difference. While Proverbs catalogues virtues and enumerates competencies, Edwards stresses not discrete acts or observances but the effortless choreography undergirding Sarah's usual round; her external movements are what Protestants deem the effects rather than the satisfying conditions of her justification. Her characteristically weightless bearing is but the visible face of her soul's multifacets. A model for what Edwards will identify as true virtue, Sarah walks in variety.

Later on in Edwards's career, it is precisely the lack of such variety that finds out the sinner. In "Sinners in the Hands of an Angry God," of course, it is the sinner's inert and pedestrian identity with himself and his therefore base and cautious clinging to the clay—to a known and visible plane—that will suggest his ultimate fate. While Sarah Pierpont moves "from place to place," her true and only home being a state of reciprocity, the sinner plays no part in the world's motions but to be vulnerable to them. Dead already, the fallen self is encumbered by an inner density and obscurity, a dark architecture that parodies Sarah Pierpont's fullness with weight and burlesques her spiritual vitality with jumpy reflexes. Selves, "engrossed by finity," in Dickinson's Edwardsean phrase, contain nothing but themselves; limited to self-love, they are greedy for themselves. But that lightness Sarah Pierpont enjoys, as Dickinson herself will testify, needs hold or hoard nothing. As Dickinson writes,

I take—no less than skies—
For Earths, grow thick as
Berries, in my native Town—

My Basket holds—just—Firmaments—
Those—dangle easy—on my arm,
But smaller bundles—Cram. (#358)

Edwards's identification of beauty with attraction and of the spiritual life as buoyant movement between disparate realms will later inform his work on both the conceptual and rhetorical levels. Edwards always assumes that relation is the stamp on excellence and that truth is a drawing together. Echoing Cotton on the coupling of graces, he writes, "one alone cannot be excellent . . . for in such a case there can be no matter of relation." Such a conviction will make it singularly satisfying to the young Edwards that it takes red and violet, the two poles of the spectrum, to make white. One great attraction in Edwards, for those who discover it, is his relish for lighting on the deeper logic behind the Creator's often counterintuitive moves. Edwards's oeuvre abounds in tensely sprung expositions, surprising bridgings, and daring landings. With considerable derring-do, he balances gravity on thin air; he finds freedom's scope within foreknowledge; he discovers Christianity's simplest axiom in Newton's Principia. Edwards shows how the God who expresses himself in complex mixtures would naturally mix his scientific and his sacred law, would naturally make the Fall feel like falling. Meanwhile, as such unlikely conceptual marriages are forged at every juncture of Edwards's work, rhetorically too, he likes to work in a variety of idioms, each governed by the law of consenting opposites. For example, in such speculative essays as "Of Being," awe must accommodate empiricist rigor and vice versa; the contemplation of nothingness, an exercise requiring that "we expel body from our thoughts" leads to where "the sleeping rocks dream." It is as if Locke and Augustine stood before one adamantine object, a metaphor mind will not penetrate because it is made of mind itself.[11] Just so, in his works of intellectual disputation, the particularity and partiality of doctrinal conviction is in a constant pas de deux with the urbanity of the international and "common sense." In his homiletics, uncanny pairings of scripture and science, colloquial directness and learned allusion spin like plates on either intellectual hand. Using multiple faculties at once, Edwards demonstrates, even as he entreats, grace's ambidextrousness.

All of these reciprocities and more are predicted in Edwards's portrait of Sarah Pierpont, whose gift is for living largely but without being large. Finally, Sarah's lightsome singing is a sign of her identity's and subjectivity's release into, and commerce with, that more diffuse and diverse environment that, here as elsewhere, is deemed God's true climate. If one effect of the Fall, as Edwards understood it, was to bifurcate and encrypt Being in temporal and spatial geologies (iron-edged, like Moore's cliffs), he lofts his saint in a more permeable region without fault lines or precipices. There, her sanctification, her outer carriage, was never misaligned with her inner justification.

Sarah has what no sinner enjoys—that elation Marianne Moore calls happiness, which she tends only to bestow on animals and baseball pitchers, but which we might as well call fun.

It should not surprise us at all that Edwards goes in, and goes in big, for such fun. His own intellectual barnstorming suggests as much, but fun is also an unmistakable aspect, and indeed persuasive evidence of a saint's justification, for Edward Taylor. Taylor, you may remember, had devoted the "Preface" of *God's Determinations* to postulating fun on a divine scale, conjuring for us just what precision of timing, just what gladness of touch was enjoyed by that Creator who fashioned a world and called it "good." By the end of the sequence, in "The Joy of Church Fellowship Rightly Attended," Taylor can report that similar pleasures now flow to the Elect: "For in Christ's Coach they sweetly sing / As they to Glory ride therein." Note that Taylor's visible saints do not just fly or strum, let forth carols or wing through clouds in a coach. Rather, as recorded by a poetic informant with, by the way, similarly excellent timing—"In Heáven soáring úp / I drópped an Eár"—they finesse both, reposing on melody, caroling buoyancy, their interior scansion exactly adjusted to the external situation. The lines that transport the saints are sprightly and ever so slightly softened with a certain mirth, yet the saints celebrated in them are no more lightweights than Sarah Pierpont. If their ease and mastery of the divine refrain is now more play than regimen, once they had not known their own strength. As Adam's progeny they *had* to have been exercised by the work of knowing. The enjoyment of grace accruing to the elect is not, in Taylor's version, relaxation but a kind of fruition or expanded range; heavenly assurance feels like know-how, like being in form, like literacy, though a literacy transcending mere mastery of the letter. Indeed, as the text sharing, or even perhaps informing, the rhetorical figures of "The Joy of Church Fellowship" reminds, the saint's soaring is like the moment, hard to isolate, when a child fully comprehends his primer text. He need not make out the letters or the words any longer; reading raises him up, carrying him and the whole alphabet away. So the Word carries mere words into the wild blue yonder, and the spirit levitates its observances. Why else would the *New England Primer* designate that the reward for spiritual literacy is a riding in style through limpid blue: "He that learns his letters fair / Shall have a coach to take the air."

American Form and the Poetics of Flight

Now, I am aware at this point that there is perhaps no Christian figure more discredited, or even ridiculous, than the figure of the airborne soul with its zither. But I hope you will bear with me nonetheless, since the persistence of the figure, as well as its devolution into cliché, has much to tell us about the persistence and appeal of a certain kind of Christian pleasure and about the history and development of a poetic ideal informed by it. This ideal honors not the metaphor itself (not, to invoke the Calvinist analogue, visible carriage) but its kinetics on loan to "the figure the poem makes." This ideal honors not meter but, as in the even more influential though enigmatic formulation, the "argument" meter makes. In Frost and Emerson, whom I just quoted, the emphasis is on a making, a mixing, or, as Cotton's terms, a "turning," that is, I have been intimating, latent in and deeded by Edwards and Taylor. Flying and singing, images of a proficient poise depend for their lift on an updraft that is not internal to, satisfied by, the figure but rather dwelling just inside, filling the sheets of, its ductility. As a form virtue takes, it is airborne; as virtue's sufficient form, it is heavy as lead.

In other words, what the flying singer provides, as Emerson might say, is the meter in which a necessarily protean virtue can make its argument. The singer is an expediency, a cipher even for virtue's triumphant ascent to a manner of being not just in, but of, time and space. Such emphasis on making will necessarily enforce circumspection as to the value of the made thing, deferring and devaluing "works" or the more meretricious realizations of style. At the same time, though, it will lift constraints on figural extravagance, elevating genre and bestowing the prestige of Bezalel on refinements of craft. Thus, Edward fashions his piece on Sarah Pierpont as a virtuoso piece, an aria or motet unabashedly elaborated in baroque detail. More formalized than a love letter, more lyrical than any theological explication, Edwards's highly stylized saint's portrait assumes that the godliness in Sarah is well served by deliberate art and that the God who made her is glorified also through the arduous discipline of the creative act. Though working in a different, homelier genre, Taylor does the same. He allows the sing-song and the charm of his refrain to coax a certain indulgence, or imaginative suspension of disbelief, requisite for full appreciation of the saint's joy (for "in Christ's Coach they sweetly sing," etc.). Taking the fabulist's latitude, Taylor bids us "come too," bids us treat ourselves. In both cases, the deployment of a particular highly stylized figure as mnemonic for grace holds literal investment in the figure at bay. Edwards's gliding saintly Sarah and Taylor's merry flying saints are effects, somewhat surprising effects, of virtue's dynamics; their graceful conduct is the result of what is conducted through them. The picture of harmony they happen to exhibit does not satisfy or resolve but rather simply betokens the force and grace of argument.

When the argument fails, to be sure, there is little to prevent the strumming seraph from lapsing into the worst kind of cliché. Such lapses are common, even among the most angelic poets. Dickinson's little tippler, for instance, swings very close indeed to kitsch; and Dickinson has, we might as well admit, a weakness for the stanza tuned to migrainal intensity. At times negligent of relation, Dickinson is not above pillaging an adjacent stanza for some rare figure and then leaving it half-developed, not felicitously "mixed" in Cotton's sense, but just abandoned to congeal in its own medium. Then, Dickinson's technique can descend to so much china painting, and her uncanny spatial effects seem merely grandiose, given what they house. There is little at such moments to distinguish Dickinson's heaven, a musicale with lanterns, from Huck Finn's same, where Miss Watson and the Widow Douglas hover and bob on the mauve and gold. However, when this does happen, what has gone wrong is telling: the effects of metaphor have overcharged and finally cauterized metaphor's life principle of relation. What remains is a stylistic or representational residue, that is, a self-perpetuating extent of mimetic half-life parodying the more vital life it affects to maintain. What remains is sanctification without justification or, in poetic terms, language attenuated in effects.

Such effects were, we might surmise, what Crane must have had in mind in "The Tunnel" when he used the images of "hair beyond extinction" and of "verdigris," the green mold on copper, to introduce Poe's language of luxurious but moribund extent. Mourning the modern dissection of language from its source in soul and following poetry's literal descent to the merely vehicular, Crane lets Poe punch tickets on poetry's last run to Gravesend. "Why do I often meet your visage here? / Your eyes like agate lanterns—on and on." These "eyes" deflect a light they do not see. They simulate quickness while they are, in fact, stone. There is, indeed, nothing behind the pupil's agate but the artful and potentially damned hand that fashioned them, as not incidentally, Poe himself had fashioned his agate-eyed mascot, Psyche, by smelting hell, Helen and Hellenism, three bewitching vehicles to one phantom, absent tenor—no there there; no meeting on a seam of encounter. Synthesizer of beauty out of classical junk, Poe functions in "The Tunnel" as one of his own effects, his human visage frozen in a rictus signifying oversignification. And what Crane sees and telescopes so brilliantly in this horrified but resolute internment of Poe with his poetics is that in, say, "The Bells," nothing changes, even though in stanza one we hear the "silver bells" that "tinkle, tinkle, tinkle"; in stanza two we hear the "mellow wedding bells" that "swell" and "dwell"; in stanza three we hear the "loud alarum bells" that "clang, and clash, and roar"; and in stanza four we hear the iron bells that "toll" and "roll." Each set of sonorities remains within its own geometry or ellipse. Each strikes the fixed set of variations in its complement of tones, heard by a hearing not likely to be changed by bells because identical with them:

> And the people—ah, the people—
> They that dwell up in the steeple,
>   All alone,
> And who, tolling, tolling, tolling,
>   In that muffled monotone,
> Feel a glory in so rolling
>   On the human heart a stone—

It is no more than poetic justice that Crane should reduce Poe's head to a prosthesis of the strap it hangs on. Poe's people do not just live "in" the steeple, rather they are *of* the steeple, clappers to sound's fuller body.

Grace and the Poise of Metaphor

Poe's style is so revealing, because it conspicuously skips the track running from Cotton through Edwards, Dickinson through Frost and Crane; it reminds us of how much these poetries actually may borrow from, and how consistent are they with, that dialectical (as opposed to rhetorical) ethos so concerned to be plain.

For what I have been describing here with Poe is an essentially rhetorical aesthetics, an aesthetics of linguistic effects that the poetics of the plain style—the poetics eventually asserted as *the* American poetics by Emerson—not only resisted but refused. "Give me truths / For I am weary of the surfaces, / And die of inanition," wrote Emerson in "Blight." And again, in "Merlin I": "The trivial harp will never please / Or fill my craving ear." And again in "Ode" where Emerson implicates his own "honied thought" along with "the priest's cant / Or statesman's rant." These are only a few instances, of course, of what those familiar with Emerson's verse will recognize, as nearly every well-known poem of Emerson's is, or contains, an animadversion against poetry. Poetry assertive of surface but with plugged up ducts, poetry shut in unity at the price of variety, poetry reaching prehensile but empty inside: all such poetry, lacking Spirit, is, as Teresa Toulouse puts it "dead formal performance."[12] Let me move toward my conclusion by suggesting that these steeple dwellers, confirming the existence of a world without inner life, are Emerson's souls, as Emerson's are heirs to those John Cotton bore in mind, grieving, when in "Christ, the Fountain of Life," he devoted twelve sermons to parsing 1 John: 5:12, "He that hath the Son, hath life; and he that hath not the Son of God, hath not life." Cotton's unjustified souls maintain an uncanny adjacency with life, not a relationship but the more mechanical dependency and contiguity of reaction to action. Like Poe's people of the steeple, Cotton's soul that "hath not life" may be, he writes, likened to a thing that "may move in its place, and yet move from some kind of outward respects; as a Watch, or a Clock it moves, but it is from the weight that lyes and hangs upon it, and so it is rather a violent motion than a natural." Such juxtaposition of Poe's poetics and Cotton's homiletics telescopes all that is actually at stake in debates on style, plain and ornate, and all that may later have given such ethical urgency to the development of various American poetics.

Metaphor is not only the favored device of Cotton's plain style; it is also, according to necessary tautology of Cotton's affectionate creed, that style's chief object. For Cotton, the graced soul is a soul adept at mixings and meltings, the soul habitually acting against its own identity or integrity. Grace works on soul as metaphoric vehicle works on tenor, orienting it toward its truer—which not to say, its most *integral* but rather its most responsive and in some ways dis-integral—bearing.[13] To cite just one of Cotton's many formulations of this process: "love, which was as heat and fire to thaw and warm, cold and hard hearts, it is as it were, cold water, which allays that heat and bitterness and harshness, which else our hearts are subject to. . . . It both thaws our cold and still hearts towards our brethren, and also puts a watery temper to cool our wrath toward our enemies; it is a mighty power of the Spirit of Grace to turn itself so many ways."[14]

The turning, grace's primary faculty for Cotton, is, of course, another name for metaphor. As we all know, trope means turn. Just so, in Cotton, grace's infusion rhetorizes the self and gives it torsion and flex, so that phenomena strictly inner or outer, spiritual or earthly, are pressed until their tough husks loosen and dissolve and identity gives itself up. If for Poe the technical grace of the poem functioned in essence to make things more and more themselves, Cotton's grace knows identity for its nemesis.

Let me, in closing, offer a brief reading of the passage from Cotton that first sparked my own interest in this subject and that sums up all that I have been suggesting in the previous pages. "This is a combination of graces," Cotton wrote,

that are not wont to be found in men thus mixed together, but it is found
in the people of God, that live a sanctified and holy life. I know not better
what to instance it, than in the liquid air, of all other things the most easiest
to be pierced through. Of itself it gives way to every creature, nor the least
fly, or least stone cast into it, but it gives way to it of itself, yet if God say
it shall be as a firmament between the waters above and the waters below, it
then stands like a wall of brass, and yields not. It will not suffer the water
in the clouds to fall down, but if it do fall to water the earth, it shall strain
through the air as through a sieve. The clouds sometimes are so full that one
would think they would burst through the air and fall upon the earth, but
God having set the air to be a firmament or expulsion between the waters
above and waters below, though of itself a very liquid thing, yet it stands like
to a wall of brass. And truly so it is with a Christian spirit.[15]

Cotton's explicit aim is to explicate Moses's kind of holiness, a holiness
capable of great strength but a strength more elemental than apparent. Like
the weather, which later supplies Taylor, Edwards, and Dickinson—not to
mention Emerson, Frost, and Stevens—with some of their own most fer-
tile figures, Cotton's Moses channels a force not mistakable for authority;
he has currency rather than identity, a capacity for flow and turn realizing
Creation's (and Christianity's) own idiom. Indeed, Moses's virtue is appropriately expressed in language mingling Genesis and John, two sources of his
liveliness. Moses's conservancy with fluid, vapor, gravity, and ground tutors
his ready acceptance of other forms; if Genesis flows through him as a force
of creative dynamism lifted above chaos, it is John that specifies the shape this
dynamism will take. And so Cotton's Moses is himself a range of possibility,
a cloud bursting with latency, a live acoustic primed to vibrate with Christ,
the Fountain's, gush of sound.

Finally, Cotton's Moses is made by and of metaphor; his outward carriage is the meter in which God makes argument. Cosmetic sanctification
and baroque embellishment—doppelgangers in the theological and rhetorical realms—will ultimately expose and discredit one another. Grace and
metaphor, committed to mutual recognizance, will, in John Cotton's words,
"poise one another." In Cotton's homiletics, as in later American poetics,
the test of grace is not unity but the variety that gives life to religious, as to
aesthetic, experience.

4

Keeping the Metaphors Alive

American Poetry and Transformation

Barbara Packer

Every lover of literature will remember Emerson's warnings to readers in "The American Scholar": "one must be an inventor to read well," and "the discerning will read in his Plato or Shakespeare only that least part,—only the authentic insights of the oracle,—and all the rest he rejects, were it never so many times Plato's or Shakespeare's." But how does one determine which parts of a great author are authentic? Easy: they are the ones that kindle one's own thoughts and bring them to expression. In the Arabian proverb Emerson quotes: "A fig tree, looking on a fig tree, becometh fruitful."[1] Armed with this principle of selection, I can search through the paragraphs of Elisa New's meditation on classic New England literature to reach the ones that are, for me, authentic and that make figs sprout again on branches the winter had left bare.

The first such sentences stood out at me in the preface New provided to her symposium presentation. In the course of discussing Emily Dickinson's poem, "There's a certain slant of light," she observed: "Meaning, in this poem by Dickinson, instructs shallow expectancy how to take in, how to internalize, patience before obscurity. . . . It reminds revelation that its origin is mystery." This seems to me profoundly true, not only of Dickinson but also of much American literature. Our professional habit as elucidators of obscure texts is so deeply ingrained that we habitually try to beam light into darkness without bothering to ask ourselves whether that was the fate the authors wanted. There is plenty of evidence that they did *not*. Emerson reminds us in "Poetry and Imagination" that "God himself does not speak prose, but communicates with us by hints, omens, inference and dark resemblances in objects lying all around us."[2] Thoreau asserts in *Walden*, "it is a ridiculous demand which

England and America make, that you shall speak so that they can understand you. Neither men nor toad-stools grow so."[3] And in the closing lines of *Song of Myself* Whitman promises that he will serve as a kind of dialysis machine for us without engaging the understanding at all:

> You will hardly know who I am or what I mean,
> But I shall be good health to you nevertheless,
> And filter and fibre your blood.[4]

The baffles Dickinson sets up to understanding are different only in degree, not in kind, from the projects of her contemporaries. All were in flight from what they saw as the shallowness of Enlightenment thought and literary styles; all wanted to recover the richness of earlier writers without giving up their hospitality to universal religion or to progressive thought. This made them, as New said in an earlier draft of her chapter, "scornful of the apparent, and committed rather to recessive, diffuse, and even obscure species of meaning." It also left them open to attacks from the conservatives—the old, eighteenth-century liberals, that is—that they were flatulent rather than inspired, occluded rather than deep, and that their obscurantism risked opening the door once again to the superstitions their fathers and grandfathers had with such courage driven out of the Commonwealth in the era of its birth.

Was there any way of deciding who was right? One litmus test proposed by the writers themselves lay in the study of a writer's metaphors. Trite metaphors suggest a mind that is either unoriginal or servile; arresting minds offer hope that the writer perceives the analogies inscribed by the First Cause on nature. "Picturesque language," Emerson argues in *Nature*, "is at once a commanding certificate that he who employs it, is a man in alliance with truth and God." And he goes on, in a passage we know from the journals to describe his own methods of composition: "A man conversing in earnest, if he watch his intellectual processes, will find that a material image, more or less luminous, arises in his mind, cotemporaneous with every thought, which furnishes the vestment of the thought. . . . This imagery is spontaneous. It is the blending of experience with the present action of the mind. It is proper creation. It is the working of the Original Cause through the instruments he has already made."[5] The problem is, as Emerson later discovered, that while the process of originating metaphors might be spontaneous, even good metaphors tended to become worn out through use. The poet needed to acquire what he called, in "Poetry and Imagination," "the habit of saliency, of not pausing but going on." And poetry itself is the effort "to see that the object is always flowing away, whilst the spirit or necessity which causes it subsists. Its essential mark is that it betrays in every word instant activity of mind, shown in new uses of every fact and image, in preternatural quickness or perception of relations." Our delight in metaphor is metaphysical to the core:

> For the value of a trope is that the hearer is one: and indeed Nature itself is a vast trope, and all particular natures are tropes. As the bird alights on the bough, then plunges into the air again, so the thoughts of God pause but for a moment in any form. All thinking is analogizing, and it is the use of life to learn metonymy. The endless passing of one element into new forms, the incessant metamorphosis, explains the rank which the imagination holds in our catalogue of mental powers. The imagination is the reader of these forms.[6]

The problem with even the best metaphors is that they tend to degenerate into clichés, which is why Emerson recommends metonymy—that is, the trope of association, not of likeness—as a way out of metaphor's petrifying powers. He thought that religious traditions were metaphors that had petrified in this way, and in the Divinity School Address he traced the bloody history of Christian theology to the fatal literal-mindedness that always seems to dog a prophet's inspired tropes. Jesus said "I am Divine," speaking in metaphors, but the next age said: "This was Jehovah come down out of heaven. I will kill you, if you say he was a man."[7]

Must it be so? Will the inspired poet always be turned into currency or made an excuse for bigotry, unless, like Shakespeare, he is content to turn his immense genius only into entertainment? Elisa New does not think so; she wishes to identify a tradition in American literature in which, as she puts it, "metaphor functions (as the Puritan saw goes) to keep open that valve between life in, and of, this world. Cleared by the grateful helix of metaphor—tenor and vehicle transfusing revelatory experience back and forth through an aperture of rare situation—the self is stirred out of a stagnancy and made a place of access and movement. Thus, too, Protestant innerness is delivered from self-absorption, and the regimens of the spirit are delivered from mere occultism or priestcraft." Evidently New shares Emerson's fears about the connection between petrified metaphors and bigotry. But how, exactly, is this transformation to be made? What keeps metaphor alive? What keeps it from becoming the "willed and meaningless repetition" that Kierkegaard and New have identified with spiritual deadness?

Part 3

LITERATURE, RELIGION, AND THE AFRICAN AMERICAN EXPERIENCE

5

Genres of Redemption

African Americans, the Bible, and Slavery from Lemuel Haynes to Frederick Douglass

Mark A. Noll

The very first published work from an African American was a long poem by a slave from Long Island, Jupiter Hammon. It appeared in 1760 and was entitled, "An Evening Thought: Salvation by Christ, with Penitential Cries." The very first stanza of this very first published work featured themes, vocabulary, and a fixation on the Bible that remained central to much African American literature from the period of the Civil War and beyond:

> Salvation comes by Jesus Christ alone,
> The only Son of God;
> Redemption now to every one,
> That loves his holy Word.[1]

Hammon's intense focus on the drama of Christian salvation marked out in miniature what would be developed at considerable length and with great variety by other African Americans in the decades that followed. In particular, his linking of the term "redemption" with the message of Scripture as God's "holy word" set out an ambitious agenda. In the mid-eighteenth century, the force of the word "redemption" still depended, as it had in its first-century usage with the Apostle Paul (e.g., Romans 3:24; Colossians 1:14), on the metaphorical application of a physical reality describing human bondage to a spiritual reality describing human salvation. In the context of the Atlantic slave trade, it was a continual struggle to secure the privileges of Christian redemption for African Americans. In the context of majority population biblical interpretation, it was almost as great a struggle for African Americans to "redeem" the Bible. Through developments that look suspiciously like divine intervention, African Americans in this era of black chattel slavery did experience Christian redemption. Then, even as the struggle for redemption from slavery went on, they themselves somehow found the energy to set about the task of redeeming the Scriptures as well. [2]

Slavery and Scripture in Antebellum America

African American Bible believers in the decades between the Revolution and the Civil War faced an unusually vigorous challenge as they brought newfound Christian faith to bear on the realities of American life. The great national confusion that bore down upon African Americans with special weight was once well described by David Brion Davis: "In the United States . . . the problem of slavery . . . had become fatally intertwined with the problem of race. Race had become the favored idiom for interpreting the social effects of enslavement and emancipation."[3] Quite apart from its devastating impact in the domains of economics and politics, the confusion spotlighted by Davis between race and slavery profoundly affected Christian interpretations of Scripture during the first decades of nationhood. A steady stream of published writings on the Bible and American slavery, which began in the eighteenth century, became from the early 1830s onward a great flood of works.[4] Authors of nearly every denominational stripe labored diligently to interpret the many scriptural passages that seemed simply to take slavery for granted as a natural part of ancient societies. By contrast, far less attention was devoted to what the Bible affirmed, also in many passages, about the equality of all races and peoples before God. As a consequence, by the time of the Civil War, the weight of American biblical interpretation was clearly tipping in favor of slavery as a biblical institution despite some serious opposition to that conclusion and even more uneasiness about the black-only form of chattel slavery that was practiced in the United States.

An indication of where this debate stood on the eve of sectional conflict is provided in two sermons preached by prominent religious leaders *in the North* that were unusual in their thoroughness but typical in their conclusions. For a fast day sermon in early January 1861, Rabbi Morris J. Raphall of New York City painstakingly examined the many passages in the Hebrew Scriptures that recorded the practice of slavery by Abraham and other leaders of God's covenant people. A month before, the Presbyterian Henry Van Dyke, also of New York, did the same with the many New Testament passages that simply accepted Roman slavery as an incontestable fact of life. The conclusions drawn by the Jewish rabbi and the Presbyterian minister spoke for a wide swath of American opinion. To Van Dyke, it was obvious that the "tree of Abolitionism is evil, and only evil—root and branch, flower and leaf, and fruit; that it springs from, and is nourished by, an utter rejection of the Scriptures." [5] For his part, Rabbi Raphall could only ask at the end of his exegetical labors, "Is slaveholding condemned as a sin in sacred Scripture? . . . How this question can at all arise in the mind of any man that has received a religious education, and is acquainted with the history of the Bible, is a phenomenon I cannot explain to myself."[6]

African American Bible believers who faced an interpretive landscape in which sober expositors like Raphall and Van Dyke came to such conclusions, despite their own sympathy for enslaved populations, were in a double bind. On the one hand, they could see more clearly than any of their peers that studying what the Bible had to say about slavery could never illuminate the American dilemma unless the Bible was also studied for what it had to say about race. On the other hand, because of the racist character of American public life, including prejudices about which writings had to be noticed and which could be safely ignored, the considerable writing that African Americans produced on the Bible and slavery received almost no general attention.

To oversimplify the fate of a broad mix of African American publications on the subject, black Americans regularly found conclusive messages in Scripture about the need for fair treatment of all humans under God. But these messages were regularly drowned out by the hubbub of white Americans laboring to interpret the Bible on the narrow question of whether the forms of slavery found in the Bible could justify the fact of slavery in the United States.

The simple point of this chapter is to suggest that a broad range of African American literature, expressed in a multitude of genres, did arise during the first ninety years of United States history to challenge proslavery interpretations of the Bible. Even if not too many whites took note, this literature possessed an unusual depth and appeared in an unusual breadth of form.

The history of African American biblical commentary on slavery was as old as the nation itself. Considering the circumstances, where opportunities for both education and church leadership were limited, it was also a history rich in specific theological argument. The pervasive Biblicism of black spirituals and black preaching provides solid evidence for how deeply Scripture had entered into African American consciousness. The record is equally clear from written sources. For example, the *Christian Recorder*, a weekly paper of the African Methodist Episcopal Church that began publication in the mid-1850s, was as evangelically Scripture-saturated as any comparable periodical in the English-speaking world. Without exception, each issue showered readers with the Scriptures: Bible-based homilies, injunctions to piety from Scripture, reports on Bible distribution at home and abroad, and frequent articles directly supporting the supernatural character and divine authority of the sacred text. Among countless instances was the issue of April 13, 1861, where on the same page the editors turned to "the Holy Word of God" to take the measure of "The Present Crisis" and also defended Scripture as the "Doctrinal Basis of Christianity" by saying that "errors of faith always lead to errors of life . . . unbelief in the doctrines of the Bible will sooner or later lead to a rejection of Christianity."[7] In fact, so securely did the Bible become *the* book for black Americans that in the years before the Civil War there seems to have been a diminishing need to rehearse explicit arguments from the Bible against slavery.

Yet if African Americans ever felt the need for arguments to match the learned exegetes who found sanction for slavery in the Bible, those arguments were ready at hand. From even before the turn of the nineteenth century, black ministers and lay Bible readers carefully challenged biblical interpretations that were held to legitimate slavery in its American forms and also developed extensive counterreadings of Scripture. The strength of those arguments is indicated by the fact that they were found in memoirs, treatises, sermons, manifestoes, and dialogues.[8]

Genres, Scripture, and the Challenge to Slavery

Memoirs

Effective engagement with the Bible was a main feature of the memoirs that many African Americans offered to the world. In that engagement, black Americans were following where a black Briton had led. The publication in 1789 of *The Interesting Narrative of the Life of Olaudah Equiano, or Gustavus Vassa, the African. Written by Himself* set a general standard but also provided particular guidance for much later use of the Bible. At a critical turning point in his own narrative, Equiano told how "the only comfort I then experienced was in reading holy scriptures." Although he did not develop extensive anti-slave arguments based on the Bible, when Equiano did argue against the slave trade, his description of "our common [human] nature" evoked biblical views of the world, and his praise of Granville Sharp, Thomas Clarkson, and James Ramsay, who had only shortly before emerged as leaders of the British anti-slave movement, took the form of quotations from Scripture.[9]

In most memoirs that followed in Equiano's train, Scripture remained more important for personal religious development than for explicit attacks on slavery. Frederick Douglass's *Narrative* from 1845 described his own intermittent attention to religion, but its sharpest comments about the Bible appeared in the famous appendix where he praised "the pure, peaceable, and impartial Christianity of Christ" in order to attack what he called "the corrupt, slaveholding, women-whipping, cradle-plundering, partial and hypocritical Christianity of this land." Douglass's 1855 account of *My Bondage and My Freedom* contained more material on how the reading of Scripture contributed to his religious development, but its most direct attention to the Bible as an attack on slavery lay in the contrast Douglass draws between the principles of Protestantism and the practice of slaveholding with respect to the slaves' desire to study the Scriptures: "to be sure, they [slaveholders] were Protestant, and held to the great Protestant right of every man to '*search the scriptures*' for himself; but, then, to all general rules, there are *exceptions*."[10]

To the extent Douglass was typical, the most direct contribution of memoirs to debates over the Bible and slavery was their narrative descriptions. Not so much direct arguments from Scripture against slavery but rather illustrations of slave appropriation of Scripture were the key.

Treatises

As with memoirs, so too African American authors of treatises that used the Bible to attack slavery could follow a notable British exemplar. In this case it was a powerful tract by Quobna Ottobah Cugoano, *Thoughts and Sentiments on the Evil of Slavery*, which appeared in two versions in 1787 and 1791. Cugoano did include biographical details of his birth in Africa, sale into slavery, and eventual manumission, but his primary burden was to mount a cascade of arguments against the slave trade and slavery. Details about how the system actually worked in Africa and the West Indies became the opportunity for explaining at great length how a right understanding of Scripture cut the moral ground out from under modern slavery. His reading of what was allowed under the law of Moses and why ancient biblical slavery differed so greatly from modern varieties depended throughout on an appropriate understanding of biblical stories like the curse of Ham or the capture by Israel of its enemies. The use of the Bible on slavery without the use of the Bible on race seemed to Cugoano like an absurdity. As he expressed his conclusion after extensive examination of many Old Testament passages: "there is nothing in nature, reason, and scripture, . . . in any manner or way, to warrant the enslaving of black people more than others."[11]

African Americans soon proved themselves adept at presenting the same kind of more or less formal arguments, which were more or less carefully applied to specific aspects of the modern slave system. Thus, in 1835, David Ruggles (1810–49), an active abolitionist from New York City, used Scripture as the foundation for a scathing indictment of the sexual license that accompanied American slavery. As the foundation for his substantial pamphlet on the immoralities occasioned by American slavery, Psalm 50:18 served as Ruggles's text: "When thou sawest a thief, then thou consentedst with him, and hast been partaker with adulterers." His indictment was based on "four of the principal facts connected with the condition of female slaves": the rise in the number of mulattoes who "incontestably demonstrate the wide spread and incessant licentiousness of the white population"; the inability of black women to resist the advances of white males since "there is no law to preserve them, and no protecting authority to which they can appeal"; the manifest temptation from "pecuniary advantage" to slave owners who tried to breed as many slaves as possible; and the fact that in American slavery "the matrimonial connection among the slaves is altogether nullified." In light of these conditions, Ruggles urged Christian believers to recognize the existence of a spiritual crisis and to meet that crisis with "evangelical weapons." One such weapon proposed by Ruggles was for "female members of our Northern Christian churches" to rise up and "slay this hydra-headed monster of corruption and wo." Ruggles asked them particularly to denounce "slaveholding" as such, but his reasoning homed in on practices associated with the American system. Women church members should especially demand that "perpetual and impenitent transgressors of the seventh [adultery] and eighth [stealing] commandments" be ejected from the churches.[12] By describing slavery as it actually existed, Ruggles felt he could exploit explicit biblical commands against adultery, as also against stealing, to demand an end to the system.

Only a few years after the appearance of Ruggles's sharply focused treatise, Henry Highland Garnet (1815–82), a Presbyterian minister, abolitionist, and temperance advocate, offered a broader account to the Female Benevolent Society of Troy, New York. This address, which argued for the intellectual distinction of black African nations and individuals in the ancient world, used the Old Testament extensively to document "the ancient frame of our ancestors." Although Garnet ranged much further afield than had David Ruggles, he also focused on the inability of Bible readers to justify a blacks-only system of slavery from Scripture. Garnet's pamphlet did move from an appeal to Scripture to an appeal to American ideals, with the hope that "the good institutions of the land" could overcome "the influence of those [people] that are evil." But at the heart of his argument was an effort to instill dignity among those whom he felt were singled out for specific prophetic attention in Psalm 63:31: "princes shall come out of Egypt, and Ethiopia shall stretch out her hands unto God."[13]

Doubtless the calmest and most learned of African American treatises of this era appeared as a long series in the *Christian Recorder* during the first half of 1861.[14] It was entitled "Chapters on Ethnology," in the exposition of which biblical accounts of early humanity were prominent. In contrast to the rhetorical flash and fire of other authors, the anonymous scholar who penned this essay developed his subject with patient care. Yet his conclusion was the same: distinctions among the races of the sort that allowed for American slavery had no basis in reliable history or proper biblical authority. Against the rising scholarly notion that humankind had descended from different species, the *Christian Recorder* responded that "the Jewish and Christian Scriptures . . . plainly teach, that mankind, of whatever race, family, or tribe, have descended from a single pair of progenitors." Details about early humans were not taught in the New Testament, except that nothing could be "more pointed and striking than the language of the Apostle Paul to the Athenians at Mars Hill, when he said: 'God hath made of one blood all nations of men for to dwell on all the face of the earth, and hath determined the times before appointed, and the bounds of their habitation'" (Acts 17:26).[15]

As with the scholarly essayist in the *Christian Recorder*, so other authors also pushed the question of whether slavery could be practiced only on a single race. By setting aside larger issues about the propriety of slavery in general, authors of these treatises hammered on the anomaly that proslavery biblical arguments almost always proceeded as if race was not a consideration when interpreting Scripture. For those with ears to hear, a whole line of African American treatises was begging to differ.

Sermons

A major study would be necessary to survey the application of Scripture in black preaching to slavery. Yet among African American ordained clergy, Lemuel Haynes (1753–1833), a Congregational minister in Vermont, was one of the most notable ministers of his era, white or black, in the subtlety with which he brought the Bible to bear on slavery. An unusually full sermon from 1813, entitled "Dissimulation Illustrated," illustrates that subtlety. Apart from what it had to say about slavery, the sermon was also of interest, because its general picture of human relationships, including slavery, was constructed of theological materials that Haynes had taken from the works of Jonathan Edwards.

As white antislave advocates had been doing since the Revolution, black abolitionists also cited inconsistencies between the United States' stated republican ideals and the practice of slavery. So it was with Haynes in 1813 when he praised George Washington for recognizing that religious virtue was required for a republic to flourish. In referring to Washington's last will and testament, Haynes proclaimed, "he was an enemy to slaveholding, and gave his dying testimony against it, by emancipating, and providing for those under his care. O that his jealous surviving neighbors would prove themselves to be his legitimate children, and go and do likewise!"

More central to this sermon, which was preached at a commemoration of Washington's birthday on February 22, 1813, was Haynes's reflections on his text from Romans 12:9: "let love be without dissolution." In particular, this passage offered him full scope to criticize the dissimulation, or deceitful hypocrisy, that he saw in both President Madison's conduct of the War of 1812 and the American support for slavery. Near the start, he paused to lay a theological foundation taken from Jonathan Edwards's theory of true virtue. To Edwards, virtue meant treating objects in accord with their intrinsic quality of being. Since God was the ultimate Being, God deserved ultimate love. But since humans were made in God's image, they too deserved to be approached with proportionate love. Without this "regard" for "beings according to their magnitude and importance," as Haynes put it, the result would be only "pretences of love to mankind, and to our country." The spiritual truth Haynes wanted to teach was that, if people attempt to love their fellow humans (lesser being) without honoring God first (highest Being), "is highly preposterous."

The reverse relationship allowed Haynes to make political points related to the War of 1812. He asked his listeners to judge whether "the warm zeal, party spirit, war and blood-shed" that then prevailed in the United States reflected the sort of benevolence to lesser being that true love to God as Highest Being should entail. Haynes obviously felt that President Madison's dragooning of New England into war with Britain failed this test of benevolence: "Benevolent affection will dispose men to make a proper estimate, or set a suitable value on things; men's lives are not to be trifled with, or vainly thrown away." Haynes, quoting the Apostle Paul's description of rulers in Romans 13, urged proper regard for proper government. But "unbounded" power was something else that revived "the old tory spirit that was among us in our old revolutionary war."

Almost as if in passing, Haynes then turned his combination of Edward-sean theology, republican ideology, and dissatisfaction with Madison into an assault on slavery. First he expressed his sympathy for impressed sailors whose liberty was forfeited and who (in republican parlance) were languishing "in slavery" to the British. But then Haynes twisted the dagger: "Our president . . . can talk feelingly on the subject of impressment of our seamen. I am glad to have him feel for them. Yet in his own state, Virginia, there were, in the year 1800, no less than three hundred forty-three thousand, seven hundred ninety-six human beings holden in bondage for life!" His conclusion tied antislavery back to the theme of his sermon: "partial affection, or distress for some of our fellow-creatures, while others, even under our notice, are wholly disregarded, betrays dissimulation."[16] In expressing its objections to Madison's war effort and as guided by the theology of Jonathan Edwards, Haynes' sermon was unusual for a black preacher of the era. Yet as many such sermons showed, the preached word of Scripture could itself become a sophisticated theological weapon against the continuation of slavery in the United States.

Manifestoes

Manifestoes employing Scripture against slavery can be differentiated from treatises and sermons by their vehemence. Although patient argument was not unknown in such works, they gained their force from fusillades of polemical fire. Lemuel Haynes had penned a work of this kind several decades before his 1813 sermon. In 1776, he had the audacity to pen an essay for the Continental Congress that began with a quotation from the famous preface of the Declaration of Independence on the self-evident fact that "all men are created Equal." In this bracing political essay, Haynes made some of the same arguments that his better-known New Divinity colleague, Samuel Hopkins, was at nearly the same time putting into his own antislave address to the Continental Congress, *A Dialogue Concerning the Slavery of the Africans*.[17] Yet even more thoroughly than did Hopkins, Haynes salted his republican antislavery with biblical antislavery. He thus made a point of quoting Acts 17:26, as the anonymous essayist in the *Christian Recorder* would also do eighty-five years later: "it hath pleased God to make of one Blood all nations of men, for to dwell upon the face of the Earth." He underscored the inconsistencies between the practices of slavery and the precepts of the gospel: "O Christianity, how art thou Disgraced, how art thou reproached, By the vicious practices of those upon whome thou dost smile!" And he provided his own paraphrase of the Pauline passage from I Corinthians 7:21 that featured so large in pro-slavery exegesis: "art thou called, being a servant? care not for it: but if you mayest Be made free, use it rather." To Haynes it was obvious that this passage communicated a clear message both spiritually and temporally: "the apostle seems to recommend freedom if attainable, q.d. 'if it is thy unhappy Lot to be a slave, yet if thou art Spiritually free Let the former appear so minute a thing when compared with the Latter that it is comparatively unworthy of notice; yet Since freedom is so Exelent a Jewel, which none have a right to Extirpate, and if there is nay hope of attaining it, use all Lawfull measures for that pur-pose.'"[18] Much of the rest of this overtly political address was also given over to reinterpreting passages that the defenders of slavery were already putting to use for their purposes.

As telling as Haynes's work was at the dawn of the new nation, it was not nearly as cutting as the pamphlet published at Boston in 1829 by David Walker (1785–1830), a free black of that city. This work, *Appeal . . . to the Coloured Citizens of the World*, was as notable for its militancy as for its explicit Christian argumentation. Its most audacious claim was Walker's prediction that, on the basis of scriptural precept, he was sure that the United States would soon be destroyed because of its sins as a slaveholding nation.

A major part of Walker's work was given over to denunciation of practices prohibited by Scripture that were intrinsic to the American system of slavery. In his view, Roman slavery "was, comparatively speaking, no more than a *cypher*, when compared with ours under the Americans." Walker cited many aspects of American slavery that he contended the Scriptures condemned. Especially galling was the treatment of slave children, which he felt involved constant violation of Jesus's command from Matthew 18:6: "whoso shall offend one of these little ones which believe in me, it were better for him that a millstone were hanged about his neck, and that he were drowned in the depth of the sea." Walker had only scorn for disregard of such passages: "now the avaricious Americans think that the Lord Jesus Christ will let them off, because his words are no more than the words of a man!!!" Such rhetoric struck fear into some white hearts, in part because of its vehemence but also because of how effectively Walker evoked the Scriptures: "will not those who were burnt up in Sodom and Gomorrah rise up in judgment against Chris-tian Americans with the Bible in their hands and condemn them?"

Walker, like Haynes and other abolitionists, did not scruple about mix-ing his arguments together. He could, thus, turn easily from scriptural norm to political ideal: "Can there be a greater absurdity in nature [than slavery], and particularly in a free republican country! . . . Americans! I ask you candidly, was your suffering under Great Britain, one hundredth part as evil and tyrannical as you have rendered ours under you?"

But the heart of Walker's inflammatory volume was similar to the main point made in many of the era's calmer treatises. Whatever one might conclude from Scripture about slavery, the Bible was unambiguous about race. Thus, Walker at one point appealed to the "Great Commission" from Matthew 28:18–20, where the resurrected Christ sent out his followers to "teach all nations . . . to observe all things whatsoever I have commanded you." Walker berated his white readers with a challenge: "You have the Bible in your hands with this very injunction—Have you been to Africa, teaching the inhabitants thereof the words of the Lord Jesus?" No, it was just the reverse. Americans "entered among us, and learnt us the art of throat-cutting, by setting us to fight, one against another, to take each other as prisoners of war, and sell to you for small bits of calicoes, old swords, knives, etc. to make slaves for you and your children." To Walker, such behavior was a direct contradiction of Scripture: "can the American preachers appeal unto God, the Maker and Searcher of hearts, and tell him, with the Bible in their hands, that they made no distinction on account of men's colour?"[19]

Even better known than Walker and his *Appeal* was Frederick Douglass and the multiple shafts he loosed against American slavery. In his newspapers Douglass regularly published biblical articles from others, and in March 1861 he himself drew on the Bible when he rounded against "The Pro-Slavery Mob and the Pro-Slavery Ministry." To Douglass in this instance, it was the way American slavery violated the spirit of the Bible that mattered most: "It would be insulting to Common Sense, an outrage upon all right feeling, for us, who have worn the heavy chain and felt the biting lash to consent to argue with Ecclesiastical Sneaks who are thus prostituting their Religion and Bible to the base uses of popular and profitable iniquity. They don't need light, but the sting of honest rebuke. They are of their father the Devil, and his works they do, not because they are ignorant, but because they are base." To African Americans it seemed clearer than to all others that slavery contradicted the Scriptures in general.

But Douglass joined many other African Americans by coming back to race as the keystone of American slavery. In this same article from 1861 he made that point with characteristic flare: "Nobody at the North, we think, would defend Slavery, even from the Bible, but for this color distinction. . . . Color makes all the difference in the application of our American Christianity. . . . The same book which is full of the Gospel of Liberty to one race, is crowded with arguments in justification of the slavery of another. Those who shout and rejoice over the progress of Liberty in Italy, would mob down, pray and preach down Liberty at home as an unholy and hateful thing."[20]

Manifestoes like those penned by Haynes, Walker, and Douglass were not always the most carefully reasoned weapons in the arsenal against slavery. But by constructing them so self-consciously out of scriptural materials, these works showed the same combination of religious and social commitments that put energy into other African American protests against the system.

Dialogue

Finally, one of the strongest theological statements against American slavery appeared early in the nineteenth century from Daniel Coker (1780–??), one of Richard Allen's first colleagues as a minister in the African Methodist Episcopal Church. Coker, who eventually migrated to Sierra Leone, published his *Dialogue Between a Virginian and an African Minister* in 1810. It advanced at least seven biblical arguments against slavery as it then existed in the United States; some of these arguments were as theologically compelling as any biblical arguments of the period.

As in many abolitionist condemnations of slavery, so also did Coker argue that the "spirit" or general principles of the Bible condemned slavery. He emphasized, for example, "the unreasonableness of perpetual unconditional slavery" in light of "the righteous and benevolent doctrines and duties, taught in the New Testament." To Coker, passages like Matthew 7:12 ("Whatsoever ye would that men should do to you, do ye even so to them; for this is the law and the prophets") pointed to only one conclusion: "It is very evident, that slavery is contrary to the spirit and nature of the Christian religion."

Arguments from broad biblical principle were not, however, Coker's main concern. Most of his *Dialogue* simply bypassed the general question of the legitimacy of slavery as such in order to focus on anti-Christian aspects of the system in practice. As an example, he complained that slaves were regularly "deprived of instruction in the doctrines, and duties of religion." Another pragmatic argument noted the damage done by slavery to American missionary efforts. To make this point, he recounted the story of a band of Native Americans who, upon being approached by American missionaries, took counsel together before concluding: "the white people made slaves of the black people, and if they had it in their power, they would made slaves of the Indians; they therefore wanted no such religion."[21] Nineteen years later David Walker would make the same observation.

Skillful as his general comments were, Coker worked even harder at reasoning directly from Scripture. By so doing, he was responsible for one of the most profound works of the period. His text was Genesis 17:13, where Abraham was commanded to circumcise his slaves ("He that is born in thy house, and he that is bought with thy money"). Proslavery Bible advocates often used this text to argue that since God regulated slaveholding by Abraham, the Father of all believers, slaveholding was legitimate for other believers in other times and places. Coker, however, went further by expanding upon the second part of the same verse: "and my covenant [says God] shall be in your flesh for an everlasting covenant." He pointed out that "this law of circumcision" was a central part of biblical religion, and that circumcision was "a token of that covenant, by which . . . the land of Canaan, and various privileges in it, were promised to Abraham and to his seed, and to all that were included in the covenant." To Coker, this last provision was critical. God's covenant promises were meant for "All . . . to whom circumcision (which was the token of the covenant) was administered." This inclusion extended to the one who "was bought with money." Therefore, all the benefits of God's covenant promises were extended to slaves whom Abraham purchased and whom he then, on God's command, circumcised. But once they were circumcised, "these persons bought with money, were no longer looked upon as uncircumcised and useless; as aliens and strangers; but were incorporated with the church and nation of the Israelites, and became one people with them." Consequently, once purchased slaves had been circumcised, they were part of Israel. And so the children of such circumcised slaves "were the servants of the Lord, in the same sense as the natural descendents of Abraham were," which meant that, as naturalized Israelites, these children of circumcised slaves could not be sold as slaves themselves (Coker quoted Leviticus 25:42 and 54, with their prohibitions against Jews enslaving other Jews). The conclusion to Coker was inescapable: "The passage of scripture under consideration was so far from authorizing the Israelites to make slaves of their servants [*sic*] children, that they evidently forbid it; and therefore, are so far from proving the lawfulness of your enslaving the children of the Africans, that they clearly condemn the practice as criminal."

For Coker, once an Old Testament slave had been circumcised, enslavement of that circumcised slave's children was impossible, because circumcision represented God's incorporation of the slave into Israel. By implication, when in the modern era Africans were enslaved and, in consequence of that enslavement, brought under the preaching of the Christian gospel, their situation became analogous to the slaves of the Old Testament. As "spiritual

Israel," Christianity bestowed all the privileges on those grafted in as converts as it offered to those who were raised in Christianity's homeland.

Coker's argument required patience to follow, since he was enlisting passages from several parts of the Pentateuch and then linking them into a single chain of reasoning. Yet it was a theologically powerful argument. In particular, he was taking seriously the principles of theological inclusion that would later prove so difficult for widely recognized theological leaders like Moses Stuart of Andover Seminary who, in an important book from 1850, addressed these same passages that Coker exegeted but did so in a manner that left American political principle triumphing over sober biblical interpretation.

At the end of his consideration of Genesis 17, Coker summarized how very different the Old Testament history was from the contemporary situation:

> The Israelites were not sent by a divine mandate, to nations three hundred miles distant, who were neither doing, nor meditating any thing against them, and to whom they had no right whatever, in order to captivate them by fraud or force; tare [sic] them away from their native country, and all their tender connections; bind them in chains and fetters; croud [sic] into ships, and there murder them by thousands, for want of air and proper exercise; and then doom the survivors and their posterity to bondage and misery forever.[22]

Coker's *Dialogue* came early in American engagement with the question of how the Bible regarded slavery. In the half-century that followed until the Civil War, few of the multitudes who worried this same question from this same source plumbed the theological depths that Daniel Coker reached.

African American interpretations of Scripture never exerted broad influence in antebellum society, but they did mount several lines of rigorous anti-slave biblical argument. The two most impressive arguments were the case for a difference between slavery in general and slavery as foisted upon only one race and Daniel Coker's contention about analogies between ancient Old Testament Israel and the contemporary Christian church. As with theological efforts that enjoyed broader influence, the ability to act upon messages purportedly from the Bible depended on the circumstances in which those messages were received and on the messages themselves. For African Americans, circumstances were as unpropitious as at least some of their arguments were strong.

Nonetheless, with such arguments, expressed in a number of genres, these writers testified to the power that the Scriptures were exerting in their redeemed lives. They also were testifying to the sanctified power of their own prose in redeeming the Scriptures.

6

Balm in Gilead

Memory, Mourning, and Healing in African American Autobiography

Albert J. Raboteau

Blessed are those who mourn, for they shall be comforted.

—Matthew 5:4

Permit me to begin autobiographically. The sun is bright. I am standing next to a wooden fence. Beyond the fence is a cow. The cow moves slowly towards me. She is called Mr. Frank's cow because she belongs to Mr. Frank, who lives next door to us. I try to feed my bottle to Mr. Frank's cow through the rails of the fence because milk comes from cows. A black dog named Sappo sits beside me. He belongs to my sisters' friend Racille. I am laughing, and Mr. Frank's cow is laughing, and Sappo is laughing, too. I run to tell my mother and my sisters.

This, my first memory, is a very joyful one. Perhaps this early experience in my hometown of Bay St. Louis, Mississippi stuck so firmly in my memory because my mother used it to wean me from the baby bottle. When we moved north not long afterwards, my bottle disappeared. When I asked for it, she told me, "Oh, Mr. Frank's cow took it." I did not quite believe her.

We moved to the North when I was two, but returned South during summers to visit relatives down home. One summer I remember especially well, the summer of my education. I remember one Sunday, when we awoke too late to attend Mass at St. Rose de Lima, the black church in Bay St. Louis. So we went to the white church, Our Lady of the Gulf. White ushers directed us to sit in back, squeezed together in a half pew. I remember going to receive Holy Communion and watching the priest carrying the host pass me by, and again pass me by, passing me by until he had given communion to all the white people. I remember stumbling back to the pew dazed, confused, shamed.

There had been two previous incidents during that same trip: my mother stopped me from drinking at a "whites only" water fountain and two white ladies objected to me wading in the bay from the white beach. But the incident that hurt me the worst was discrimination at the Communion rail. Even at seven I knew it was a sacrilege.

Forty years later on a research trip to Charleston, South Carolina, I decided to attend Mass in the historic cathedral downtown. Arriving late, I sat in back. When it came time to receive Communion, I stood in line amidst a sea of white faces. I felt as if something were holding me back. I turned from the line. I talked to myself and turned back, but I could not make myself go. I left the church and on the sidewalk outside I began to cry—a grown man shedding tears that had not fallen forty years earlier that summer down home.

Memory and the Roots of Racial Identity

That summer I was initiated into the racialized character of American society through my own particular experience, not just of being racially other, but of being identified as pejoratively other. This experience, accompanied by deep feelings of shame, loss, and rejection, constitutes a significant dimension of identity formation for African Americans (and other racialized minorities) as persons and as a group. The moment(s) of racial trauma live on in memory. Even when seemingly forgotten, an incident, remark, or situation can precipitate the feelings of a past experience of racism. These hidden wounds affect white Americans also, as Thandeka poignantly demonstrates in her book, based on her interviews with whites about their memories of racial identity formation, *Learning to Be White*. When asked, "How and when did you learn that you are white?" a significant number of her respondents spoke of painful memories of loss, shame, guilt, and betrayal, associated with close childhood interracial friendships that their parents broke or forced them to break. Recalling these childhood memories caused some to react emotionally with tears or with anger.[1]

Groups, like persons, have memories that serve to constitute their identities as groups. Moreover, our nation, constituted by diverse ethnic, racial, and religious groups achieves a unified identity, not only through a set of shared principles articulated in civic institutions but also through memory. A prime source of identity for a nation is history, construed as a set of interlocking stories that we tell one another about our origins and our past. I mean the mythic history that establishes our sense of national origin, destiny, and purpose

(Lincoln's "mystic chords of memory"). Our sense of common history changes over time to accommodate our expanding awareness of the variety of who we are ethnically, racially, and religiously. Usually the expansion of our historical vision occurs in response to social pressure from some group whose story has been left out of the national story. So responding to successive and vociferous complaints by African Americans, Native Americans, Asian Americans, Hispanic Americans, and women, books, curricula, and the media, both elite and popular, changed. The astounding flexibility of our culture to include the stories of the invisible or the forgotten, disguises the fact that their stories have been included but not fully incorporated. We, black and white, suffer a form of partial amnesia, which distorts our perceptions, because we have not adequately remembered and mourned what we have suffered. I am talking about a mourning that is not an episode but an attitude, a state of awareness, the "melancholy of race" as Anne Cheng calls it in her strikingly original and insightful book of that name, or perhaps even a profound sense of *penthos*, the term the Greek Fathers used for a condition of repentant sorrow over the brokenness within and without.

I experienced a surprising and powerful example of the need for memory and mourning during black history month several years ago. PBS broadcast a documentary on the murder of Emmett Till, focusing not only on his death but also on the crusade of his mother Mamie Till Mobley to achieve justice in her son's case. A few minutes after the program ended, the telephone rang and a voice at the other end of the line asked to speak with me. It was a college classmate whom I had not seen in years, a Jesuit priest and psychologist. He began to sob uncontrollably as he stammered out an explanation that he had just seen the Till film. He could not stop crying because he was so upset at the atrocity he had glimpsed, a crime committed fifty years ago but recalled by vivid images on the TV screen. He called because he was so upset by what he had seen; he was alone and he thought of me (perhaps because we first met when I was only a year older than Till at the time of his murder).

During that same week a radio interview on NPR featured a panel discussion of race relations during which a black participant (a historian) broke down in tears when he recalled the question his parents had never been able to answer for him as a child: "Why did white people hate us so? When they lynched us, why did they mutilate our bodies?" His tears brought to mind Howard Thurman's assertion that black people carry the memory of lynching in their bodies and that the nation as a whole still has not come to terms with lynching. In Brooklyn, St. Paul Community Baptist Church sponsors an annual pilgrimage to the ocean in Far Rockaway to mourn for the millions of Africans who died in the transatlantic slave trade. "We have not properly mourned nor repented past atrocities afflicted upon us a people of color," the pastor of St. Paul's explains, "clearly, a trauma of this magnitude in the life of a people must be acknowledged and mourned."

Our nation has need of tears, tears for all those lynched, maimed, whipped, shamed, and debased by our history of race hatred. Our country has need of tears for those who suffered and for those at whose hands they suffered. For they, by denying the humanity of others, denied their own. We remain connected to the past by memory, and the nation, like individuals, must come to terms with the past. There is a way out of the evasion and willed amnesia of our racial trauma stories, recalling them to memory. African American autobiography offers one such way as a telling of memories, an expression of mourning, and, by means of telling and mourning, a method of healing the wounds, personal and social, inflicted by racism.

Autobiography in the African American Experience

The earliest African American autobiographical narratives emerged in the late eighteenth century in the context of two transatlantic movements: Evangelical revivals and British antislavery. Evangelical figures, including George Whitefield, who appears prominently in several of the narratives and Selena Hastings, the Countess of Huntingdon, whose Connexion ordained and supported John Marrant, were noteworthy examples of a transatlantic Evangelical network that supported the publication of early black narratives as well as the poetry of Phillis Wheatley. The *Baptist Register* and the *Methodist Magazine*, British journals, followed the example of the earlier Moravian *Periodical Accounts* by publishing narratives of the lives of African American preachers, such as David George and George Leile, and reporting news of their ministries in Virginia, Nova Scotia, Jamaica, and Sierra Leone. Black ministers' accounts of their own conversions and the expansion of Christianity among slaves and free blacks served to validate the authenticity of the revival and to illustrate the universality of its blessings. The earliest black autobiographies, those of James Albert Gronniosaw, John Marrant, and Olaudah Equiano, are spiritual, as well as slave, narratives in which the experience of conversion is a central theme, because their authors propose a strong convergence between freedom from spiritual and bodily bondage.

These narratives, addressed to a biracial but overwhelmingly white audience, also served to advance the cause of antislavery, especially, the campaign to end the Atlantic slave trade. They constituted testimonies of black humanity equivalent to the famous Wedgewood plate design depicting a chained African kneeling with hands clasped surrounded by the words "Am I not a man and a brother?" Equiano's narrative, the most critically acclaimed, was particularly effective in offering a native African's account of being kidnapped as a child into slavery, his experience of the horror of the Middle Passage, his enslavement in the West Indies and Virginia, his picaresque career as a seaman (including a voyage to the North Pole), his eventual emancipation, settlement in England, and evangelical conversion, and his collaboration with Granville Sharp and others in the antislave trade campaign.

Equiano or Gustavus Vassa established several rhetorical strategies that would be deployed again and again by black autobiographers. The first was to cast the drama of African humanity and African freedom against the backdrop of the Bible. The second, stemming from the first, was to articulate the chosenness (of the narrator and African American Christians) to convict Anglo-Europeans of their sin (to civilize and humanize them). The third was to discern in the events of their own lives (and the life of their people) a providential and universal message of reconciliation. Equiano begins his account with a recollection (possibly fictional) of his Ibo (Nigerian) homeland in which he reiterates three times in three pages the analogy between the "manners and customs of my countrymen and those of the Jews, before they reached the Land of Promise, and particularly the patriarchs while they were yet in that pastoral state which is described in Genesis—an analogy, which alone would induce me to think that the one people had sprung from the others." The import of this pastoral image is to reverse the supposed inferiority of Africans in comparison with Europeans: "I remember we never polluted the name of the object of our adoration; on the contrary it was always mentioned with the greatest reverence; and we were totally unacquainted with swearing, and all those terms of abuse and reproach which find their way so readily and copiously in the languages of more civilized people." The sin of blasphemy pales in comparison to those committed by Christian Europeans involved in the wholesale desecration of "God's own image carved in ebony" known as the Atlantic slave trade. Repeatedly in his narrative, Equiano explicates the ironic and tragic conflict between Christian ideals and Christian practice as suffered by enslaved Africans.

The authenticity of his witness is buttressed by his own Christianity, providentially ordered by God. After a prolonged spiritual struggle, described at length in the culminating moment of his narrative, Equiano experiences conversion and grasps the pattern of meaning in his life: "Now every leading providential circumstance that happened to me, from the day I was taken from my parents to that hour, was then in my view, as if it had but just then occurred. . . . I was sensible of the invisible hand of God, which guided and protected me when in truth I knew it not." Foreshadowing this providential moment, Equiano had explained the significance of his African name (changed by different slave masters to Jacob, Michael, and Gustavus Vassa) in the beginning of his text. Olaudah "in our language signifies vicissitude, or fortunate: also, one favoured and having a loud voice and well spoken." His autobiography is the loud and well-spoken demonstration of divine providence leading him to proclaim amidst the struggle against slavery that "the worth of a soul cannot be told. May the Lord give the reader an understanding in this."[2] Equiano's text constructs a map of meaning out of the circumstances of his life, condemns the evil of slavery, exemplifies African humanity, depicts the image of God carved in ebony, and, through his particular story, powerfully evokes the universal truth that "God has made of one blood all the nations of the earth."

Another antislavery campaign, this time to abolish slavery in the United States, inspired the publication of black autobiographies in the form of slave narratives. The greatest of these, the narrative of fugitive slave Frederick Douglass appeared in 1845. Douglass first came to the notice of abolitionist circles as an eloquent platform speaker, and his published narrative was meant to extend the powerful effectiveness of his oratory through the printed page. Douglass's public condemnation of slavery was both liberating and dangerous, since he was still a slave, adding to the authenticity of his voice. His narrative begins with his memory of two childhood incidents that introduced him to the meaning of slavery. The first, the whipping of his Aunt Hester, demonstrated the brutality of the slave owners, the second, the singing of the slaves, demonstrated their response to being enslaved:

> I have often been awakened at the dawn of day by the most heart-rending shrieks of an own aunt of mine, whom he [the master] used to tie up to a joist, and whip upon her naked back till she was literally covered with blood. No words, no tears, no prayers from his gory victim, seemed to move his iron heart from its bloody purpose. The louder she screamed, the harder he whipped, and where the blood ran fastest, there he whipped longest. . . . I remember the first time I ever witnessed this horrible exhibition, I was quite a child, but I well remember it. I never shall forget it whilst I remember any thing. It was the first of a long series of such outrages, of which I was doomed to be a witness and a participant. It struck me with awful force. It was the blood-stained gate, the entrance to the hell of slavery, through which I was about to pass. It was a most terrible spectacle. I wish I could commit to paper the feelings with which I beheld it.[3]

Notice Douglass's insistence on the presence of this memory and his desire to communicate the feel of his childhood terror to the reader. The same reach toward immediacy of recall attaches to his second initiatory memory, the sound of slaves singing:

> I did not, when a slave, understand the deep meaning of those rude and apparently incoherent songs. I was myself within the circle; so that I neither saw nor heard as those without might see and hear. They told a tale of woe which was then altogether beyond my feeble comprehension; they were tones loud, long, and deep, they breathed the prayer and complaint of souls boiling over with the bitterest anguish. Every tone was a testimony against slavery, and a prayer to God for deliverance from chains. The hearing of those wild notes always depressed my spirit, and filled me with ineffable sadness. I have frequently found myself in tears while hearing them. The mere recurrence to those songs, even now, afflicts me; and while I am writing these lines, an expression of feeling has already found its way down my cheek. To those songs I trace my first glimmering conceptions of the dehumanizing character of slavery. . . . Those songs still follow me, to deepen my hatred of slavery, and quicken my sympathies for my brethren in bonds. If any one wishes to be impressed with the soul-killing effects of slavery, let him . . . place himself in the deep pine woods, and there let him, in silence, analyze the sounds that shall pass through the chambers of his soul.[4]

Horror and pathos are the two dominant emotions Douglass calls up from childhood and tries to impress upon the empathy of his readers in order to initiate them into his childhood experience of slavery.

It is irony, however, arising out of a deep anger, that is Douglass's chief weapon for moving the reader to a deeper understanding of the contradiction between slavery and Christian America. The irony starts with the book's subtitle, "An American Slave, Written by Himself." The text, studded with examples of irony, ends with an appendix condemning "the corrupt, slaveholding, women-whipping, cradle-plundering, partial, and hypocritical Christianity of this land" and concludes with a biting parody (supposedly written by a northern Methodist minister) of "Heavenly Union," a hymn popular in antebellum Southern churches. But the most resonant and complex personal irony for Douglass was the very fact of his literacy, the source of his discontentment as a slave and the tool of his self-fashioning. Having furtively learned to read at the age of twelve, thanks to the help of several poor white children, Douglass encountered two antislavery essays in *The Columbian Orator*, which precipitated what I would identify as his "conversion experience" (instead of his famous apostrophe to Freedom on the banks of the Chesapeake Bay):

The reading of these documents enabled me to utter my thoughts, and to meet the arguments brought forward to sustain slavery; but while they relieved me of one difficulty, they brought on another even more painful. . . . As I read . . . that very discontentment which [my master] had predicted would follow my learning to read had already come, to torment and sting my soul to unutterable anguish. As I writhed under it, I would at times feel that learning to read had been a curse rather than a blessing. It had given me a view of my wretched condition, without the remedy. It opened my eyes to the horrible pit, but to no ladder upon which to get out.[5]

Release from his inner turmoil came in the form of two kindly Irish dockworkers who advised him to run away to the north where he would be free. Douglass recalled his new found determination: "From that time I resolved to run away. I looked forward to a time at which it would be safe for me to escape. I was too young to think of doing so immediately; besides I wished to learn how to write, as I might have occasion to write my own pass. I consoled myself with the hope I should one day find a good chance."[6] The die was cast. Literacy enabled him to fashion freedom out of slavery.

Douglass continued to write; he edited a newspaper, agitated for civil rights for former slaves and for women, and published two more autobiographies before his death in 1895. He lived into elder statesmanship, long enough to see the disappointment of Reconstruction's failure and the rise of Jim Crow. During the nadir of race relations at the turn of the nineteenth century, a new voice emerged upon the national scene. W. E. B. DuBois attempted to explain the psychological and social costs of "the color line" in his classic text, *The Souls of Black Folk* (1903). *Souls* is not, strictly speaking, an autobiography but rather a collection of essays and one short story, most of which are autobiographical. The first chapter begins, for example, with a vivid recreation of the initiatory moment of racial discrimination in DuBois's life:

It is in the early days of rollicking boyhood that the revelation first burst upon one, all in a day, as it were. I remember well when the shadow swept across me. . . . In a wee wooden schoolhouse, something put it into the boys' and girls' heads to buy gorgeous visiting-cards . . . and exchange. The exchange was merry, till one girl . . . refused my card . . . peremptorily with a glance. Then it dawned upon me with a certain suddenness that I was different from the others; or like, mayhap, in heart and life and longing, but shut out from their world by a vast veil. I had thereafter no desire to tear down that veil, to creep through; I held all beyond it in common contempt, and lived above it in a region of blue sky and great wandering shadows. That sky was bluest when I could beat my mates at examination-time, or beat them at a foot-race, or even beat their stringy heads.[7]

One observes in the language of DuBois the adult the anger of DuBois the child, avenging his racial rejection upon the closest whites.

DuBois's analysis of the effects of discrimination hinges on two famous metaphors, the "veil" and "double-consciousness." Both take on multiple meanings in his text. The veil represents "the color line" that segregates blacks culturally and socially from whites. The veil also signifies the caul that covers the face of some infants at birth, indicating, according to folk tradition, that they possess second sight, as does the seventh son of a seventh son. For DuBois, African Americans exist behind the veil, which he intends to lift, if ever so briefly in *Souls*, and they are gifted with second sight, an insight into the reality of America that white people lack. Double-consciousness is an internal condition of the black person produced by American discrimination that "yields him no true self-consciousness, but only lets him see himself through the revelation of the other world. It is a peculiar sensation, this double-consciousness, this sense of always looking at one's self through the eyes of others, of measuring one's soul by the tape of a world that looks on in amused contempt and pity. One ever feels his two-ness—an American, a Negro; two souls, two thoughts, two unreconciled strivings; two warring ideals in one dark body, whose dogged strength alone keeps it from being torn asunder."[8]

DuBois's diagnosis of the black American psyche has become so canonical that I occasionally ask my students whether it in fact only describes DuBois's particular experience and ought not to be projected onto the rest of us. My question is usually met with consternation. DuBois continues his analysis on what seems to me to be firmer cultural and social ground:

> The history of the American Negro is the history of this strife, this longing to attain self-conscious manhood, to merge his double self into a better and truer self. In this merging he wishes neither of the older selves to be lost. He would not Africanize America, for America has too much to teach the world and Africa. He would not bleach his Negro soul in a flood of white Americanism, for he knows that Negro blood has a message for the world. He simply wishes to make it possible for a man to both a Negro and an American, without being cursed and spit upon by his fellows, without having the doors of Opportunity closed roughly in his face. This, then, is the end of his striving: to be a co-worker in the kingdom of culture; to escape both death and isolation, to husband and use his best powers and his latent genius.[9]

DuBois clearly envisions the healing of double-consciousness as, in part, a cultural project, and his text attempts to reveal the richness of the culture produced by black folk. The main cultural expression of African Americans, indeed the main contribution of America to world culture, DuBois asserts, is the slave spiritual. And in a brilliant stroke of writerly will, he yokes together the words of European and Euro-American poets and philosophers with bars of music from various African American "Sorrow Songs," as epigraphs to each chapter of *Souls* (except the last), creating a visual emblem of the two cultures distinct, equal, complementary parts of one epigraphic text. The concluding chapter, "Of the Sorrow Songs," breaks the pattern by pairing the poetic verses of one spiritual, "Lay This Body Down," with the music of another spiritual, "Wrestlin' Jacob," indicating the integrity of the cultural contribution of black folk and pride at the cost of its creation. The veil has been lifted. The final paragraph bears out such a reading, as DuBois turns directly to white Americans and reveals the second-sight that comes from those born with(in) the veil:

> Your country? How came it yours? Before the Pilgrims landed we were here. Here we have brought our three gifts and mingled them with yours: a gift of story and song—soft, stirring melody in an ill-harmonized and unmelodious land; the gift of sweat and brawn to beat back the wilderness, conquer the soil, and lay the foundations of this vast economic empire two hundred years earlier than your weak hand could have done it; the third, a gift of the Spirit. Around us the history of the land has centred for thrice a hundred years; out of the nation's heart we have called all that was best to throttle and subdue all that was worst; fire and blood, prayer and sacrifice, have billowed over this people, and they have found peace only in the altars of the God of Right. Nor has our gift of the Spirit been merely passive. Actively we have woven ourselves with the very warp and woof of this nation, we fought their battles, shared their sorrow, mingled our blood with theirs, and generation after generation have pleaded with a headstrong, careless people to despise not Justice, Mercy, and Truth, lest the nation be smitten with a curse. Our song, our toil, our cheer, and warning have been given to this nation in blood-brotherhood. Are not these gifts worth the giving? Is not this work and striving? Would America have been America without her Negro people?[10]

DuBois hopes for the day when "America shall rend the Veil and the prisoned shall go free." The DuBois of *Souls* remained hopeful. But his hope was shadowed by mourning over the wounds of race. In 1899, his eighteen-month-old son Burghardt died of typhoid fever. DuBois had searched in vain for one of the two or three black doctors in Atlanta, since white doctors refused to treat blacks. In the chapter "The Passing of the First Born," he described his reaction to the death of his son:

All that day and all that night there sat an awful gladness in my heart—nay, blame not if I see the world thus darkly through the Veil—and my soul whispers ever to me saying, 'Not dead, not dead, but escaped; not bond, but free.' . . . Well sped, my boy, before the world had dubbed your ambition insolence, had held your ideals unattainable, and taught you to cringe and bow. Better for this nameless void that stops my life than a sea of sorrow for you.

But then DuBois pulls back and strains toward hope:

Idle words, he might have borne his burden more bravely than we . . . and found it lighter too, some day; for surely, surely this is not the end. Surely there shall yet dawn some mighty morning to lift the Veil and set the prisoned free.

And then he turns back again:

Not for me, I shall die in my bonds, but for fresh young souls who have not known the night and waken to the morning. . . . Some morning this may be, long, long years to come. But now there wails, on that dark shore within the Veil, the same deep voice *Thou shalt forego!* And all have I forgone at that command and with small complaint, all save that fair young form that lies so coldly wed with death.[11]

What happens to hope deferred? Where is it kept? For DuBois, a primary repository for hope was the kingdom of culture (not the kingdom of heaven), where, above the veil, "I sit with Shakespeare and he winces not." There he can move across the color line "arm in arm with Balzac and Dumas" and "summon Aristotle and Aurelius and what soul [he] will, and they come all graciously with no scorn nor condescension." From the heights of a liberal education blacks would gain the perspective to "sight the Promised Land." He believed in the necessity of a liberal arts education for African Americans to develop the talent, vision, and character necessary to protest, politically and socially, the color line. Though DuBois respected the historic leadership of some black clergy, he had little faith in the contemporary black church, which he thought had lost its ethical compass, and tossed aimlessly between the Scylla of pessimistic bitterness in the North and the Charybdis of "hypocritical compromise" in the South. But he did have faith in "the deep religious feeling of the real Negro heart, the stirring, unguided might of powerful human souls, who, have lost the guiding star of the past and are seeking in the great night a new religious ideal." Daring to define that new ideal as desegregation, DuBois predicted that "some day the Awakening will come, when the pent-up vigor of ten million souls shall sweep irresistibly toward the Goal, out of the Valley of the Shadow of Death, where all that makes life worth living—Liberty, Justice, and Right—is marked 'For White People Only.'"[12]

In the 1950s the awakening that DuBois envisioned seemed finally to dawn as a nascent civil rights movement, heartened by its victory in the U.S. Supreme Court's Brown vs. Board of Education decision, felt the time had come for America to rip the veil apart. James Baldwin, in a series of brilliant essays, published in *Notes of a Native Son* (1953), *Nobody Knows My Name* (1962), *The Fire Next Time* (1963), and *No Name in the Streets* (1972), charted the course of the movement autobiographically and politically.

Baldwin insisted that the personal pain, the emotional stunting, and the psychic damage caused by racism devastated both black and white Americans, who were inextricably bound together by history and memory. Unless blacks accepted the whiteness within themselves and unless whites accepted the blackness within themselves, Baldwin argued, racial reconciliation was impossible. Though the effort is a joint one, it is black Americans who have taken the initiative by naming and exposing the evil of racism, by revealing their experience of its corrosive power, and by testifying to the necessity of mournful remembering if healing is ever to occur.

Baldwin speaks eloquently of these issues in many of his essays but exemplifies them most effectively, in my judgment, in his first novel, *Go Tell It on the Mountain* (1953). The story of one day in the life of a fourteen-year-old black boy John Grimes, the novel is a profound meditation on the meaning of black history and the mystery of human suffering. The novel opens on the morning of John's birthday and closes the next morning after his "rebirth" on the floor of a storefront sanctified church in Harlem. The book also tells the stories of John's relatives: his stepfather Gabriel, his mother Elizabeth, and his Aunt Florence. Their stories occupy the second part of the book, "The Prayers of the Saints," and through them Baldwin encapsulates the history of black Americans, from the post-Emancipation rural South to the urban ghetto of the twentieth-century great migration. Threatened by racial oppression and violence from without, the lives of John's family are riven from within by pride, jealousy, misunderstanding, and the failure to love. Their stories come to a focus upon him as he is struck down by the Spirit at a tarrying service in the Fire-Baptized Church his family attends. He falls not only under the weight of sin but also under the burden of the history of his people's suffering.

It is precisely this suffering that John desperately seeks to escape, that is, the misery, poverty, and oppression of his environment. But the more he struggles on the "threshing floor," the deeper he falls; there is no escape, except to go through. John is being claimed by a spiritual force larger than his own ego, a force that pushes him onto a journey across an ancient landscape populated by prophets, apostles, and martyrs. In his trance he confronts an army of people. They are the wretched of the earth, the poor, those who suffer. And he is in their company; there will be no escape. Their sufferings will be his. Then suffering becomes a sound, a sound "he had heard all his life," a sound he not only recognizes but now internalizes:

> And now in his moaning . . . he heard it in himself—it rose from his bleeding, his cracked-open heart. It was a sound of rage and weeping which filled the grave, rage and weeping from time set free, but bound now in eternity; rage that had no language, weeping with no voice—which yet spoke now to John's startled soul, of boundless melancholy, of the bitterest patience, and the longest night; of the deepest water, the strongest chains, the most cruel lash; of humility most wretched, the dungeon most absolute, of love's bed defiled, and birth dishonored, and most bloody, unspeakable, sudden death. Yes, the darkness hummed with murder: the body in the water, the body in the fire, the body on the tree. John looked down the line of these armies of darkness, army upon army, and his soul whispered: *Who are these? Who are they?* And wondered: *Where shall I go?*[13]

John struggles to escape but hears a voice telling him "Go Through. . . . Ask Him to take you through." Then "he saw before him the fire, red and gold, and burning in a night eternal, and waiting for him. He must go through this fire and into this night." Then John glimpses the Lord, "and the darkness, for a moment only, was filled with a light he could not bear." And in that moment he was set free: "the light and the darkness had kissed each other and were married now, forever, in the life and the vision of John's soul."[14]

John has been grasped by his people's history, and in being grasped, engulfed by that company of sufferers, he comes to comprehend the paradox that it is precisely these wretched of the earth who are the chosen ones of God. Complementing the vision of the suffering, violent, and bloody history of black Americans comes another vision. In a passage filled with allusions to Scripture, the spirituals, and gospel songs, Baldwin reads in John Grime's experience the history of suffering and triumph of those who have gone before:

> No power could hold this army back, no water disperse them, no fire consume them. . . . They sang, where the darkness gathered, where the lion waited, where the fire cried, and where the blood ran down. . . . They wandered in the valley forever; and they smote the rock, forever; and the waters sprang, perpetually, in the perpetual desert. They cried unto the Lord forever, and lifted up their eyes forever, they were cast down forever, and He

lifted them up forever. . . . Job bore them witness, and Abraham was their father. Moses had elected to suffer with them . . . Shadrach, Meshach, and Abednego had gone before them into the fire, their grief had been sung by David and Jeremiah had wept for them. Ezekiel had prophesied upon them, these scattered bones, these slain, and, in the fullness of time the prophet, John, had come out of the wilderness, crying that the promise was for them. They were encompassed with a very cloud of witnesses: Judas, who had betrayed the Lord; Thomas, who had doubted Him; Peter, who had trembled at the crowing of a cock; Stephen, who had been stoned; Paul, who had been bound; the blind man crying in the dusty road, the dead man rising from the grave. And they looked unto Jesus, the author and the finisher of their faith, running with patience the race He had set before them; they endured the cross, and they despised the shame, and waited to join Him, one day, in glory, at the right hand of the Father.[15]

In this striking passage Baldwin casts the meaning of African American history within the biblical story of salvation in language that echoes the idiom of black religious culture.

The gospel to be "told on the mountain" is that salvation does not lie in wealth, power, or the attempt to evade suffering at all costs. Rather it is the lesson of African American history that the rejected are the "chosen," not because they suffer but because suffering can be transformed into a source of wisdom, maturity, authenticity, and truth; or as Martin Luther King, Jr., would put it, "suffering can be redemptive." Tried by fire, they may achieve the moral and emotional strength to draw out of their suffering profound lessons about human life, truths that can only come from suffering, lessons that permitted them not only to endure but also to transcend the power of evil. As John Grimes realized, light and darkness had kissed and now no man could cut down his soul.

Baldwin, himself a sanctified preacher on the street corners of Harlem at the age of fifteen, had left the church and Christianity by the time he wrote *Go Tell It On the Mountain*. Like Ivan Karamazov he found the "price of the ticket" too high to pay. But he never forgot the "authenticity" of the sound of the storefront church and the history that produced it. In *The Fire Next Time*, he wrote that coming to grips with this past of suffering and transcendence, not erasing it as the Nation of Islam attempted to do, was necessary to achieving authenticity and maturity. It was necessary to internalize the meaning of that past for interracial community to become a possibility, a hope he so eloquently posed in the penultimate sentence of the book: "If we—and now I mean the relatively conscious whites and the relatively conscious blacks, who must, like lovers, insist on, or create, the consciousness of the others—do not falter in our duty now, we may be able, handful that we are, to end the racial nightmare, and achieve our country, and change the history of the world."[16]

One battle of the civil rights struggle, which Baldwin interpreted so perceptively, was chronicled by Melba Pattillo Beals in *Warriors Don't Cry*, a harrowing firsthand account of the attempt by nine black teenagers to integrate Central High School in Little Rock, Arkansas in 1957. It took Beals thirty years to finish the book she started to write at the age of eighteen, because the pain of her memories defeated each of her earlier attempts. As a child Beals accidentally wandered into a whites-only ladies room and was rescued from the threats of several white women by her Grandmother India. Even as her grandmother confronted the hostility of the white women, Melba noticed the quiver in her voice and was shocked to realize that her forceful grandmother was afraid. This incident foreshadowed the inability of her family to protect her from the violence she would experience as one of the "Little Rock Nine." Enduring physical assault, rejection, insults, and hatred day after day from her white classmates for an entire school year, Beals was forced to become a warrior in the battle for "the integration" as her people called it. With the help of her mother, her grandmother, one white National Guardsman temporarily assigned to guard her, and one white classmate, she lasted out the year (as did seven of the other children.) But the accumulated pain of her daily torture got so intense that she had to admit to her diary: "I think only the warrior exists in me now. Melba went away to hide. She was too frightened to stay here." Writing the book constituted one way for Beals to lay to rest the ghosts of that trauma, ghosts that still came alive for her and the others when they visited Central High years later, celebrated as honored guests and ceremonially greeted by the student body president, a bespectacled black youth wearing a mourning coat.

The fact that Melba Beals survived a difficult birth was interpreted by her grandmother as a confirmatory sign of her providential role in the integration movement. But Beals's uncertainty about the costs and extent of the integration's "victory" complicates the story and lends all the more rhetorical power to the questions she poses at the conclusion of her book: was the physical and emotional scarring worth it and did (do) the adults really understand the effects of using children "as tender warriors" then and now "on the battlefield to achieve racial equality?"[17]

A different dimension of the nation's racialized history troubled the life of James McBride, the son of a black father and a white Jewish mother. Raised in Queens with eleven brothers and sisters, McBride grew up during the "Black Power" era and was troubled by his interracial identity and by his mother's insistence on ignoring issues of race. Hence the book's title, *The Color of Water*: when asked, "what color is God?" she answered "the color of water." Around the age of twelve, McBride's racial identity crisis led him to create an imaginary world, in which he "believed [his] true self was a boy who lived in a mirror." He alternately loved and hated the boy in the mirror, who was free and did not have a mother who was white: "yet I myself had no idea who I was." Gradually he began to learn that his mother's reticence about her past was due to the pain of her memories. The daughter of an immigrant Orthodox Rabbi, she had abandoned her crippled mother and younger sister to escape the cruelty of her father and his plans to marry her off. She was shunned by her entire extended family for eventually marrying a black man whom she met and fell in love with, McBride's father. As his mother's story, set in alternating chapters with his own, develops, two parallel but overlapping histories emerge, McBride's search for his family and his mother's increasingly articulate memory of hers.

As an adult, McBride goes south to Suffolk, Virginia where his mother was raised to interview people who might remember his mother and his grandparents. After listening to stories of local blacks and Jews who remembered his family well, McBride had an unexpected experience of what I would call transgenerational recall. Awakening suddenly at four o'clock in the morning he walked along a wharf overlooking a river:

> It suddenly occurred to me that my grandmother had walked around here and gazed upon this water many times, and the loneliness and agony that Hudis Shilsky felt as a Jew in this lonely southern town—far from her mother and sisters in New York, unable to speak English, a disabled Polish immigrant whose husband had no love for her and whose dreams of seeing her children grow up in America vanished as her life drained out of her at the age of forty-six—suddenly rose up in my blood and washed over me in waves. A penetrating loneliness covered me, lay on me so heavily I had to sit down and cover my face. I had no tears to shed. They were done long ago, but a new pain and a new awareness were born inside me. The uncertainty that lived inside me began to dissipate; the ache that the little boy who stared in the mirror felt was gone. My own humanity was awakened, rising up to greet me with a handshake as I watched the first glimmers of sunlight peek over the horizon.[18]

No less than John Grimes, James McBride was seized by the memory of his people, significantly by the presence of his Jewish grandmother and so received his identity.

Last year I co-taught, with my colleague in English, Valerie Smith, a seminar at Princeton on "Spiritual Aspects of African American Autobiography" in which we read the books I discuss in this chapter and several others, including Richard Wright's *Black Boy, American Hunger*, Malcolm X's *Autobiography*, and Jan Willis's *Dreaming Me*. The students, half of them black and the other half white, wrestled with the texts all semester, each of them making two presentations. During the next to last class, one student used a surprising metaphor in her class presentation to describe what we had been doing all semester. She said, "we have been breaking apart the bread of the texts and offering each other communion." Her metaphor was intentionally Eucharistic based upon liturgical *anamnesis*, "calling to mind" the ritual repeating of Christ's action of offering and blessing the bread as his body and the wine as his blood at the Last Supper in obedience to his command to "do this in memory of me." As she continued, a murmur of recognition and approval emerged from the class and, when she had finished, a burst of applause. She enabled all of us to glimpse a more profound vision of the transformative power of memory and mourning.

7

THE RACE FOR FAITH

Justice, Mercy, and the Sign of the Cross in African American Literature

Katherine Clay Bassard

To be inside and outside a position at the same time—to occupy a territory while loitering skeptically on the boundary—is often where the most intensely creative ideas stem from. It is a resourceful place to be, if not always a painless one.[1]

—Terry Eagleton

Race, Faith, Theory

My primary title, "the Race for Faith," revisits and revises the title of black feminist literary critic Barbara Christian's 1987 essay, "The Race for Theory." In it, Christian gave voice to the misgivings of many scholars of color about the political ramifications of the escalation of theoretical discourses marshaled in the late 1980s and early 1990s—a proliferation, I might add, that forever divided generations of scholars into "before theory" and "after theory." It is within this framework that she coins the term "the race for theory," intended to signify both the prior acts of African American theorizing within dynamic forms of narrative and literary representation ("the race *for* theory") and the tendency of certain critical enterprises to enact the very oppressions they purport to solve ("the *race* for theory"). In the first use of the term, Christian notes that "people of color have always theorized—but in forms quite different from the Western form of abstract logic. And I am inclined to say that our theorizing (and I intentionally use the verb rather than the noun) is often in narrative forms, in the stories we create, in riddles and proverbs, in the play with language, since dynamic rather than fixed ideas seem more to our liking." Moreover, she voices a suspicion of Theory (capital "T") as yet another attempt to divide into haves and have nots, insiders and outsiders, privileged and "others":

> The race for theory, with its linguistic jargon, its emphasis on quoting its prophets, its tendency towards "Biblical" exegesis, its refusal even to mention specific works of creative writers, far less contemporary ones, its preoc-cupations with mechanical analyses of language, graphs, algebraic equations, its gross generalizations about culture, has silenced many of us to the extent that some of us feel we can no longer discuss our own literature, while others have developed intense writing blocks and are puzzled by the incomprehensibility of the language set adrift in literary circles.

What interests me in this passage is that she couches the dominance of critical theory in religious terms: "emphasis on quoting its prophets," "tendency towards 'Biblical' [capital "B"] exegesis," and so on. Put simply, Christian feels that "the new emphasis on literary critical theory is as hegemonic as the world which it attacks." Morever, this theoretical hegemony is created, authorized even, through sacred uses of language:

> I see the language it creates as one which mystifies rather than clarifies our condition, making it possible for a few people who know that particular language to control the critical scene—that language surfaced, interestingly enough, just when the literature of peoples of color, of black women, of Latin Americans, of Africans began to move to "the center." Such words as *center* and *periphery* are themselves instructive. . . . Because I went to a Catholic Mission school in the West Indies I must confess that I cannot hear the word "canon" without smelling incense, that the word "text" immediately brings back agonizing memories of Biblical exegesis, that "discourse" reeks for me of metaphysics forced down my throat. . . . "Periphery" too is a word I heard throughout my childhood, for if anything was seen as being in the periphery, it was those small Caribbean islands which had neither land mass nor military power.[2]

Barbara Christian sees a similarity in the positioning of the colonized subject as other to both the academic deployment of critical Theory and colonial Christianity. Similarly, in his review essay "Traces of God," Bruce Ellis Benson remarks on the blindness of theorists to the type of critique that Barbara Christian puts forth; for example, Derrida's equation of *differance* with justice reveals to Benson an inattentiveness to the oppressive uses of deconstruction. In his words, "at best I think we can say that deconstruction *has the potential to be a powerful tool of justice but has just as great a potential to be used for injustice.*" Moreover, Benson argues that the same holds true for religious discourse: "But, if it is difficult to act as a moral person without doing violence, can one believe as a religious person without doing violence? Derrida doesn't think so. The reason is that the same sorts of potential for violence characterize religious belief."[3] This, I think is the spirit, if not the letter, of Barbara Christian's analysis that brings both theory and Christianity under critique for African Americans and other oppressed peoples, as both literary theory and religious discourse address issues of violence and justice, dehumanization and equality.

Thus the beginning point for the following reflections is the uneasy alliance between "race," "faith," and "theory" as evidenced in African American literary representations of the cross of Christ. As an African American Christian scholar, addressing issues of faith and literary representation often feels like assembling a coalition of the not-so-willing. Indeed, the nominative "African American Christian scholar" is replete with apparent contradictions or, at best, tensions, as those tensions play out within a field of social inequality and historical injustice.

The more personal impetus for this series of readings came from watching Mel Gibson's *The Passion of the Christ* and hearing a colleague remark that the film was "a moving crucifix." I began to feel, as a Protestant who had grown up under the sign of the empty cross as the only authentic representation of Christian faith, that I had been missing something. I remember an incident in my small Baptist church when a member had returned from Mexico with a large crucifix that she insisted be placed within full view in the sanctuary. I remember the ensuing discussion: "Jesus isn't on the cross anymore. He's been resurrected." I also remember a feeling almost of offense at the grotesque figure described by someone as "bleeding from every pore." The Protestant insistence that the physical representation of the crucified Jesus compromises the second commandment—"Thou shalt not make unto thee any graven image"—and downplays the historicity of the resurrection was at the center of the discussion. In other words, the empty cross represents for believers not the absence of Jesus but his presence—both physically ascended into heaven "seated at the right hand of the father" and dispersed through the Holy Spirit and the church (the Body of Christ) into the world. The central evidence upon which Christianity rests is an *empty* tomb, an *absent* body, as the sign of ultimate power and redemption.

Related to this in my thinking is the significance of the empty cross for African Americans and others for whom the racial or ethnic representation of Jesus remains a troubling issue. While no one spoke of it that day in the discussion at my church, the absent body of Jesus allows one to skirt the issue of race. The visual representation of Christ necessitates a racialized (and we could say as well-gendered) body. The irony for me is that, in insisting on the empty cross as a way of signaling ethnic and cultural inclusiveness or a fully realized resurrection, we also lose contact with the suffering (as well as resurrected) body. In other words, while the absent body signifies presence for the faithful it opens a space for potential misreadings that actually undermine the entire redemptive project. If the need for social justice and equality demands the reappearance of an oppressed body, the demands of mercy and atonement appear to inscribe a counternarrative of redemptive invisibility.

I want to turn now to the African American literary tradition and trace a series of engagements with Christianity through the figure of the cross. My argument begins with the observation that a demystifying of the cross in cultural and theoretical discourse is equated with a disassociation of the cross with the passion of Christ—his suffering and resurrected body. This disembodiment of the central symbol of Christianity increasingly renders the cross as a cultural and linguistic sign in an effort to bring about social justice and equality. Ironically, the vanishing body of Jesus leaves an empty signifier whose reembodiment is both demanded and displaced by those from dispossessed communities. In other words, African Americans that reembody the cross with a black messiah find themselves performing a counterreformation move that cuts across the central tenets of Protestantism. To show the outworking of this dilemma that I am calling the problem of justice and the sign of the cross, I will look briefly at three historical textual moments in the African American literary tradition from the preemancipation period to the Harlem Renaissance before treating in more depth and detail Richard Wright's classic protest novel *Native Son* (1940) and Toni Morrison's *Paradise* (1997) from black postmodernity. What I hope to show is the way that these writers' engagements with Christianity—all of them quite serious, though they ultimately come to various positions of belief and unbelief—evidence a shift in the figuration of the cross from a more orthodox African American Protestantism to a displacement of its meanings out onto the African American (women's) community itself. I regard this movement as largely historical in nature, although there are other factors of gender and even individual authors' visions at stake. Moreover, the historical progression I sketch here incorporates the disappearance, refiguration, and (re)appearance of the body as a contestation over the meaning of Jesus as Messiah in both spiritual and material senses—what I refer to as an agent of mercy (spiritual) and justice (material).

In the case of what to do with the crucifix in my African American Baptist church, we decided to display it, not in the sanctuary but in a corner of the fellowship hall.

Justice, Mercy, and the Sign of the Cross in African American Literature

Before turning to the literary texts, I would like to outline three cultural and theological concepts that frame the readings to follow: Martin Luther's "theology of the cross," Wilson Jeremiah Moses's concept of "black messianism," and the historical emergence of representations of the black Christ culminating in the 1960s with James Cone's black theology of liberation. In May 1518, Luther wrote his *Heidelberg Disputation* and revealed to the world his theology of the cross: "crux sola est nostra theologia." The centerpiece of these twenty-eight theses is the contrast between "the way of glory" and "the way of the cross." To summarize Alister McGrath's reading of the *Heidelberg Disputation*, the theology of the cross is concealed revelation: "in that it is God who is made known in the passion and cross of Christ, it is *revelation*; in that this revelation can only be discerned by the eye of faith, it is *concealed*." Further, the revelation can only be discerned "in the sufferings and the cross of Christ, rather than in human moral activity or the created order." Thus the knowledge of the hidden God is a matter of faith and, most importantly for my purposes here, "God is particularly known through suffering."[4] In "The African American Experience and the Theology of the Cross," John Nunes notes that, historically, the theological practice of African Americans has been "crypto-Lutheran," and despite negative connotations, the way of the cross is embedded as "deep, durable faith" in African Americans.[5] However, Joel B. Green and Mark D. Baker point to the selectivity of images of Christ offered to conquered and colonized peoples; while the conquistadores resonated with images of the conquering, triumphant Messiah, the suffering Jesus on the cross was reserved for colonized others. Green and Baker write, "Especially among those who are the bearers of power and privilege in particular social contexts, the cross is sometimes deployed as a model for others. . . . 'Your pain, your loss,' this typology seems to urge, 'is an opportunity for you to identify with the passion of Jesus.' On the other hand, 'our victories, our imperial dominion is nothing less than a reflection of the divine conquest over the forces of evil.' Green and Baker further point out the significance of the cross in underwriting western concepts of justice, especially the notion of penal substitutionary atonement, which underlines the dilemma of Wright's *Native Son*.[6]

The application of the suffering servant typology onto enslaved African Americans gave rise to the tradition of black messianism. In his classic book *Black Messiahs and Uncle Toms*, Wilson Jeremiah Moses notes that "people develop a messianic view of themselves because of the historical experience of being oppressed as a group. Messianic traditions persist because the heritage of oppression persists." Stating that "no group of Americans have had a more deeply rooted or more stubbornly maintained messianic tradition than black Americans," Moses identifies four types of messianic representation: the expectation or identification of a personal savior; the concept of the redemption mission of the black race; journalistic and artistic presentations of certain black individuals as symbolic messiahs; and "Prophetism" or "prophetic movements." For Moses, the black messianic tradition is organized around two types of representation, that is, Uncle Tom and Nat Turner:

> It is these two jarringly opposed symbols that the messianic myth has joined together in dynamic tension. Black messianism has not simply identified the victimized African with such obvious Biblical motifs as the "Man of Sorrows" or the "Suffering Servant." . . . While the Uncle Tom tradition of turning the other cheek achieved undeniable importance in the passive-resistance tactics of the civil rights movement, the Nat Turner model soon began to provide a more acceptable self-image, even for moderate and gradualist political activists.[7]

The need for a "more acceptable self-image" can be traced to the emergence of the black Christ as religious and cultural icon in African American theology, art, and literary representation. Tracing the image from the earliest beginnings to contemporary culture, Kelly Brown Douglas notes that the black Christ image emerges in the 1960s with James Cone's black theology of liberation, although "different aspects of Christ's Blackness were highlighted from time to time throughout black history." As Douglas points out, "the Blackness of Christ in the Black church community has had more to do with Christ's commitment to Black freedom than to Christ's appearance."[8] As I will show, while literary embodiments of Christ appear during the preemancipation period, it is not until the Harlem Renaissance that African American writers began to identify Christ as black co-sufferer, following the artistic representations of Jacob Lawrence and Romare Bearden. These representations of the black theology Jesus are behind Rev. Misner's understanding of the cross in the centermost scene of Morrison's *Paradise*.

In order to situate Wright and Morrison within a larger context of African American literary community, I will sketch in broad strokes the progression of representations of the cross as both a fully embodied signifier and increasingly disembodied sign as Protestant concepts of atonement and mercy give way to more secular concerns of social justice and agency. The brief outline of how such a tradition would look is as follows:

1. Messianic Hope: represented by Phillis Wheatley's poetry and into the nineteenth century, which Sandy Dwayne Martin refers to as the era of "black Christian consensus." As messianic hope, Wheatley represents Jesus's suffering on the cross simultaneously as the fulfillment and extension of God's mercy and thus the promise or hope of social justice. This corresponds to the first category in Moses's definition as it relies on the concept of the expectation of a personal savior or deliverer.

2. Messianic Fulfillment: represented by Frederick Douglass and Harriet Jacobs in their slave narratives of 1845 and 1861, respectively. Here, the physically free body of the fugitive slave is troped not as a suffering messiah but as a resurrected Christ, as in Douglass's statement: "it was a glorious resurrection from the tomb of slavery to the heaven of freedom." In this sense, Douglass and Jacobs implicitly refute the sacrificial image of Uncle Tom in Stowe's novel by depicting messianism as a realized physical and material emancipation

3. Messianic Desire: here I read James Weldon Johnson writing during the Harlem Renaissance, as Jesus is represented less as the embodiment of spiritual atonement and more as the problem of racial representation and identification. In this phase the fulfillment of messianic desire is contingent on the identification of Christ with specifically African American suffering. Here, the nineteenth-century notion of the black redemptive mission becomes specifically embodied as the black male lynching victim by poets like Countee Cullen and Langston Hughes.

4. Messianic Deferral: Wright's *Native Son* inverts the mercy-justice paradigm of the black Christian consensus by foreclosing the issue of justice for black men in racialized America. Because there is no social justice, mercy is also rendered suspect. Social injustice, represented by the white indictment of African Americans for the "sin" of blackness, displaces the desire for mercy onto human rather than divine agents. This corresponds to what Moses calls "messianic symbolism," the representation of certain individuals as messiah.

5. Messianic Displacement: in Toni Morrison's *Paradise* this represents a post-postmodernist "After Theory" movement in which the vanquished messiah becomes reembodied within the community of outcast women who represent the meeting place of justice and mercy. Here the convent functions as a prophetic community with a "special mission from God."[9]

I want to make a brief distinction between what I am calling "hope," "desire," "deferral," and "displacement." Hope, as I use it here, refers to an expectation for which the prior conditions have already been met, as in "faith is the sub-stance of things hoped for, the evidence of things not seen" (Hebrews 11:1). It is not wishful thinking but the stance that signifies the fulfillment of pre-conditions and is therefore forward-looking. Desire, as I use it here, refers to a situation in which the fulfillment of desire is contingent upon conditions that may or may not have been met. It looks, therefore, both forward and backward. Deferral refers to a pattern of regression in which the fulfillment of desire is always placed just out of reach, which throws the subject inward. Displacement in my lexicon refers to the redirection of the fulfillment of desire away from the future onto a fully realized present temporality.

Protestant Crucifix: Messianic Hope in Wheatley's Poetry

Two poems from Phillis Wheatley's *Poems on Various Subjects Religious and Moral* (1773) will suffice to demonstrate the fully embodied messianic vision behind her poetics. The first is "To the University of Cambridge in New-England" where Wheatley, "an *Ethiop*," admonishes students at Harvard and future leaders of what will become the United States to

> Improve you privileges while they stay,
> Ye pupils, and each hour redeem, that bears
> Or good or bad report of you to heav'n.

Important for my purposes here is the central stanza in which Wheatley directs the students' (and the reader's) gaze to contemplate Jesus on the cross:

> See Him with hands out-stretcht upon the cross;
> Immense compassion in his bosom glows;
> He hears revilers, nor resents their scorn:
> What matchless mercy in the Son of God!
> When the whole human race by sin had fall'n
> He deign'd to die that they might rise again,
> And share with him in the sublimest skies,
> Life without death, and glory without end.

The imperative to "see Him" brings before the reader a visual image of Christ's sacrifice that necessitates a contemplation of his physical body, "with hands out-stretcht upon the cross." In the remainder of the poem when Wheatley chides the Harvard pupils to use their immense privilege in responsible ways, it is on the basis of this image of "matchless mercy in the Son of God!"[10] The extension of God's mercy fully realized in the crucified Christ becomes the ground for any reading of the poem as a plea for social justice.

The elegy "On the Death of the Rev. George Whitefield," Wheatley's first published poem, was published as a broadside in 1770 to commemorate the death of the famous evangelist. It versifies a typical Whitefield sermon "freely offer'd to the num'rous throng:"

> Take him, ye wretched, for your only Good;
> Take him, ye hungry Souls, to be your Food;
> Take him, ye Thirsty, for your cooling Stream;
> Ye Preachers, take him for your joyful Theme;
> Take him, my dear *Americans*, he said,
> Be your Complaints in his kind Bosom laid;
> Take him, ye *Africans*, he longs for you,
> *Impartial Saviour* is his Title due.
> If you will walk in Grace's heavenly Road,
> He'll make you free, and kings, and Priests to God."[11]

What Wheatley puts on Whitefield's lips is a sermon with a sweeping egalitarian vision: "Take him my dear Americans." "Take him, ye Africans." By referring to Jesus as "*Impartial Saviour*" she is envisioning a messianic order where both Africans and white Americans "shall be sons, and kings, and priests to God." The "see Him" from "To The University of Cambridge" has become the "Take Him" here, as Wheatley imagines a universalist gospel the acceptance of which forms the ground for justice in the social order. The body of Christ is signified here not by an actual body on the cross but by references to the Eucharist: "Take him ye hungry Souls, for your Food; / "Take him, ye Thirsty, for your cooling Stream."

"Glorious Resurrections": Resurrection Typology in Two Slave Narratives

Wilson Jeremiah Moses's argument that antebellum black messianism rests on the two poles of the Uncle Tom and Nat Turner figures fails to take into account the ways in which slave narrators like Frederick Douglass and Harriet Jacobs mediated their christological representations through a third trope of empowerment: the New Testament insistence on the bodily resurrection of Jesus. If Stowe's Uncle Tom refigures the suffering, "masochistic martyr" Christ of the crucifixion and Nat Turner's self-portrait in his *Confessions* embodies the "retributive messiah" of the Second Coming, the male fugitive slave of Douglass's 1845 *Narrative of the Life of Frederick Douglass* and Jacobs' 1861 *Incidents in the Life of a Slave Girl* points to an alternative possibility.[12] In this sense, slavery itself is the "cross" born by enslaved African Americans who, in the state of liberation, become empowered Christ figures. In his

Narrative, after defeating the slave breaker Mr. Covey in a physical show of force, Douglass uses the language of resurrection to describe the mental and emotional transference from slave to free: "He only can understand the deep satisfaction which I experienced, who has himself repelled by force the bloody arm of slavery. I felt as I never felt before. It was a glorious resurrection, from the tomb of slavery to the heaven of freedom. My long crushed spirit rose, cowardice departed, bold defiance took its place; and I now resolved that, however long I might remain a slave in form, the day had passed forever when I could be a slave in fact."[13] Although he has not yet physically escaped slavery, by aligning his deliverance with the resurrected Christ rather than the suffering messiah, Douglass is able to bypass the type of representation that Stowe would popularize in *Uncle Tom's Cabin*.

Harriet Jacobs makes a similar move in chapter 4 of *Incidents in the Life of A Slave Girl* in which she recounts the escape of her uncle Benjamin. Presented as a male slave narrative within a female slave narrative paradigm, "The Slave Who Dared to Feel Like a Man" is both an affirmation and a displacement of the male fugitive slave experience made popular by Frederick Douglass. Like Douglass, Jacobs emphasizes Benjamin's physical fighting off of the master. However, she reserves the resurrection language for his actual escape to the North. His miraculous and mysterious escape from prison, the various sightings of Benjamin which have characters remarking that he looks "like a ghost," and the prohibition against touching him all utilize language of the resurrected but preascension Christ.[14]

In using resurrection language, Douglass and Jacobs steer their fugitive slave messiahs between the "retributive and masochistic" dimensions that Moses identifies. Yet however much the male fugitive slave might represent the goal of future deliverance for all African Americans, the slave as messiah is only a self-deliverer; whatever the symbolic value of the fugitive slave, deliverance remains individual in nature and only representative of future expectation.

"Were You There?": Messianic Desire in James Weldon Johnson's "The Crucifixion"

James Weldon Johnson composed the poems that make up *God's Trombones* from the vague and shadowy memories he had of sermons heard in childhood. "The Crucifixion" is positioned before the Exodus poem "Let My People Go" and "The Judgment Day." That Johnson positions the poem out of biblical narrative order is significant as, again, the cross is viewed as a statement about the possibility of justice for African Americans, the precursor to both their social liberation represented by the Exodus story and the ultimate judgment of American oppression on Judgment Day. The close identification between the speaker and Christ is seen in the use of possessives to begin each of the first three stanzas: "Jesus, my gentle Jesus"; "Jesus, my burdened Jesus"; "Jesus, my sorrowing Jesus." This continues in other places in the poem: "My blame-less Jesus"; "my loving Jesus"; "my sweet King Jesus"; "My lamb-like Jesus"; "my darling Jesus"; "my lonesome Jesus," and so on. The culmination of this personal identification occurs in the line, "They crucified my Jesus." That the speaker identifies personally with the suffering of Christ comes as no surprise. What is of interest is in stanza seven:

> Up Golgotha's rugged road
>   I see my Jesus go.
>   I see him sink beneath the load,
>   I see my drooping Jesus sink.
> And then they laid hold on Simon,
> Black Simon, yes, black Simon;
> They put the cross on Simon,
> And Simon bore the cross.[15]

The three-fold repetition of "I see" again brings the body of Christ in view. The emphasis on Simon's blackness and the transfer of the cross to him meta-phorically inverts the substitutionary sacrifice: it is not the (black) speaker's identification with Christ that is important but rather Christ's identification with the suffering of black people. Christ's ability to represent not only the mercy associated with the visual, graphic imagery in the rest of the poem ("the Roman spear plunged in his side"; "the blood came spurting from his wound," etc.) but also the justice of blacks who also "bear the cross" is conditioned on this close association with Simon of Cyrene. The penultimate stanza—

> And the veil of the temple was split in two,
> The midday sun refused to shine,
> The thunder rumbled and the lightning wrote
> An unknown language in the sky

—pictures the scene as an unwriting or rewriting of the text of the crucifixion in a way that translates into African American desire for justice.

In the last stanza, Johnson responds to the call from the well-known African American spiritual:

Were you there when they crucified my Lord?
Were you there when they crucified my Lord?
Oh, sometimes it causes me to tremble, tremble, tremble.
Were you there when they crucified my Lord?

Johnson answers the call in the affirmative with these words:

Oh, I tremble, yes, I tremble,
It causes me to tremble, tremble,
When I think how Jesus died;
Died on the steeps of Calvary,
How Jesus died for sinners,
Sinners like you and me.

The positive affirmation that "yes, I tremble" places the speaker in the scene experientially through his own salvation and vicariously through the figure of Simon. The tremble of messianic desire holds the promise of a liberated body because of Jesus's identification with black suffering.

Interestingly enough, Johnson does not represent Jesus as black in the way of Langston Hughes in "Christ in Alabama" or Countee Cullen in "The Black Christ." In "Christ in Alabama," "the unique suffering of the Gospel is replaced by the repeated suffering of the lynched black man."[16] Both of these poems figure the body of a black male lynching victim as the crucified Christ.

Richard Wright's Double Cross in *Native Son*

In tracing this line of descent from hope to desire to deferral, there is no more important work than Richard Wright's *Native Son* (1940). Written after the optimism of the Harlem Renaissance had subsided, Wright set out to shift the scene of the discussion of black Americans from the rural south to the urban landscape of the North. In so doing, he shifted the terms of the meaning of the possibility of justice for blacks in white-dominated America. The problem of justice and mercy is figured in *Native Son* as a "double cross," a literal and figurative doubling of the meanings associated with Christianity in a racist society. Writing after the figurations of lynching as crucifixion and before Cone's black theology of liberation, the images available to Wright become refracted through the prism of the empty cross(es) in *Native Son*. Set in Chicago, *Native Son* is the story of Bigger Thomas, a twenty-year-old African American man who accidentally kills the daughter of his wealthy employer, Mr. Dalton. Terrified of being found in her bedroom, he accidentally smothers her, then disposes of her dismembered body in a furnace. While on the run, he discovers a sense of power and agency he had never experienced before and begins to internalize the idea of his criminality as an act of creative agency. In the process of trying to collect ransom for the "missing" Mary, he kills a second time—this time brutally raping and murdering his African American girlfriend Bessie and stuffing her body down an elevator shaft of an abandoned building. Bigger is finally caught, arrested, and finds himself in the hands of the criminal justice system. Ironically, when the remains of Mary are found among the ashes in the furnace, she is presumed to have been raped as well. Bigger ultimately is tried for the wrong crime with the wrong body (Bessie's) used as evidence against him. Despite a valiant attempt by his Marxist lawyer, Max, he is convicted and sentenced to death.

Bigger Thomas's plight turns on what Green and Baker call "autobiographical justice," which is based on the view "that individuals perform acts of transgression, so that individuals (or individual entities) ought to be examined and punished for their complicity." The idea of individual responsibility or accountability is deeply rooted in Christian notions of salvation and redemption and underwrites the penal system's focus on people as individuals "not as persons embedded within social systems."[17] Wright's naturalism in *Native Son* is an exploration of this very dilemma.

Wright's Marxism and atheism would seem to close the issue of his views of religion in general and Christianity in particular. In books 1 and 2, the expected dismissals of a weak Christianity, which only renders inner city poor blacks docile and ineffective, is the rule. Yet at the end of book 2, with Bigger's arrest, and throughout book 3, "Fate," Wright launches a serious engagement with Christian doctrine and the meaning of the cross. Book 2 ends with Bigger represented as a Christ figure: "Two men stretched his arms out, as though about to crucify him; they placed a foot on each of his wrists, making them sink deep down in the snow. His eyes closed, slowly, and he was swallowed in darkness." The image is unmistakable: Bigger, surrounded by whiteness, snow, police, and so forth, is the innocent sufferer for the "sin" of blackness. The equation of black suffering with Christ goes as far back as Frederick Douglass's *Narrative* almost a century before *Native Son* and is not surprising. What is surprising is that all of book 3 will continue to struggle over the meaning of the cross, whose image explodes in a kind of refractive hall of mirrors as Wright deploys images of sacrifice and substitution to explore the issue of justice in the light of mercy and forgiveness.

The Christic references continue in book 3 as we are told that Bigger, dragged from one police station to another, "steadfastly refused to speak" and "would not even drink water." Yet these equations of Bigger with Christ do not hold in the novel but give way when Bigger, facing the death penalty, is visited by Reverend Hammond, his mother's pastor. The first words out of Hammond's mouth are "Mah, po' boy! May the good Lawd have mercy on yuh." The offer of mercy, however, is interpreted by Bigger as condemnation and "made him feel as condemned and guilty as the voice of those who hated him." Hammond offers Bigger not the justice he craves but also a narrative: "lemme tell yuh why yuh's here. Lemme tell yuh a story tha'll make yo' heart glad." Rather than make his heart glad, the story of Creation, the Fall, and Christ's redemption has the opposite effect on Bigger:

> The preacher's face was black and sad and earnest and made him feel a sense of guilt deeper than that which the murder of Mary had made him feel. He had killed within him the preacher's haunting picture of life before he had ever killed Mary; that had been his first murder. . . . To those who wanted to kill him he was not human, not included in that picture of Creation; and that was why he had killed it. To live, he had created a new world for himself and for that he was to die.[18]

The narrative represents Bigger's "crime" as the murder of the only narrative that offers him anything like hope and redemption. It is this inability to place himself within the cultural symbolic and within the framework of humanity that becomes Bigger's undoing. Bigger has a dim awareness of a crime or sin prior to the murder for which he is on trial (the accidental death of white Mary Dalton) or the one he actually committed (the deliberate murder of black Bessie). He misnames it as the killing or murder of a picture, a narrative that represented both a "haunting picture of life" and the promise of life itself: "How could he believe in that which he had killed? He was guilty." It is important to note that the annihilation of this image of life occurs because of society's dehumanization of Bigger through racism; he experiences himself as "unCreated" and, because he views himself as outside the paradigm of Creation, he is outside the hope of redemption as well. Bigger reads the Creation-Fall-Cross narrative through the lens of the nonhuman. Significantly, to be outside the narrative is to be outside even the potential not only for grace but also for transgression. It is a situation in which his guilt is necessary to prove his humanity.

In this context, Rev. Hammond's prayer for "mercy" reads as a condemnation of his very existence as not-human. It is at this point that Hammond presents to Bigger "a small wooden cross with a chain upon it" saying, "Ah'm holdin' befo' yo' eyes the only thing tha' gives a meanin' to yo' life. Here, lemme put it roun' yo' neck. When yuh git alone, look at this cross, son, 'n' b'lieve." The cross lying next to his skin causes him to feel, according to the narrator, "that life was flesh nailed to the world, a longing spirit imprisoned in the days of the earth."[19]

Unlike the representations of the cross by Wheatley or Johnson where the body of Christ is present ("See Him"; "I see") the cross that Hammond presents to Bigger is an empty signifier, because Bigger is already outside the narrative that would stabilize its meaning. There is no messianic hope, and, for Bigger, messianic desire for justice is always deferred, because the desire or even need for mercy is suppressed. The narrator explains Bigger's reaction to Rev. Hammond this way: "He feared and hated the preacher, because the preacher had told him to bow down and ask for a mercy he knew he needed."[20] The wooden cross with a chain is contrasted with another cross that comes into Bigger's field of vision, and it is here that the deconstruction, or double cross, occurs:

> He felt hot spittle splashing against his face. Somebody tried to leap at him, but was caught by the policemen and held back. As he stumbled across the street, above the heads of the people, loomed a flaming cross. At once he knew that it had something to do with him. But why should they burn a cross? As he gazed at it he remembered the sweating face of the black preacher in his cell that morning talking intensely and solemnly of Jesus, of there being a cross for him, a cross for everyone, and of how the lowly Jesus had carried the cross, paving the way, showing him how to die, how to love and live the life eternal. But he had never seen a cross burning like that one upon the roof. Were white people wanting him to love Jesus too? He heard the wind whipping the flames. No! That was not right; they ought not burn a cross. . . . The eyes and faces about him were not at all the way the black preacher's had been when he had prayed about Jesus and His love, about His dying upon the cross. The cross the preacher had told him about was bloody, not flaming; meek, not militant. It had made him feel awe and wonder, not fear and panic. It had made him want to kneel and cry, but this cross made him want to curse and kill.[21]

The doubling of the crosses in "Fate" represents the deconstruction of the meaning of Christianity within the field of white supremacy and racism. In trying to sort out this duality, Bigger "felt betrayed": "With bated breath he tore his shirt open, not caring who saw him. He gripped the cross and snatched it from his throat. He threw it away, cursing a curse that was almost a scream."[22]

Several policemen and guards react to try to get Bigger to "take up his cross": one returns it to his cell only to have Bigger toss it away again. There is an interesting moment in which one of the guards outside Bigger's cell "piously touch[es] his fingers to his forehead, his chest, his left shoulder, and then his right; making the sign of the cross." With this silent gesture, one that evokes a crucifix where Christ's suffering is fully embodied to view, the emptiness of the cross(es) in Bigger's experience stands in bold relief. It is the disembodiment of the cross, its inability to signal the preacher's narrative in any meaningful way for Bigger that causes his ultimate rejection of the hope of either justice or mercy. When he is confronted with the reality that was "not the cross of Christ, but the cross of the Ku Klux Klan," he is faced with the vulnerability of the cross as an open sign.[23] That it could signify simultaneously love and hate, humility and arrogance, life and destruction ultimately renders it without meaning. This is not a deconstruction that liberates Bigger but one that plunges him into despair. The cross as "word" is as vulnerable as any other sign to misappropriation and misinterpretation.

Yet Wright does not leave things there, and the idea of the cross, particularly the ideas of substitution and sacrifice, continue to play out in "Fate." If the cross as "word" is reduced to a mere cultural sign whose emptiness signifies not the risen Christ but his absence, the cross as Flesh continues to surface as the deferral of messianic redemption. It is here that I believe Wright wrestles more seriously with Christianity than critics have given him credit for. Jan, the young communist and Mary's boyfriend who befriends Bigger, is the second visitor to his jail cell. Significantly, in an effort to cover up his crime, Bigger had earlier tried to frame Jan for Mary's murder. Jan's words to Bigger are encoded with images of sacrifice: "I—I just wanted to come here and tell you that I'm not angry and I want you to let me help you. I don't hate you for trying to blame this thing on me. . . . Maybe you had good reasons. . . . I don't know. And maybe in a certain sense, I'm the one who's really guilty."[24] Jan's embodiment of Christlikeness is described by the narrator as "the word had become flesh." Later in the same scene, Jan confesses, "I can't take upon myself the blame for what one hundred million people have done." Similarly, Mr. Dalton, Mary's father and the wealthy philanthropist for whom Bigger had worked, remarks, "Do you want me to die to atone for a suffering I never caused? I'm not responsible for the state of this world. I'm doing all one man can." This theme of one representing the "guilt" of many is also ascribed to Bigger: "Had he not taken fully upon himself the crime of being black? Had he not done this thing which they dreaded above all others? They should go home contented, feeling that their shame was washed away." The language of substitution, sacrifice, and atonement (Bessie's body substituted for Mary's as evidence of the crime, for example) point to the deferral of messianic hope and desire in the narrative. The answer to the question posed by both Jan and

Mr. Dalton seems to be that however much human sacrifice and generosity can approximate Christlikeness, they only gesture toward the messianic and, in fact, highlight its absence. There is a kind of despair at the end of "Fate" that leaves Bigger outside the Symbolic, outside either justice or mercy, "trying to remember where he had heard words that would help him. He could recall none. He had lived outside the lives of men. Their modes of communication, their symbols and images, had been denied him."[25]

(Re)Embodying Jesus: Messianic Displacement in Paradise

Tell us what it is to be a woman so that we may know what it is to be a man. What moves at the margin. What it is to have no home in this place. To be set adrift from the one you know. What it is to live at the edge of towns that cannot bear your company.

—Toni Morrison, Nobel Prize Lecture, 1993

Set in Oklahoma, *Paradise* opens in 1976 when the men of Ruby, an all-black town, invade a neighboring former convent that has become a haven for women in flight from abuse and troubled circumstances. The Ruby men, themselves descendants of former slaves who settled first in Haven then in Ruby in a gesture of self-determination and black liberation, formulate their ideas of justice through a grid of color and gender difference. If justice and mercy work at cross purposes in *Native Son*, they collide in *Paradise*, and at the center of the collision is the cross. This time, however, notions of sacrifice and redemption, rather than eternally deferred, are displaced within the narrative as messianic desire, refigured through acts of feminine embodiment.

The first prominent mention of the cross in the novel is in the opening section where the men are stalking the women in the convent with the intent of killing them: "the outline of a huge cross comes into view. Clean as new paint is the space where there used to be a Jesus." The missing space of Jesus can be read as remnants of the convent that had been replaced by a Protestant mission to Native American girls. Earlier in an internal monologue which catalogues the objects that come into view as the men scour the convent looking for victims, we get the following description: "a fedora tilted on the plastic neck of a female torso, and, in a place that once housed Christians—well, Catholics anyway—not a cross of Jesus anywhere."[26] The missing Jesus represents the vacating of the masculine body to clear the cross to serve as a site of female reembodiment.

The most important scene involving the cross, however, occurs in the centermost chapter, "Divine." The chapter opens at the wedding of Arnette and K. D., where the Methodist pastor Rev. Pulliam delivers a judgmental speech on love meant to shame and demean rather than uplift the wedding attendants. Earlier the reader's gaze has been directed toward "a three-foot oak cross. Uncluttered. Unencumbered. No gold competed with its perfection or troubled its poise. No writhe or swoon of the body of Christ bloated its lyric thunder." Having been "targeted" by Pulliam's sermon, the Baptist pastor, Rev. Misner, who is to perform the wedding ceremony, decides on a response: "Misner walked away from the pulpit, to the rear wall of the church. There he stretched, reached up until he was able to unhook the cross that hung there. He carried it then, past the empty choir stall, past the organ where Kate sat, the chair where Pulliam was, on the podium, and held it before him for all to see—if only they would."[27]

In a gesture reminiscent of Phillis Wheatley's "See Him" and "Take Him" in the eighteenth century, Misner's silent presentation of the cross is an urgent plea for a sort of spiritual or "second" sight on the part of the congregation. Like Luther's theology of the cross, it is a "concealed revelation" that Misner holds up to the congregation, hoping that they will be able to reembody the empty cross through their own experiences of suffering and oppression. Yet, unlike Wheatley who directs the reader's gaze to "Him with arms out-stretcht upon the cross," Misner offers the uncluttered and unencumbered cross with neither body nor spoken text. In a sense, this failure to "take a text" becomes his undoing. In seeking to counter Pulliam's mishandling of "the Word," Misner relies upon "the Sign." In Misner's mind, he is holding up the empty cross precisely in hopes that the people will perform their own reembodiment and reread it through the text of their own oppressed bodies. In a long interior monologue, the reader is privy to his thoughts while the stunned wedding guests look on in silence:

> See? The execution of this one solitary black man propped on these two intersecting lines to which he was attached in a parody of human embrace, fastened to two big sticks that were so convenient, so recognizable, so embedded in consciousness *as consciousness*, being both ordinary and sublime. See? His woolly head alternately rising on his neck and falling toward his chest; the glow of his midnight skin dimmed by dust, streaked by gall, fouled by spit and urine, gone pewter in the hot, dry wind. . . . See, how this official murder out of hundreds marked the difference; moved the relationship between God and man from CEO and supplicant to one on one? The cross he held was abstract; the absent body was real, but both combined to pull humans from backstage to the spotlight, from muttering in the wings to the principal role in the story of their lives.[28]

The invitation to "See? . . . See?" is predicated on Misner's representation of Jesus as black ("one solitary black man," "his woolly head," "the glow of his midnight skin") in the tradition of the black theology of liberation. Because for him the identification of Christ with an executed black man is a foregone conclusion, he is able to offer the cross as an agent simultaneously of mercy and justice. The problem for Rev. Misner is that the embodiment of Christ as a realization of black suffering is only in his imagination: "But Rev. Misner could not speak calmly of these things. So he stood there and let minutes tick by as he held the crossed oak in his hands, urging it to say what he could not: that not only is God interested in you; He *is* you. Would they see? Would they?"[29]

The conflation of human and divine is what I mean by messianic displacement, a displacement gestured to by Wright but left incomplete and incompletable in the figures of Jan, Mr. Dalton, and Max. What is important here is that the congregation fails to see exactly what Misner sees; the cross cannot speak for itself, but because it is vacant, it becomes a projection screen for each viewer's preoccupations and predispositions. Unable to hear the "lyric thunder" of the empty cross, the congregation resents the silence, which they fill in with "coughs and soft, encouraging grunts." The silent and empty representation incites alternately shame, terror, and a judgmental attitude. In a way Steward's remark may be the most accurate of all—"whatever Rev. Misner was thinking, he was wrong. A cross was no better than the bearer."[30] Misner's attempt to will the congregation to see what he sees fails; two hundred years after Wheatley's offer to "Take Him," Misner's black Christ has no takers and yields no deliverance or hope for justice. It is the failure of this moment, I believe, that sets the stage for the retributive justice enacted by the men of Ruby on the female scapegoats of the convent. The failure of Misner's bodiless, wordless cross to definitively convey mercy leads to a misfiring of justice.

In a review of Terry Eagleton's *After Theory*, Eugene McCarraher ponders what is to come after Eagleton's declaration that "the golden age of cultural theory is long past," speculating that the space vacated by theory in the academy could well be filled by theology: "So, if cultural theory occupies the place once filled by theology, and if 'the age in which culture sought to play surrogate to religion is perhaps drawing to a close,' shouldn't theology be one of those 'new topics' explored in the wake of postmodernism?" It seems that Toni Morrison's answer in *Paradise* is yes. Having explored the terrain of new historicism in *Beloved* (1987) and deconstruction in *Jazz* (1992), *Paradise* appears to be Morrison's foray into the theological. As McCarraher concludes, "revolution is indissoluble from resurrection."[31] The question is, what Body do we imagine rising from the grave?

8

FORMS OF REDEMPTION

John Stauffer

Following the ideals of freedom released by the American Revolution and evangelical religion, slavery and racial prejudice became the dark underside of the American dream. James Madison referred to slavery as America's "original sin"; it was the obstacle to white Americans' pretensions of perfection, the barrier blocking their path to the millennium. The tragic result of this formulation, as David Davis has shown, was to identify African Americans as the "Great American Problem." The road would be clear, the new age in sight, were it not for the presence of blacks. Such beliefs affected many white and even a few black abolitionist writings and lay at the heart of the many proposals for colonizing blacks outside the United States. Hence the victims of slavery became, in his psychological inversion, "the embodiment of sin."[1] This idea that blacks embodied sin helped justify slavery and racial oppression. The three chapters under review (Chapters 5–7) all explore how black writers responded to this psychological curse—that is, how it felt to be "a problem."[2]

Redemptive Reading: African Americans and the Abolitionist Movement

Mark Noll looks at how African American writers "redeemed" Biblical defenses of slavery during the first ninety years of U.S. history. He organizes his chapter around five genres: memoirs, treatises, sermons, manifestos, and dialogue. By structuring the chapter in such a way, he is able to show how genre and form shape the message. Memoirs illustrated how former slaves appropriated scripture. Treatises exposed how proslavery biblical arguments ignored race when interpreting scripture. The sermon became a sophisticated weapon against the continuation of slavery. Manifestos emphasized the link between religious and social commitments. And dialogue, especially Daniel Coker's "Dialogue Between a Virginian and an African minister," offered one of the "strongest theological statements against American slavery," according to Noll, even though it appeared in 1810.

Noll provides a wonderful summary of the uses and limits of black writers seeking to redeem scripture, and I would like to add to it. What Noll gives up by organizing his chapter around genre is a clear sense of change over time in black resistance to slavery and proslavery theological arguments. In reading Noll's account, one might conclude that the "black Founders" in the Age of Revolution were as rhetorically radical and militant against the sin of slavery and proslavery theology as antebellum black abolitionists, such as Frederick Douglass, Henry Highland Garnet, and Theodore Wright. Yet there was a significant shift in attitudes and beliefs among black leaders from the Revolution to the Civil War.

There were a number of reasons for this. Enlightenment thought during the Revolutionary era was torn between "the ideal of the autonomous individual," which was antithetical to slavery, and the "ideal of a rational and efficient social order," which feared the social chaos that would result from ending slavery too quickly. As a result, there were few recorded instances of whites or blacks advocating an *immediate* end to all sin and thus immediate and universal emancipation. The first abolition societies refused to accept African Americans as members; and Quakers, the first white abolitionists, generally did not welcome free blacks into their churches and homes. White abolitionists sought gradual means for ending slavery, primarily through colonization.[3]

The first generation of black abolitionists were also influenced by Enlightenment thought, though the degree to which they shaped it has not been fully explored. In general, they accepted patient and gradual abolition and emigration to Africa (though not through the American Colonization Society) as a *pragmatic* solution to racism and unfreedom. Black leaders tended to act deferentially toward white abolitionists. They were willing to compromise their desire for immediate emancipation and equality in exchange for some semblance of safety and the prevention of bloodshed.

A few examples highlight black leaders' faith in a pragmatic solution to slavery in the post-Revolutionary era. Phillis Wheatley, in her 1775 poem, "To His Excellency General Washington," reveres Washington as a champion of freedom, yet, unlike the later generation of black activists, she makes no mention of him owning slaves and not advocating abolition. The very structure of Wheatley's poetry—formal closed couplets—underscores her emphasis on order and deference to authority. In 1794 Absalom Jones and Richard Allen used deferential language to protest slavery and racial oppression. "We do not wish to make you [whites] angry," they wrote, "but excite your attention to consider how hateful slavery is in the sight of that God, who hath destroyed kings and princes or their oppression of the poor slaves."[4] This was a rhetoric of control rather than defiance. In 1799 Jones and seventy-three other blacks elaborated on their reform vision in a petition to the president, Senate, and House of Representatives: "we do not ask for an *immediate* emancipation of *all*, knowing that the degraded state of the *many*, and their want of education, would *greatly disqualify* for such a change." For these black Founders, self-help and education were prerequisites to liberty and equality. And they urged a gradual end to slavery: "we desire that you exert every means in your power to undo the heavy burdens and *prepare the way* for the oppressed to go free, that every yoke may be broken."[5] In 1797 Prince Hall told his black brethren to be "patient" in their hopes for emancipation. As late as 1813, James Forten referred to "white men" as "our protectors" in his pleas for "rational liberty."[6] These black writers, having witnessed the passage of gradual emancipation laws throughout the north, had reason to believe that slavery would gradually and eventually end throughout the nation. Their rhetoric of deference was, in other words, smart politics.[7]

These examples of deference also reflect the *newness* of antislavery thought and the desire for an orderly transition from slavery to freedom. Throughout history, few people have accepted their condition as slaves without rebelling in some way, but, until the Age of Revolution, rebels sought to invert the master-slave hierarchy instead of advocating universal freedom.[8] The St. Domingue rebellion of 1791, which was influenced in Enlightenment beliefs in the rights of man, marks a major shift in the rise of antislavery thought and the strategy of rebellion; it was the first instance that we know of in which slave rebels also advocated universal freedom, and it can thus be seen as the first instance of immediatism—that is, arguments for an immediate end to slavery.[9]

Immediatism represented both a shift in strategy and a change in outlook. While white gradualists embraced colonization and boycotts as a means to end slavery, black gradualists accepted voluntary emigration and deferred to white authorities as a pragmatic attempt to retain their tenuous freedom and prevent a race war. Immediate abolitionism advocated a total and swift transformation of society. It also reflected a shift from Enlightenment to Romantic worldviews, from a "detached, rationalistic perspective on history and progress to a personal commitment to make no compromise with sin." Immediatism was an expression of inner freedom and triumph over worldly conventions; it reflected an eschatological leap, a sharp break from linear notions of progress and history, and assumed that a new age was dawning. It was thus an appropriate doctrine for a new Romantic age.[10]

Immediate abolitionism brought blacks and whites together as allies and friends in a way that had not occurred before.[11] They advocated racial equality and worked to achieve it, and there was a moral certainty to their immediatist outlook, which was absent among gradual abolitionists. While gradualists were willing to compromise with sin, immediatists believed that the nation would soon become all one thing or all the other, to paraphrase Lincoln, and so one needed to do the right thing right now. With such moral certainty came an acceptance of social chaos and eventually violence; moral certainty of any kind can more easily lead to chaos and bloodshed than order.[12]

As Noll elegantly notes at the end of his chapter, African American writers "testified to the power that Scriptures were exerting in their redeemed lives. They also were testifying to the sanctified power of their own prose in redeeming Scriptures." He adds that black protest against proslavery theology "never exerted broad influence in antebellum society," he says; few "whites took note." But Noll downplays the significance of black protest. If one looks at the influence of black interpretations of scripture on white abolitionists and the abolition movement as a whole, then blacks' influence looms large. As a number of historians have recently noted, David Walker's *Appeal* and *Freedom's Journal*, the nation's first black newspaper, vigorously attacked proslavery interpretations of Scripture and exerted considerable influence on William Lloyd Garrison, the emergence of his *Liberator*, and the rise of the American Anti-Slavery Society. If we acknowledge the crucial influence of African Americans on the abolition movement as a whole, then it is easier to argue that they exerted a broad influence in antebellum society. The abolition movement transformed Northern attitudes about slavery—especially the rise and spread of political abolitionism to which blacks were especially attracted. If political party platforms are any indication, most Northerners countenanced slavery in the 1820s to 1840s. But by 1860, most Northerners sought to prohibit the spread of slavery and believed that containing it would lead to its ultimate extinction.[13]

The policy of containment was, of course, a central platform of the Republican Party; it stemmed from Northerners' belief that God and the Bible opposed slavery. As Lincoln put it in 1857: "If slavery is not wrong, nothing is wrong."[14] Blacks' struggle to redeem themselves and scripture from slavery mirrored the national redemption of the "original sin" of slavery, as James Madison noted.

Lincoln's second inaugural address became one of the most power-ful theological weapons against the continuation of slavery in the United States. After stating that "both [Northerners and Southerners] "read the same Bible, and pray to the same God," Lincoln makes it clear that he believes God opposes slavery: "Fondly do we hope—fervently do we pray—that this mighty scourge of war may speedily pass away. Yet if God wills that it con-tinue, until all the wealth piled by the bondman's two hundred and fifty years of unrequited toil shall be sunk, and until every drop of blood drawn with the lash, shall be paid by another drawn with the sword, as was said three thousand years ago (in Psalm 19), so still it must be said 'the judgments of the Lord, are true and righteous altogether.'"[15]

Frederick Douglass heard Lincoln's speech and thought it sounded more like a sermon than a state paper. He then attended the reception at the White House, and when Lincoln saw him, he asked Douglass how he liked his inau-gural address, adding: "there is no man in the country whose opinion I value more than yours." "Mr. Lincoln, that was a sacred effort," Douglass replied.[16] It was his third visit to the White House to meet with Lincoln, and the fact that Lincoln would place such currency on Douglass's opinion points to the black influence in shaping American attitudes about slavery, sin, and scripture.

Interestingly, Noll does not comment on how African Americans sought to refute Genesis 9:20–27, the so-called Curse of Canaan, in which Noah cursed Ham's son Canaan to perpetual slavery. Few passages in the Torah or Christian Bible have had such pernicious influence on race relations. Not only Southerners but many Northerners and Jews such as Morris Raphall, whom Noll quotes, repeatedly invoked Noah's curse to justify racial slavery. The Louisiana proslavery writer and physician Samuel Cartwright published a popular book of essays in 1842 to show how the biblical curse correlated with anatomical evidence of black inferiority. And in *The Bible View of Slav-ery* (1861), Raphall offered one of the most influential defenses of slavery in which he drew heavily on Genesis 9:20–27. The black intellectual Alexander Crummell noted the influence of the curse in 1862: "the opinion that the sufferings and the slavery of the Negro race are the consequence of the curse of Noah is a general, almost universal, opinion of the Christian world." This opinion, Crummell added, "is found in books written by learned men; and it is repeated in lectures, speeches, sermons, and common conversation. So strong and tenacious is the hold which it has taken upon the mind of Chris-tendom, that it seems almost impossible to uproot it. Indeed, it is an almost foregone conclusion, that the Negro race is an accursed race, weighed down, even to the present, beneath the burden of an ancestral malediction."[17] The

Curse of Canaan became an ideal way to remain faithful to scripture while endorsing black slavery and oppression. Acceptance of the curse continued into the twentieth century, despite the fact that it was not originally a racist text. Interpretations of Ham and his descendents as black became prominent with the rise of the Atlantic slave trade.[18]

Frederick Douglass was one of the most effective black critics of proslavery interpretations of the Bible. In his speech (and pamphlet), "The Claims of the Negro Ethnologically Considered," he revised ethnology in order to critique scriptural doctrine: he argued, following his friend James McCune Smith, that Egyptians—whom he called the originators of western culture—were in essence Africans, which subverted the racist biblical doctrine that identified Ham and his descendants with Africans.[19]

Memory and Mourning: The Transformation of African American Autobiography

Albert Raboteau draws on the power of memory and mourning as a source of redemption for blacks and whites in the United States. He borrows from Anne Cheng's *The Melancholy of Race* and provides rich and subtle readings of African American autobiography, which offer a way out of our willed amnesia of racial trauma. The memories of former slaves include expressions of mourning and revisions of memories (or re-memory, to borrow from Toni Morrison) and, thus, provide a way to heal the personal and social wounds inflicted by racism. Using memory as an antidote to racism is an especially rich thesis given that the willed amnesia of past sins is a prerequisite of racism, as numerous scholars have noted.[20] Black autobiographers saw themselves as truth-tellers, seeking to expose the sins of the past in order to understand and reform the present and past sins in order to understand the reform of the present moment.

I very much like Raboteau's uses of these autobiographies and his selection of texts. He begins with Olaudah Equiano, includes Douglass and DuBois, and ends with Baldwin, whose work emphasizes the need for blacks and whites to come together to confront their past and begin the process of mourning and redemption.

Equiano established several rhetorical strategies that would be deployed repeatedly by black autobiographers, as Raboteau notes. He casts the drama of African humanity and freedom against the backdrop of the Bible. He defines African American Christians as a "chosen" people who convict Anglo-Europeans of their sin of slavery in order to civilize and humanize them. And he discerns in his own life a providential and universal message of reconciliation.

I would also emphasize that Equiano's messages of reconciliation, his universal condemnation of slavery, and his use of the Bible to buttress African freedom emerges *after* his conversion experience. Before he becomes born again through Christ, he condones slavery in Africa and participates in the slave trade to make money and free himself. His conversion totally transforms him: "I saw the Lord Jesus Christ in his humiliation, loaded and bearing my reproach, sin, and shame. I then clearly perceived, that by the deed of the law no flesh living could be justified. I was then convinced, that by the first Adam, sin came; and by the second Adam (the Lord Jesus Christ), all that are saved must be made alive. It was given me at that time to know what it was to be born again."[21] In being born again, Equiano is purified and redeemed, which then leads him to attack the institution of slavery everywhere and embrace universal freedom.

Raboteau shows how Douglass brilliantly used horror, pathos, and especially irony to move his readers to a deeper understanding of the contradiction between slavery and Christian America. In reading this analysis, I was struck by how, in Douglass's other two autobiographies, memory functions much differently. Despite Douglass's emphases on memory and history in *My Bondage and My Freedom*, he places even more weight on the future—here a millennial future—whereas slavery is defined as bondage to the past: "The thought of only being a creature of the *present* and the *past* troubled me, and I longed to have a *future*—a future with hope in it. To be shut up entirely to the past and present is abhorrent to the human mind; it is to the soul—whose life and happiness is unceasing progress—what the prison is to the body; a blight and mildew, a hell of horror."[22] A life without progress, "shut up entirely to the past and present," was tantamount to "hell," an internalization of white attitudes. Slavery was like facing death with no possibility of a future or afterlife. Douglass's comparative focus on the future in *My Bondage* partly reflects his identity as a journalist, which was absent when he published his 1845 *Narrative*. While historians are primarily concerned with origins, journalists are interested in outcomes, as David Nord has noted, and for Douglass, the outcome he prophesied was an apocalyptic end of slavery.[23]

Douglass's attitude toward the past and memory changes again in *Life and Times of Frederick Douglass* (1881, 1892). Here he is concerned not so much with slavery but with his life as a freeman. He no longer believes that God can change the world or affect the laws of nature. In *Life and Times* he castigates blacks for believing that they could procure "help from the Almighty." By remaining true to their faith, blacks were "false" to fact and thus to history, he argues. Material facts and the laws of nature now trumped "all the prayers of Christendom."[24]

Raboteau pays more attention to the continuities rather than the changes over time of memory and mourning, which makes good sense in the scope of his chapter. But I would have also liked a little more distinction regarding the way the transformative power of memory and mourning changed, as it did for Douglass. He notes that James Baldwin, in *Go Tell It On the Mountain*, casts the meaning of African American history within the biblical story of salvation, "just as black narrators have done since the late eighteenth century in language that echoes the idiom of their religious culture." His reading of Baldwin is superb and developed from his essay "The Conversion Experience." Perhaps in a future essay Raboteau will grapple with how stories of salvation changed from the eighteenth to the twentieth century.

The Spirit of the Body: Religious Faith and Social Justice

In Chapter 7, Katherine Bassard traces a series of engagements with Christianity through the figure of the cross. She argues that a disembodied cross becomes a cultural "sign" that participates in efforts of social justice and equality. The vanishing body of Jesus "leaves an empty signifier whose reembodiment is both demanded and displaced by those from dispossessed communities." Focusing on Phillis Wheatley, Frederick Douglass, Harriet Jacobs, James Weldon Johnson, Richard Wright, and Toni Morrison, Bassard points to a shift in the figuration of the cross from a comparatively orthodox African American Protestantism to a displacement of its meanings onto the black community.

By focusing on meanings of the cross, Bassard shows how faith relates to activism over time. The various representations of the cross evolve from "a fully embodied signifier" to an "increasingly disembodied sign as Protestant concepts of atonement and mercy give way to more secular concerns of social justice and agency."

Inspired by Wilson Moses's work, Bassard articulates five stages of evolution in representations of the cross:

1. In the "Messianic Hope" of Phillis Wheatley, Jesus's suffering is "the fulfillment and extension of God's mercy and thus the promise or hope of social justice."

2. Frederick Douglass and Harriet Jacobs embrace "Messianic Fulfillment," whereby the body of the fugitive becomes a symbol of the resurrected Christ.
3. James Weldon Johnson's "Messianic Desire" is contingent on the identification of Christ with black suffering.
4. The "Messianic Deferral" of Richard Wright represents a failure and
   thus a deferral of mercy and social justice.
5. In Toni Morrison's work of "Messianic Displacement," the vanquished
   messiah becomes reembodied within the community of outcast women.

The schema works very well as an organizing principle, opening up enormous
possibilities for understanding the link between symbolization, black activism, and Christian doctrine.

Bassard compares Wheatley's two poems, "To the University of Cambridge, in New-England" and "On the Death of the Rev. Mr. George Whitefield," to show the links between Christ on the cross and social justice. She
distinguishes between Wheatley "seeing" Christ in the first poem and "taking" Christ in the second. To "see" Christ necessitates a contemplation of
his physical body and emphasizes God's mercy and a vision of future social
justice. In "taking" Christ, which refers to the Eucharist ("Take him, ye starv-
ing sinners, for your food"), Wheatley imagines a "universalist gospel," which
becomes the grounds for imagining immediate emancipation and social justice. This is a superb reading of Wheatley, but it is important to note that
Wheatley's "sweeping egalitarian vision" in the poem of Whitefield occurs
in *heaven*, not on earth. "You *shall* be sons, and kings, and priests to God,"
Wheatley has Whitefield say. Wheatley's "messianic hope" collapses the distinction between heaven and earth, but she conceptualizes the millennium as
occurring at some point in the distant future. Bassard seems to want to see
Wheatley's millennium as at hand and thus her reform vision as immediatist.
But if Wheatley's millennium is underway in her Whitefield poem and she
envisions immediate emancipation and equality on earth, then why does she
ignore Whitefield's acceptance of slavery and his Georgia plantation, on which
he owned about seventy-five slaves? And why does she not admonish her other
heroes, such as George Washington, for owning slaves. Indeed the very category
Bassard assigns to Wheatley, "Messianic Hope," suggests a future vision and a
gradualist approach to reform, whereas the "Messianic Fulfillment" of Frederick Douglass reflects faith in an impending transformation.[25]

Douglass employs "the language of resurrection to describe the mental
and emotional transference from slave to free," as Bassard notes. Douglass
becomes an empowered Christ figure who refuses to compromise with the sin

of slavery; his new age is at hand, so there is an urgency to his message that is lacking in Wheatley's poem. Douglass conceptualizes both the cross and the millennium differently than Wheatley does, which leads to different understandings of reform and social justice. For Douglass, revolutionary forms of resistance would help pave the way to the new age.

In her reading of Douglass, Bassard could have drawn from *My Bondage and My Freedom*, where Douglass acknowledges, in a way, that he *becomes* the symbol of Christ; he describes how, as a young boy, he received a bad wound while warring "with Uncle Abel's son, 'Ike,'" "which made a *cross* in my forehead very plainly to be seen now." It was as though God had given his seal of approval to physical resistance, which Douglass accepts throughout *My Bondage and My Freedom*.[26]

There are superb readings throughout Bassard's analysis, though I would have liked some analysis of how Catholics read the "sign" of the crucifix. She describes Protestants as representing the sign of the cross in ways that approach those of Catholics. Did black Catholics become more like Protestants in their representations of the crucifix? What is the relationship for Catholics between the crucifix and pleas for justice—formally, linguistically, and socially? And what role did black Catholics play in the emergence of the figure of a black Christ in black liberation theology? As Raboteau notes in his essay on black Catholics, about 4 percent of black Americans are Roman Catholics and 2 percent of American Catholics are black. And throughout U.S. history black Catholics have been an important part of the Catholic Church, especially in states like Maryland, Louisiana, and Mississippi.[27]

Bassard ends her chapter by quoting Eugene McCarraher to suggest that "after theory" comes theology. Such a trajectory is suggested in the novels of Toni Morrison, who moved from exploring poststructuralism in *Jazz* to theology in *Paradise*. "Revolution is indissoluble from resurrection," Bassard notes, quoting McCarraher, and then adds: "The question is, what Body do we imagine rising from the grave?" To this I would add another question, with which Noll, Raboteau, and Bassard all implicitly grapple. It concerns the location of God's kingdom and thus the relation between religious faith and social justice: "What kind of Spirit do we imagine inhabiting our bodies?" What does it look like and what forms does it take?

Part 4

Literature, Religion, and American Public Life

9

HAMLET WITHOUT THE PRINCE

The Role of Religion in Postwar Nonfiction

Alan Wolfe

In 1956, the sociologist C. Wright Mills published *The Power Elite*, a book that would go on to become one of the leading best sellers in the history of the field, still earning royalties in 2005.[1] (I should know; I get a small portion of those royalties from my afterword to the edition published in 2000.) *The Power Elite* was very much a product of its time; its account of the way business and the military cooperated with Congress anticipated President Eisenhower's warnings in his farewell address about the "military-industrial complex." The cold war loomed over Mills's book, as did all those transformations in American life that resulted in concentrated big business, complacent labor unions, an anticommunist foreign policy, and a public tasting its first fruits of consumerism.

Yet in one important way, *The Power Elite* was not a product of its time at all. The 1950s was a decade in which mainline Protestant denominations, which had not yet begun to lose so many of their members, were still influential; Secretary of State John Foster Dulles, a typical Millsian man of power, was also a Presbyterian church elder. Catholics were deeply ensconced in forms of parish life that dominated their predominantly Catholic neighborhoods and held tenaciously to rosaries, blessings, and confession. Jews were by and large observant and had not yet begun to intermarry in significant numbers. Conservative Protestants were taking the first steps toward the political influence and visibility, which would all but define contemporary American politics. On all these topics, *The Power Elite* did not comment. Mills grew up in Texas, where his mother raised him Catholic, even to the point of having him serve as an altar boy, but by his high school years Mills's atheism was already pronounced, a commitment that stayed with him throughout his life. (Ironically, though, Mills would later be adopted by many mainline Protestants as having offered the definitive word on America's political and economic condition.) If Mills himself was not religious, however, he was also one of America's leading interpreters of Max Weber, the greatest sociologist of religion the world has produced and, hence, not ignorant of the subject. Sociologists communicate through their silences as well as their words, and Mills's silence toward religion is striking.

One might respond by pointing out that *The Power Elite* was concerned with the highest reaches of influence in American life and that, for all their resonance among ordinary Americans in the 1950s, religious institutions were not part of America's ruling class (even if missionary Christianity had played an important role in the creation of the American empire that Mills was attacking). Yet what then is one to make of *White Collar*, Mills's 1951 disturbing account of middle-class life in America?[2] Here is a book concerned with alienation, false consciousness, the lack of autonomy, and the corruption of character, yet nowhere can one find a word about either religion's contribution to the state in which Americans had presumably found themselves or the suggestion that religion might offer a way out of that state. (At least Marx, from whom Mills learned so much, denounced religion as the opiate of the people.) Mills, Morris Dickstein has written, "was an almost novelistic observer of social change," but that modifying "almost" has a lot of work to do; *White Collar* has no traces of Albert Camus or Saul Bellow, that is, no existentialist dilemmas or spiritual anxiety.[3] Its chapter on the professions deals with doctors, lawyers, professors, and businessmen but not with the clergy. Mills worries about conformity but has nothing to say about creed. It is as if Americans go to inferior schools that fail to teach them critical thought, work for big organizations that frustrate their independence, and vote for candidates who perpetuate their woes, without ever attending church, confessing their sins, or asking God for meaning.

The failure of Mills to take religion seriously is even more striking given what happened to him, and to his country, in the wake of his tragic death in 1962 at the age of forty-five. Anticipating that the complacency of the 1950s might come to an end, Mills warned the emerging New Left not to place too much of its hopes on labor, and for that, he is rightly considered to have influenced the 1960s student movements; what made the New Left new was its search for agents of historical change outside the working class. Yet a substantial part of what we now mean when we talk about the 1960s is the spiritual searching that took so many into mind-altering drugs, ecstatic experience, or even religion itself, and not just, by the way, the Eastern versions; Jesus people were as much part of the 1960s as members of the SDS (Students for a Democratic Society) were. This Mills did not anticipate. Compared to Eisenhower or even Adlai Stevenson, Mills was quite radical. Compared to the Doors, Bob Dylan, or Timothy Leary, he seems quite conventional.

In this chapter I want to address the way a number of America's leading nonfiction writers of the 1950s and 1960s dealt with the religion of their time. (I have chosen nonfiction because I am a social scientist, not a literary critic, and because the authors I will be treating had, unlike many of today's leading social scientists, huge audiences and consequently some impact on American culture.) Mills offers one way of responding to religion, and that is to all but ignore it. A second response is to recognize religion but to nonetheless use it as a stand-in for other, presumably more important, forces. And the third is to focus directly on religion in order to make it a subject of equal importance to foreign policy or business domination. While the third of these approaches offers obvious advantages given the omnipresent role religion played in the United States in the 1950s and 1960s, none of the leading social scientists of the period got all the details right, especially that assembly of forces that would lead, in the first years of the twenty-first century, to national politicians courting the votes of conservative religious believers. Nonfiction, particularly the kind written by social scientists, has high standards to meet, including faithfulness to empirical reality, conceptual clarity, and general readability. On all those standards, this literature ranks high, higher, alas, than it does on one additional standard, the ability to foreshadow the direction society will take.

Religion in Modern American Nonfiction

For all his popularity, C. Wright Mills was not the number one best-selling sociologist of his day; that honor belongs to David Riesman. A frequent critic of Mills, Riesman's politics were more centrist and would eventually become quite conservative (although his turn to the right took place at a time when Riesman was not as prolific as he was once and so his conservatism is not widely known). Perhaps because he was less the rebel than Mills, Riesman was treated as something like America's primary clinician; his picture would appear on the cover of *Time*, and his words became the subject of widespread national self-analysis. No other book became as central to that self-analysis as *The Lonely Crowd* (coauthored with Reuel Denney and Nathan Glazer), which first appeared in 1950.

Unlike Mills, for whom psychology was a byproduct of political economy, Riesman was a serious student of psychoanalysis—Erich Fromm was the

man who had treated him—and as a result, Riesman was more familiar with
central European thought than the quintessential American Mills. (Mills had
written his doctoral dissertation on American pragmatism.[4]) Hence Riesman
spends considerable time on such psychologically charged subjects as parental
roles, childrearing practices, peer group influence, anomie, and adjustment.
The subject of *The Lonely Crowd*, moreover, has a strong psychological com-
ponent; Riesman's task is to explain nothing less than "character," both that
of individuals and, it follows, of the nations that compose them. By page five,
Riesman has cited not only Fromm but also George Santayana, Erik Erikson, and Gardner Murphy, as well as Henry Fielding's *Tom Jones*. There will
be discussions of work and politics in *The Lonely Crowd*, but they will take
second place to a concern with individuals and how they search for meaning
in their lives.

Erik Erikson would go on to write a famous book about Martin Luther,
and Luther's spirit hovers over *The Lonely Crowd* as well.[5] "Character," as
Riesman uses the term, is a translation of *beruf* or calling, that is, a central, if
not the central, concept of Lutheran theology. The "inner-directed" individual steps right out of the Reformation, reaches American shores in the form
of the Puritans and grows to maturity (or *bildung*) in the nineteenth-century
atmosphere of hard work and individual aspiration only to be threatened in
the twentieth century by the cloying conformity of "other-directed" clones.
And Martin Luther as translated into sociology by Max Weber is not the only
religious resource upon which *The Lonely Crowd* relies; the spirit of Alexis
de Tocqueville, who paid special attention to the religion he found on these
shores, hovers over the book as well. Without the sociology of religion, in
short, *The Lonely Crowd* could not have been written.

Yet while Riesman tells us in great detail about the inner lives of Americans, he tells us almost nothing about their spiritual lives. What we learn of
inner-directed people is that their sex lives are generally inhibited, their taste
in food tends toward the simple but elegant, they are suspicious of too much
leisure time, and in their hobbies they aspire to be craftsmen; we learn nothing at all about their choices of sacred music or their attitudes toward liturgy.
For all his differences with Mills, Riesman joins his silence toward faith. In
The Lonely Crowd, religion is entirely in the background and never struts
upon the stage. There is one reference to Catholics involving the veto power
of the Church and one reference to Jews (who are equated with Negroes
and Italians rather than with Protestants and Catholics) and their pride in
their ethnicity.[6] Churches and synagogues do not make an appearance in *The
Lonely Crowd*. Except for leisure time, the focus of the book is on weekdays.

It is as if Sundays did not exist for the Americans of the immediate postwar period. Riesman, it must be added, would address the question of religion in other of his writings, including the essays later published in *Individualism Reconsidered*, and he would pay special attention to Catholic colleges and universities in a book he would later write with Christopher Jencks on American higher education. But his most famous book is also the one that pays less attention to a phenomenon widely considered important by the Americans whose behavior he put under the microscope.

Riesman would insist throughout his remaining years that he never meant to pass value judgments on "inner-directed" and "other-directed" Americans. Yet his book frequently suggests a preference for the former over the latter, which is certainly the way *The Lonely Crowd* would be read by future generations of Americans. One who read him very carefully was the social critic Betty Friedan, who cited Riesman four times in *The Feminine Mystique*.[7] Friedan was not, like Mills and Riesman, an academic, although she had studied psychology in graduate school in Berkeley before dropping out, but she was well-read in the social sciences and her ambitions were not unlike those of Riesman and her Nyack, New York neighbor Mills.[8] For Friedan, Riesman's emphasis on autonomy was central to her insistent call for women to break out of the chains of patriarchy in which American society had ensnared them. (At the same time, Friedan was critical of Riesman for his suggestion that women might best seek autonomy by helping their husbands with their careers.) Held captive by "the feminine mystique," women, especially middle-class suburban women, were "other-directed." If they took steps to educate themselves and seek status as professionals, they could become "inner-directed."

Give Friedan this much credit: she does discuss religion. It would be difficult, given her perspective, not to; by the time her book was published in 1963, religion's role in reinforcing traditional gender roles was fairly pronounced. Strenuous opposition to the ordination of women as clergy was present, not only in Catholicism, Orthodox Judaism, and conservative Protestantism, but even in liberal, mainline denominations, such as the Episcopal Church. Had one sought texts reinforcing the need for women to stay at home to be full-time mothers, the publishing houses of nearly all of America's religions would have offered them. According to many a pastor of the period, a woman seeking equality with her husband was not only destined to unhappiness but was also committing a blatant sin against God's commands. One hesitates to rank America's postwar institutions by their degree of what we would now call sexism, but religious institutions, despite the fact that they would, over the course of time, empower many women, would certainly rank high on the male privilege scale.

Friedan's discussion of religion touches none of this, for she is content to mention a few anecdotes before moving on to presumably more important subjects. She does note the existence of a religious revival in America, but, rather oddly, by this she means not the rise of the evangelicals but the attraction of ministers to psychoanalysis. One Catholic woman she discusses dropped out of the labor force at the urging of her priest (although she remained active in local politics). Another, a trained physician, opted to be a doctor's wife rather than a doctor, presumably to keep a more Jewish home; no particular reason for citing this woman's Jewish faith is mentioned.[9] And that is pretty much it. *The Feminine Mystique* examines women's magazines, sex education manuals, Freud's baleful legacy, and Margaret Mead's writings. It does not concern itself with sermons, Sunday school, or Bible class.

Compared to what passes for social science today, there is much to admire in the work of Mills, Riesman, and Friedan. They are first-rate writers, all of them. They have powerful stories to tell and they tell them in ways that still make for engaging reading. Yet their failure to treat a sociological reality as omnipresent to the American experience as religion is inexcusable. These are writers well versed, not only in Tocqueville and Weber but also in Sigmund Freud, Perry Miller, Emile Durkheim, and Lionel Trilling (who makes a few appearances in *The Lonely Crowd*). Alongside of them stood contemporaries in the social sciences—for example, the Harvard political scientist Louis Hartz—who did give religion in America the attention it was due. I cannot think of a single good reason why, given their concerns, religion did not play a greater role in their books. Ambitious books with ambitious agendas, their aim was nothing less than to render comprehensive the American condition. To do that without religion is like Hamlet without—well, you know how that sentence ends.

On the Margins: Religion and the Modern Writing of American History

Perhaps because they deal with the American past and therefore have fewer excuses to ignore religion, historians were more likely than sociologists to touch on religious themes in their work. As is true of social scientists of the 1940s and 1950s such as Mills and Riesman, some of America's leading historians, including Arthur Schlesinger, Jr., and Richard Hofstadter, were not the monograph-writing, stick-close-to-the-sources, and never-become-too-controversial kinds of historians that would flourish in the American university by century's end. They were stylists with literary ambitions, and their books were intended not only to reach large numbers of readers but also to comment on current affairs in the guise of historical analysis. Yet while they did treat religion more explicitly than their colleagues in the social sciences, they essentially "secularized" religion, modifying it to be part of a larger story that had no particular religious meaning.

Arthur Schlesinger, Jr.'s call to arms, *The Vital Center*, was published in 1949. At one level an effort to reclaim America's progressive past but at another a warning to the left not to be seduced by communism, Schlesinger's book was dark in tone, a sharp contrast to what Schlesinger condemned as the hopeless naïveté of popular front liberalism. At the time he wrote the book, Schlesinger was in a "God that Failed" mood, yet for all the book's attempt to deal with the troubled soul of American liberalism, God himself plays relatively little role in the book; religion does not even merit a mention in the index.

Still, the influence of one important religious figure, Reinhold Niebuhr, was noticeable throughout the book. The admiration was reciprocal; Niebuhr would thank Schlesinger for his contribution to *The Irony of American History*, published three years after *The Vital Center*. Schlesinger adopted from Niebuhr the mood of "moderate pessimism" that defined his vital center. Immoderate pessimism took the form of a reactionary conservatism that would stand in the way of America realizing its objectives; excessive optimism had too few qualms about human nature to be sufficient in the face of totalitarianism. Against both, Schlesinger quoted the most famous lines that Niebuhr ever wrote: "Man's capacity for justice makes democracy possible, but man's inclination to injustice makes democracy necessary."[10] The trick was to find a way of being hopeful without appearing naïve, and for that task, Niebuhr's thought fit the bill.

However much they may have learned from each other, however, Schlesinger and Niebuhr endorsed moderate pessimism for very different reasons. For Schlesinger, moderate pessimism served the primarily political aim of avoiding authoritarian temptations coming from either the right or the left. For Niebuhr, by contrast, "the real difficulty in both the communist and the liberal dreams of a 'rationally ordered' historic process is that the modern man lacks the humility to accept the fact that the whole drama of history is enacted in a frame of meaning too large for human comprehension or management." Extremist politics, in Niebuhr's view, are not just a danger to democracy; they also express pride and in that sense are sinful. Totalitarianism—or even liberal planning that takes insufficient account of ironic experience—is a violation of God's charge to us, a language Niebuhr was happy to use even if Schlesinger did not. Christianity offers us the sense of irony that politics cannot, because "the whole drama of human history is under the scrutiny of a divine judge who laughs at human pretensions without being hostile to human aspirations."[11]

To give credit where credit is due, *The Vital Center* was correct to warn liberals against a totalitarian longing and even more correct to turn to thinkers inspired by Europe's tragic history as an alternative to ever-present American optimism; for a book written to address an immediate audience, it stands the test of time remarkably well. Yet for all the role that Niebuhr played in the book, Niebuhr's actual religion played little role at all, as if Niebuhr had been led to his pessimism by reading existentialism rather than by reflecting on Christ's message to human beings. In that sense and for that reason, Schlesinger, while acknowledging the importance of religious thinking, nonetheless reduced religion to an essentially secular phenomenon, clearly an improvement over ignoring the subject completely but not much of one compared to the serious theology produced in the United States at that time by the brothers Niebuhr or (a few years later) by Paul Tillich.

Niebuhr organized his reflections on America's destiny around the idea of irony, a notion very much part of the postwar period's zeitgeist. Irony played a considerable role in the work of Lionel Trilling, of course, but similar concerns, as Benjamin DeMott once pointed out, also motivated two of Trilling's Columbia University colleagues.[12] One was a sociologist, Robert K. Merton, who, among his other activities, helped develop theory and methods in sociology that contributed to the isolation and alienation of C. Wright Mills. A brilliant writer fascinated by literature, quite unusual for a sociologist with his technical skills, Merton early in his career argued that human activity was replete with "unanticipated consequences," thereby insuring that appearance and reality are never quite in agreement.[13] The other was the historian Richard Hofstadter, who devoted his career to showing the extent to which people seeking one objective wound up realizing another. Thus farmers praising the purity of rural life were actually entrepreneurs—Hofstadter obligatorily cites Riesman's inner-directed character—who wound up destroying whatever rural traditions America had.[14] And thus progressive reformers might have thought of themselves as doing good, but their naïveté frequently led them into trouble they did not even recognize.

It was inevitable that Hofstadter's appreciation for irony would lead him to the subject of religion, a subject of great interest to those always on the lookout for unanticipated social consequences, such as Sinclair Lewis in

Elmer Gantry. Along with David Riesman and Nathan Glazer, Hofstadter contributed an essay to *The Radical Right*, originally published in 1955 and one of the first books in the postwar period to take note of what would eventually become the Moral Majority and the Christian Right. Hofstadter's chapter, "The Pseudo-Conservative Revolt," as its title suggests, did not take the professed conservatism of the American right seriously; those attracted to the right, as the authors of the collection more generally pointed out, were engaged in a significant loss of status as the modern world passed them by, and their response was a radical protest against all those forces in modern America they feared, such as the university or the cosmopolitan Eastern establishment. Hofstadter shared this outlook, and while he wrote in his 1962 reflections on his essay that he regretted using the term "status politics," he left little doubt that for the new American right "politics becomes an arena into which the wildest fancies are projected, the most paranoid suspicions, the most absurd superstitions, the most bizarre apocalyptic fantasies."[15]

Toward the end of his 1962 reflections, Hofstadter made reference to Dr. Fred Schwartz's Christian Anti-Communism Crusade and the Rev. Billy Hargis, Jerry Falwells, and Pat Robertsons of his era. Those references would be considerably expanded in an essay published a few years later that would lead off Hofstadter's 1964 book, *The Paranoid Style in American Politics*. In this essay, Hofstadter discovers American religious history; before his thirty-five pages are done, he has written about a 1798 sermon of Jedidiah Morse, the Populist Party's anti-Catholicism, the anti-Masonic movement in the United States, Mormonism, Illumism, Maria Monk, Lyman Beecher, the Millerites, and the alleged Jesuit conspiracy against America. Compared to what social scientists were writing at the time, Hofstadter understands the role that religion has played in shaping American politics and culture.[16]

Hofstadter, however, treats the Christian right in a manner similar to the way Arthur Schlesinger treats Reinhold Niebuhr, as instrumental to a purpose having little or nothing to do with religion per se. That purpose was to identify a paranoid strain in American political culture, the persistent idea that the lives of ordinary Americans are distorted by vast conspiracies they cannot see, led by evil men intent on destroying America to promote their particular un-American agendas. As it happens, such conspiracy theorizing is not foreign to many attracted to the Christian right; as the historian Paul Boyer, writing generally in the Hofstadter tradition, would later show, the apocalyptic scenarios of Hal Lindsay's *The Late, Great Planet Earth* and the even-more-popular "Left Behind" series of Tim LaHaye and Jerry Jenkins, are part of a long-standing genre of American religious thought.[17] Yet

Hofstadter ignored such examples from American religion to focus on politics; it was the "anti-Communism" part of Fred Schwartz's organization that attracted him and not the "Christian" or "crusade" part. Hofstadter was trying to understand Joe McCarthy, a not very devout Catholic from Wisconsin, and for that purpose, an investigation into the Protestant dispensationism of the South and West was unnecessary.

Hofstadter was by no means alone in his approach to the new American conservatism; Daniel Bell's contribution to *The Radical Right* was called "The Dispossessed," a term that captures the degree to which the sociologists and historians of the period believed that the extreme right, backward looking in purpose, was out of step with the generally positive social transformations of modern America.[18] But in assigning conservative religion to the margins of society, writers such as Bell and Hofstadter also failed to appreciate the staying power of the conservative forces they were among the first to analyze. Like C. Wright Mills, Richard Hofstadter died far too young; he passed away in 1970 at the age of fifty-four. Had he lived until the present time, he would no doubt be surprised to discover that conservative Christian religious believers, embodying all the features of the paranoid style of politics he so well described, would be found, not in the rural byways of West Virginia and Arkansas, but in prosperous exurban communities working for global corporations, sending their children to competitive colleges and universities, and considering themselves, and not liberals such as Hofstadter, the true guardians of America's moral conscience.

A Unique American Piety

There were those who ignored religion. They were those who noticed it but reduced its power to other forces, especially politics. And then there were those who made religion central to their understanding of how American society functioned.

No nonfiction writer was more important in the postwar period in offering a framework for the mutual interaction between religion and American culture than Will Herberg. The child of Russian immigrant Jews, Herberg was an early precursor of today's neoconservatives: active in the Young Worker's League, he would later write for *The National Review* and other conservative publications. He also became a professor of Jewish thought at a predominantly Methodist institution, Drew University in New Jersey. But his greatest claim to fame was *Protestant, Catholic, Jew*, his 1955 book that did so much to help Americans understand their melting pot, the Judeo-Christian tradition, assimilation, and civil religion, all of them the great themes of religious speculation in the postwar period.

Herberg's was a book on religion as if David Riesman had written it; Herberg understands that terms such as "inner" and "other" direction have religious roots and he uses them accordingly. The resulting picture is not very flattering. "Being religious and joining a church," Herberg writes, "is, under contemporary American conditions, a fundamental way of 'adjusting' and 'belonging'; through the built-in radar apparatus of other-direction it becomes almost automatic as an obvious social requirement like entertainment or culture."[19] Americans, as Herberg makes clear in this passage, were widely attracted to religion; they identified strongly with their faith, attended church or synagogue, made friends and business contacts through their congregations, and looked for signs of religious commitment on the part of their leaders. To read Herberg is to enter a completely different world than when reading Mills; everything missing in the latter assumes a prominent role in the former. With Herberg, postwar American sociology finally achieved its classic work on religion. *Protestant, Catholic, Jew* lacked the historical research and comparative perspective of Max Weber and the theorizing of Emile Durkheim. But after the book appeared, no one writing seriously about the United States could ignore what Herberg had found.

If Herberg's Americans were attracted to religion, however, they were not all that religious. Americans were focused on religion's functionality, that is, on what it could for do for them. But this came at considerable cost to religion's seriousness of purpose. Echoing H. Richard Niebuhr's famous lament—"a God without wrath who took man without sin into a kingdom without justice through the ministrations of a Christ without a cross"[20]— Herberg wrote of a "religion without serious commitment, without real inner conviction, without genuine existential decision." His view toward American religion was as dark as Schlesinger's views toward extremist politics: "What should reach down to the core of existence, shattering and renewing, merely skims the surface of life."[21] Add Herberg to the long list of social critics distracted by the seeming breezy cheerfulness of life in the United States. We needed a good dose of Kierkegaardian struggle and we got the power of positive thinking instead.

Herberg's *Protestant, Catholic, Jew* proved that religion could be treated with many of the same skills of acute sociological analysis and dramatic storytelling that led C. Wright Mills to talk about the military or Betty Friedan to dissect the condition of middle-class women. After Herberg, no one could seriously offer the American equivalent of Mr. Thwackum's famous words in

Tom Jones: "When I mention religion, I mean the Christian religion; and not only the Christian religion, but the Protestant religion; and"—well, you know how that sentence ends as well.[22] America was now not only a religious nation but also a religiously pluralistic one. However much religions may differ with each other, they share in common the challenge of adapting to American culture. Unlike any other book of its time, *Protestant, Catholic, Jew* anticipated the difficulties American religions would have in maintaining their traditions in a society that values tradition so little. The debt that later writers on these topics have to him, especially including myself, is considerable.[23]

But if Herberg anticipated some things, he did not anticipate everything. Interestingly enough it was Herberg's reliance on David Riesman's sociology, which gave his book so much of its power, that becomes the clue to the huge changes in American religion that Herberg missed. Persuaded that Americans believe in order to belong, Herberg insisted on the importance of religious organizations, especially, in a country still predominantly Protestant. "The denomination," he wrote, "is a stable, settled church, enjoying a legitimate and recognized place in a larger aggregate of churches, each recognizing the proper status of the other." Denominationalism, for Herberg, was as American as apple pie: "so firmly entrenched is this denominational idea in the mind of the American that even American Catholics have come to think in such terms."[24] If *Protestant, Catholic, Jew* were the title of the overall book, a Herbergian approach to Protestantism would be called "Methodist-Episcopalian-Baptist" or one dealing with Jews would no doubt possess the title "Reform-Conservative-Orthodox."

Herberg was clearly caught up in the sociological spirit of his time, the one that was persuaded of the existence of an "organization man" wearing a "gray flannel suit." But in fact the sociologists of the 1950s were wrong to assume that organizational conformity was the key to American culture and Herberg was wrong to assume the importance of denominations. There has always existed in American religion an antiinstitutional impulse, one that ignores the denomination in favor of the congregation—"all religion is local," as a follower of the late Tip O'Neill would have put it—or is even capable of resisting the congregation in favor of "home churching," the believer's equivalent of home schooling. It is not sociology that explains contemporary American religion so much as psychology. Americans do not believe in order to belong; they believe in order to be. If religion means organization and doctrine, Americans are not all that religious. If it means purity of heart and sincerity of spirit, they are religious beyond recognition.

The locus of the anti-institutional trends in American religion can be found among the evangelicals, long attracted to "free churches" with weak or nonexistent ties to denominations found in faraway New York or Nashville. Herberg was enough of a scholar to recognize the existence of evangelicals in the United States; he knew that there was "an anti-theoretical, anti-liturgical bias" in American religion that made "emotional richness" its core task.[25] But when Herberg discussed the existence of a religious revival taking place in the United States, he had in mind the theologians on the East Coast, not the revivalism of Billy Graham. (Herberg's one mention of Graham criticized him for his "individualistic piety" and his "smug and nagging moralism."[26]) The great surprise in reading *Protestant, Catholic, Jew* now is the lack of attention paid to conservative religion then. Herberg was a better student of American religion than Hofstadter, yet he joined Hofstadter in ignoring a development of major importance for America's future. If anything, in fact, Hofstadter, who feared the religious right, paid more attention to conservative Protestantism than Herberg, who lamented so strongly the loss of a serious religious movement in the United States.

Whether evangelicalism constitutes that serious religious movement is another matter entirely. Although Herberg paid insufficient attention to conservative Protestantism, his general analysis helps explain why softer forms of born-again revivalism, as opposed to harder forms of political fundamentalism, have characterized so much of our recent history; between the lines of *Protestant, Catholic, Jew* one can detect the emergence of *The Purpose Driven Life*. Evangelicalism may have only a lukewarm affinity with denominationalism, but it has fallen in love with the mega church, where only on the rarest of occasions is fire-and-brimstone preaching about sin and hell the Sunday norm. Although Herberg paid little attention to religious music, he would, one assumes, be mildly amused by the popularity of contemporary Christian rock. Yes, he wrote, religion is pervasive in American culture, but "the only question is: What kind of religion is it? What is its content? What is it that Americans *believe* in when they are religious."[27] Those questions are still pertinent today, and the answers are by no means obvious. Evangelicalism in particular is more popular than ever, its influence felt not only in matters of faith but also throughout the world of sports, entertainment, inspirational literature, and even diet books. Its very popularity, however, suggests that it is a religion of a very specifically American sort that, for all the attention it pays to emotional satisfaction, pays relatively little attention to matters of theology, creed, and liturgy. Herberg never anticipated its staying power, but he was able to grasp the form that would enable it to stay.

The Role of the Secularization Thesis

It is probably fair to say that the novels of the 1950s and early 1960s did a better job recognizing the importance of religion than did the work of social scientists; J. F. Powers was the best sociologist of American Catholicism of his time, and a preoccupation with religious themes appeared in even the earliest works of Bernard Malamud, John Updike, Flannery O'Connor, J. D. Salinger, and others too numerous to mention. It is not as if religion's place in American culture was terra incognita. The 1950s and 1960s were years in which the economy began to grow and Americans spent considerable amounts of time building families and careers. Yet these years also passed in the immediate shadow of the evil of totalitarianism and never could escape the possible mushroom clouds hanging over them, disturbing realities that captured the imagination of fiction writers more thoroughly than they did the data analyzed by sociologists. Surely nonfiction writers aspiring to capture the era's mood should have paid far more attention to religion than they did.

Without question, part of the reason why insufficient attention was paid to religion at this time, as Andrew Delbanco notes in his response to this essay, lies in the fact that the dominant religion in America was Christianity, while many of its critics (with the exception of Mills) were Jewish. To come to terms with American religion meant learning about and accepting something so far removed from the backgrounds of second-generation Americans from Eastern Europe that they could, in a sense, be forgiven. In addition, it is common for the children of immigrants to reject the religion of their parents; in becoming successful American writers and critics, they were distancing themselves from their own religion and in that way distancing themselves from all religion.

Still, I believe that there is an additional reason why critics of this period tended to shy away from the subject of religion; as marginalized as Riesman and Mills may have been from trends that would lead social science in the direction of natural science, they were not marginalized from the tendency of all social scientists to accept what is called "the secularization hypothesis." In the 1950s and 1960s, it was, so to speak, an article of faith to conclude that modernity would leave little room for faith. Once people in rich liberal democratic societies understood the benefits of reason and rationality, their religious beliefs, if they existed at all, would be safely tucked out of sight. The secularization thesis did not necessarily lead to the conclusion that religion would simply expire; in some versions, particularly those associated with the sociologist Peter Berger, it would continue to have important functions as a mechanism for creating meaning in the world.[28] But it would always be on the defensive, something left over after more important matters of politics and economics dominated the attention of individuals.

Adherence to the secularization thesis was probably strongest among some of the contributors to *The Radical Right*, who predicted the decline not only of religion but also of all ideological belief systems. But it could be found among all the authors I have discussed in this chapter, including even Herberg, who wrote that "it is this secularism of a religious people, this religiousness in a secularist framework, that constitutes the problem posed by the contemporary religious situation in America."[29] Even if they understood religion to be all around them, these writers were not convinced that religion would be there, at least not in any really strong form, in the future, and they were writing for the future as well as the present (a characteristic they shared with the faithful). Wanting to be on the right side of history, they wound up on the wrong side; predicting the future is something that all social scientists, no matter their methodological and theoretical predispositions, frequently cannot do.

None of this, of course, is an argument against the kind of nonfiction writing produced by the social scientists of the 1950s and 1960s. Although their work would be dismissed as popularization by the social science mandarins of the period, it is, in fact, the mandarins whose work has been all but forgotten and the books of people like Mills and Riesman that remain. What is most admirable about their work is that these writers were—I almost hate to use the term—"inner-directed." They were perfectly prepared to ignore the academic conventions of their time in favor of books that reflected both objective efforts to understand the world and the subjective interests and concerns of the people who wrote them. If there is criticism to be made of them, it is that they were not inner-directed enough; by sharing in a general consensus about religion's relative unimportance, they weakened their analysis and revealed not especially pleasant prejudices. Still, their work stands out for its acute depictions of the American condition; by calling attention to one of their most conspicuous weaknesses, I wish only to underscore the strength of what they accomplished.

10

"The Only Permanent State"

Belief and the Culture of Incredulity

Andrew Delbanco

In Chapter 9, Alan Wolfe makes a strong case that many of the key figures of American intellectual life in the 1950s and 1960s—C. Wright Mills, Richard Hofstadter, David Riesman, Daniel Bell, Betty Friedan, Arthur Schlesinger, among others—either missed or misused religion in their otherwise powerful analyses of American society. By the early '60s, Bell and Hofstadter realized that they were witnessing the emergence of a new kind of radical conservatism that was making inroads into American political life, but they underestimated the significance for this movement of its evangelical religious element and regarded the whole phenomenon as a "rear-guard action" doomed to fail before the irresistible force of modernity. Even Will Herberg, author of *Protestant, Catholic, Jew: An Essay in American Religious Sociology* (1955), failed to see that local denominational allegiances were receding before the sweeping fundamentalist Protestantism that has since evolved into the single most potent force in American spiritual and political life.

I think Alan Wolfe is generally right. He is right, that is, about the seriousness of the oversight. What I would like to offer by way of response are a few supplementary comments along with a brief reflection on the question of whether American intellectual life is much different in this respect today.

One of Wolfe's striking points is that even writers with a profound sociological imagination, such as David Riesman, were unable to apply their own insights into the American hunger for peer-group approval to the millions of people who found this hunger satisfied, or at least appeased, in communities of faith. In Riesman's own tenth anniversary preface to *The Lonely Crowd* (first published in 1950), he took stock of its initial reception and used the occasion to dissent from Freud's doctrine that childhood experience determines human development, proposing instead that the peer group and the school exert a shaping influence during adolescence. But Riesman still did not ascribe comparable power to the churches—a surprising omission since in many religious traditions adolescence and young adulthood are regarded as the likeliest seedtime of faith and the best time for voluntary commitment to a confessional community. Riesman does hint in his 1960 preface that he mistrusts his own understanding of the significance of religion, at least for those Americans whom death has placed beyond the reach of the pollsters:

> When we were working on *The Lonely Crowd* [this is not the royal "we," but a reference to Riesman's collaborators, Reuel Denney and Nathan Glazer], we were frustrated by the paucity of historical materials in many areas we deemed relevant; for instance, we could not find reliable evidence as to what religion meant for the different social strata when Tocqueville was here in the 1830's. We could get data on church membership and activities, on various revival movements, and on theological disputes, but little that gave us the firm sense of the emotional weight of religion for men as well as women, adults and children, the more and the less respectable classes, the newer and the older denominations.[1]

Since Riesman wrote those words, there has been impressive progress toward recovering what the historian David Hall has called "lived religion" by scholars who have searched the archives for memoirs, letters, conversion relations, and the like, but the inner life of believers, past and present, remains an exceptionally elusive matter.

In the 1950s, those who did look for it, did not, as Wolfe says, always look for it on its own terms. They tended to think about religion in relation to social movements that seemed to feed on religion or turn it to political use. His most striking example is Hofstadter's *Anti-Intellectualism in American Life* (1962), which assessed evangelicalism as an enemy of mind and a friend of groupthink. For Hofstadter, who had begun writing in the heyday of McCarthyism and finished in its aftermath, the revival meeting was, in effect, a training ground for demagogues. And Hofstadter's contemporary, Arthur Schlesinger, Jr., who had written an important history of the Jacksonian period (*The Age of Jackson*, 1945) with little reference to the churches or the religious sources of social reform, only got religion when he discovered Reinhold Niebuhr as a useful ally in the urgent work of warning liberal intellectuals to break off their romance with the Soviet Union. Wolfe also points out that while Herberg's *Protestant, Catholic, Jew* helped put flesh on the bones of the then-skeletal idea of something that was starting to be called the "Judeo-Christian" tradition, it presented religion mainly as a mechanism for social adjustment. On this view, the three great Western religions, as they had evolved in America, were doctrinally loose and ultimately more about belonging to this world than preparing for the next.

With these points in mind, I would like to emphasize something about which Wolfe does not particularly comment—that is, the fact that the intellectual moment he is writing about was fundamentally a New York moment and that many, if not most, of its leading figures (with the notable exception of C. Wright Mills, who was brought up Catholic) were, in some genealogical or self-identifying sense, Jews.

Long before the ascendancy of the Jewish writers who made twentieth-century New York the intellectual capital of the United States, the face of the city was already turned toward Europe, from which it imported a certain anticlericalism. Consider the nineteenth-century poet Nathaniel Parker Willis, a refugee from transcendental New England, who remarked, with relief, that in New York

> Religion seems very ill-planned!
> For one day we list to the pastor,
> For six days we list to the band![2]

Though I would not want to trivialize the role of religion in New York, which is the hometown, after all, of such clerical leaders as Harry Emerson Fosdick, Adam Clayton Powell (both senior and junior), and Stephen Wise, it seems fair to say that religion has never played the central role in Gotham that it did in America's previous intellectual capital, Boston.

In this context, if we look at Herberg's trio of Protestant, Catholic, and Jew and think of them as relational terms, it is important to recognize that they were also hierarchical terms. In the 1950s, upper-crust Protestants still held sway over the nation's leading institutions, certainly including New York institutions, such as its law firms, hospitals, and leading university, Columbia. Catholics were still struggling for respectability in the board rooms and higher reaches of American politics, even after the Harvard-finished Jack Kennedy accomplished in 1960 what Al Smith had been unable to achieve in the 1920s. As for the Jewish presence in this largely Protestant world, although my university is famous for such figures as Meyer Schapiro and Lionel Trilling, when my brother applied in 1960 for admission to the Columbia medical school, rumor had it that there was still an informal Jewish quota. (He may have sneaked in under cover of his Italian-sounding surname.) Trilling was the first Jew to receive tenure in my own department in what was still, in some respects, an Episcopalian institution, and the closest that the leading

New York intellectuals of that time, Irving Howe and Alfred Kazin, came to the Puritan-descended Protestant establishment was when they were invited late in life to Harvard for a week to deliver a series of public lectures.

As for Jewish-Catholic relations, the memory of Father Coughlin and Pope Pius XII was still fresh in the 1950s. I remember from my own childhood a book on my mother's bookshelf, Paul Blanshard's *American Freedom and Catholic Power* (1949), which was widely read at a time when the notion of an international Catholic conspiracy was at least as alive as was the notion of an international Zionist conspiracy. My own first experience with overt anti-Semitism came in the 1950s in third grade in my suburban New York public school when a Catholic friend told me that he could no longer be friends with a Christ-killer. As an undergraduate at Harvard in the 1970s, I became aware of a certain covert anti-Semitism in the high-church Protestant final-club crowd, and as a junior faculty member in the 1980s, I encountered it among faculty colleagues, both blue bloods and *arrivistes*. For more than a quarter century past 1950, tensions persisted between Jews and Christians even in America's leading institutions, and I am not certain that they have entirely dissipated.

So there was a certain wariness, shall we say, on the part of America's minority intellectuals toward America's majority religion. But perhaps more important for Alan Wolfe's narrative, New York Jews were not necessarily committed in any deep sense to their own religious heritage. In most cases they had watched the Holocaust from afar, and, with the founding of the Jewish state in Palestine, were likely to feel distant, estranged, or at least confused about their relation to the horror and hope of Jewish history. As for their personal piety, they were likely to agree with the pogrom survivor in Saul Bellow's 1953 novel *The Adventures of Augie March*, who had witnessed a laborer in the old country "pissing on the body of his wife's younger brother, just killed." After the things he had seen, this character admonishes his friends and family not to dare to "talk to me about God." And yet, as Bellow remarks, "it was he who talked about God, all the time."[3]

As for the New York intellectuals, when they talked about God it was less likely to be the God of Abraham than what Richard Crossman called the "God that failed."[4] At least until the Molotov-Ribbentrop pact of 1939— and, for some of the faithful, long after—the historical dialectic as revealed by Marx seemed a more sustaining faith than the Christian idea of a merciful redeemer who saves through his own martyrdom. After Auschwitz, though the romance with Marxism may have been fading, Christianity itself was an unbearable affront to the six million victims of the greatest slaughter ever perpetrated in Christendom. Jewish readers reacted ambivalently at best when the Jewish-American writer Edward Lewis Wallant, in his 1961 novel *The Pawnbroker*, celebrated the idea of redemptive sacrifice in what amounted to a Christian allegory of deliverance from the psychological legacy of the holocaust.

Another reason that Wolfe's writers were unserious about religion is that they took seriously the Tocquevillean idea that America's historical distinctiveness was to have escaped the cycle of religious conflict in which so many lives in the Old World had been consumed. This idea, sometimes called American exceptionalism, had its roots in Tocqueville's insight that the United States, having skipped the violent transition to bourgeois rule that disturbed Britain and convulsed France and having been founded on the principle of church and state separation, had wisely consigned religion to the private sphere. Since religion had been banished from public affairs, secularly inclined American intellectuals came to feel that religion was, in effect, none of their business.

Their business was chiefly politics—that is, the structures and mechanisms of power and the ideology or, as Tocquevilleans from Louis Hartz to Sacvan Bercovitch would have it, the absence of ideology that forms the context in which power is exercised in American society. Religion seemed irrelevant in just the sense that the founding fathers intended it to be. A straight line can be traced from Thomas Jefferson's view that "it does me no injury for my neighbour to say there are twenty gods, or no god," to Dwight Eisenhower's often cited (and possibly apocryphal) remark that "our country makes no sense unless it is founded on a deeply felt religious faith—and I don't care what it is." [5] If this sort of genial latitudinarianism left plenty of room for a multitude of private religious convictions, it was somehow the basis for the singular public faith that Robert Bellah, in a famous 1967 essay, identified as the American "civil religion."[6]

Everyone remembers the general thrust of Bellah's essay, but it may be useful to recall its particular and prophetic suggestion that the nation might split apart into factions of what Bellah called "liberal alienation" and "fundamentalist ossification" with respect to the "beliefs, symbols, and rituals" that constituted the civil religion. This prophecy has been strikingly borne out. Liberals today have lost their grip on those symbols and rituals, while conservatives, in league with their Christian evangelical allies, have invested them with a religious fervor of quite astonishing intensity. For a child of the '60s like myself, who still thinks of those symbols as shared by the progressive left, I was startled to hear on the radio not long before the 2005 congressional elections a report of a fundraising event on behalf of Tom DeLay. My generation remembers Odetta and Mahalia Jackson singing "He Holds the

Whole World in his Hands" at civil rights rallies, but here was the same song, rendered in a version that sounded like a cross between the Lawrence Welk singers and the Robert Shaw Chorale, coming after DeLay's speech calling for liberal judges to be banished and gay marriage to be banned.

When Alan Wolfe looks back to the 1950s, he uses the tough word "inexcusable" to describe the indifference of liberal intellectuals toward religion. I have tried to suggest some contexts, if not excuses, for that indifference. I would like also to suggest that, since then, indifference or insouciance has hardened into hostility. In most of our leading universities today, suspicion runs deep toward religion in all its forms, whether theistic or civil. Most intellectuals I know are appalled by the kind of transcendental nationalism that I take to be what Stanley Hauerwas and Ralph Wood have in mind when they speak of the "Constantinian" character of American Christianity. After years of amicable separation, the idea of reconciliation between church and state in America now raises the specter of God-fearing judges issuing Christian fatwas. Here I should add that many of today's American Jewish intellectuals, especially those in the academy, also evince growing hostility to the increasingly religious character of the state of Israel.

Under these conditions, neutrality has given way to animosity. I think, for instance, of Richard Rorty's rather harsh response to George Marsden at a recent symposium (proceedings published in *Hedgehog Review*, Fall, 2000) on the state of American higher education. In response to Marsden's critique of the modern research university as an institution that has lost its moral bearings, Rorty shuddered at the thought of religion sneaking back into the academy and declared it a blessing that universities had taken over from churches as sanctuaries of rational thought.

In view of the fact that he was the grandson of Walter Rauschenbusch, Rorty may have been a particularly vexed example, but his is now the default position of most academic intellectuals for whom religion is an embarrassment at best and a menace at worst. I sometimes suspect that more sensitive interpreters of American religious life are to be found in Hollywood (I think of Robert Duvall's 1997 film *The Apostle* and even—this citation may be surprising—Steve Martin's 1992 movie *Leap of Faith*) than in all our elite universities combined. Yet there are some signs that the times may be changing. Stanley Fish, who is nothing if not savvy about academic trends, was asked by a journalist, at the time of Jacques Derrida's death, what would be the next big thing in literary studies after the decline of theory, and, without hesitation, he gave a one-word answer: religion.

With Fish's prediction in mind, I would like to end, if I may, on a partly personal note. It was my good fortune, after my New York upbringing, to study at Harvard with Alan Heimert, who, like his mentor Perry Miller, was a nonbeliever who was able to expound with sympathetic passion what Miller had called the "Augustinian strain of piety" in early America. When I was Alan's student, he endured a good deal of professional scorn for his view that the American Revolution and American democracy itself, could not be understood without comprehending the force of religion in shaping the republic. Some of his contemporaries, and many Americanists of the succeeding generation, forgot or discounted Whitman's insight that "at the core of democracy, finally, is the religious element."[7] Today, I think, any responsible academic dean or department chair should be concerned if his or her institution does not have a strong contingent of religion scholars, who, with Tocqueville, understand that "it is by a sort of intellectual aberration, and . . . by doing moral violence to their own nature, that men detach themselves from religious beliefs . . . [that] incredulity is an accident; faith is the only permanent state of mankind."[8]

If, as it seems today, Tocqueville was right, we can only hope that he was also right in believing that the American experiment in toleration will not prove finally incompatible with the very essence of religious passion. There are still many believers who are as sure as one of the early Puritans (Nathaniel Ward) that whoever "is willing to tolerate any Religion, or discrepant way of Religion, besides his own . . . either doubts of his own, or is not sincere in it." For such believers, belief itself is, by definition, intolerant of disbelief or what might be called mis-belief. And we know this is equally true of some of the secularized faiths of modernity, such as Marxism, which have their own scriptures, their own eschatology, and their own bloody histories of persecuting heretics.

Nearly seventy years ago, in *Civilization and its Discontents*, Freud identified guilt as the most important problem facing civilization. Today, I wonder if we might not rather say that our greatest problem is finding a way to satisfy the human craving for belief while containing the proselytizing and purifying passion of true believers. Riesman and Hofstadter and the rest can be excused, I think, for failing to see that problem as clearly as we are compelled to see it today.

Part 5

Theology and American Literature

11

How the Church Became Invisible

A Christian Reading of American Literary Tradition

Stanley Hauerwas and Ralph C. Wood

It is surely a scandal that "a nation with the soul of a church," as G. K. Chesterton famously described our country, should have produced so few writers who are Christian in any substantive sense of the word.[1] Emerson, Thoreau, Dickinson, Melville, Poe, Hawthorne, Twain, James, Frost, Faulkner: nearly all of our eminent writers are heterodox at best, atheist or even nihilist at worst. Only such major-minor writers as Flannery O'Connor and Walker Percy can be called distinctively Christian: writers whose artistic vision and work derive from the scandalous claims of God's own self-identification in the Jews and Jesus and the church. The perhaps obvious answer to this conundrum is that brilliant minds gifted with artistic imagination have seen biblical faith for the delusion that it is and thus have refused to make its false claims essential to their work. Our task is to make the countercase that our major writers have little substantive regard for Christianity, because our churches have made it virtually impossible for them to do so. Despite our nation's inveterate religiosity, exceeded perhaps only by that of India, we maintain that the church has become virtually invisible in America. It has so fully identified itself with the American project that our artists have had little cause to heed any unique and distinctively Christian witness in the churches. After accounting for this strange invisibility, we will examine some of the ways in which Christians remain profoundly indebted to our national literary tradition despite its sub-Christian character. Finally, we will look at two instances of overtly Christian kinds of fiction that we believe to be exemplary for a church tasked with making its witness in the one nation founded almost entirely on an Enlightenment basis.

Literature and the Gospel of U.S. Culture

Our first claim is that the Christian witness in American literature has been watery and thin because our churches, Catholic and Protestant alike, have made the gospel of Jesus Christ seem all too much like the gospel of the United States. The trumpets of ecclesial America have been virtually indistinguishable from the nation's own buglers, leaving our major writers but little cause to make Christ and the Kingdom central to their work. What a Jewish rabbi once declared about his own faith we believe to be true also for us Christians: "While America has been good for Jews," he said, "it has been bad for Judaism."[2] It is surely a good thing that Jews have not been subjected to American pogroms and holocausts and that their talents and capacities have been allowed to flourish here as virtually nowhere else in the world. And yet this new birth of freedom from persecution and for prosperity has often meant the ruin of Judaism as a radically communal and countercultural way of life: the life of the synagogue, the life devoted to things higher than, other than, and even opposed to mere individual flourishing, and the life of communal worship and service given to the one true God: Yahweh.

So it is with us Christians. Were it not for our brave ancestors who, at great risk, left the old world for the new, many of us would still be pounding rocks in Europe, living in perpetual peonage to our backs rather than our brains. Like our Jewish counterparts, however, we have come to equate American opportunity with the human good, yet with a notable difference: we have made American opportunity virtually coterminous with Christian freedom. *Contra* Chesterton, therefore, our churches have had the soul of a nation. Rarely has the Christian herald sounded the good and therefore dangerous news that, though they indeed intersect and at times overlap, the Christian church and the American nation will always remain alternative regimes, often scandalously in conflict with each other. The city of God and the city of man cannot be conflated, as Augustine rightly insisted more than 1,500 years ago.

The acculturation of the Gospel is not unique, of course, to Christianity in America. As the Catholic theologian Henri de Lubac discovered, the early church regarded the Eucharist as the *mystical* body of Christ while the gathered community was understood as the *real* body of Christ. The Real Presence lay not in the bread and wine alone so much as in this body of believers whose transubstantiation into a reconciled community was enabled by their partaking of the mystical meal. It transformed *them* into Christ's actual presence in the world, empowering them to live according to a drastically different Story than the world lives by. There they celebrated the true Narrative of the entire cosmos as it is sacramentally compressed into the singular Supper of suffering and death and resurrection. Gradually, however, these terms were reversed, so that the Eucharist alone was understood to be the *real* Presence, while the Christian community became the far vaguer—and often invisible—thing called the *mystical* Body of Christ. The long-term result was that the Eucharist eventually became known as "the medicine of heaven," an almost pharmaceutical remedy against sin, often taken without great regard for the communal reconciliation and transformation which it originally enabled.[3]

Not long after the Emperor Constantine issued the Edict of Milan in 313, making Christianity a tolerated faith, the church soon became the official cult of the Roman Empire. This reversal of the original order of things, according immense political power to Christians, also changed the locus of their confidence in God. Prior to Constantine's establishment of the church as the state religion, John Howard Yoder notes, Christians were convinced that God's action was to be discerned primarily in the church, even as they also believed that God remains at work in the world. In the face of the world's terrible enmity, Christians had little confidence that God ordered the affairs of the Roman state; on the contrary, the Gospel alone sustained them as a community facing governmental torment. After Constantine, however, Christians became confident that God was active chiefly in the world, while only secondarily present in the church. By the time of Theodosius II, only a century later, the reversal had been made complete: it was now a civil offense *not* to be a pro-Nicaea Christian. From having suffered as a persecuted minority, to being tolerated as an accepted plurality, finally to reigning as the established majority religion, Christianity became the religious arm of the empire. The gospel had thus been fundamentally transformed from a nonviolent faith to be embraced only by conversion into a coercive faith wherein to be Christian was the enforced obligation of every citizen of Byzantium.[4]

This little discourse on the Constantinian shift, as it has come to be called, may seem to stand at a far remove from our concern with American religion and literature, especially given the fact that, once the effort of the Puritans and Anglicans to create a state church had ended in the eighteenth century, our national project was built on the explicit disavowal of any established religion, even Christianity. We believe, on the contrary, that the American churches have enjoyed a cultural establishment that, for being so subtle, may be far more pernicious than the old-style conflation of realms. Jefferson, for example, assumed that the nation would retain a Christian majority whose morality would undergird the enlightened political wisdom of such miracle-and-doctrine denying deists as himself. Among the chief purposes of the state, according to Jefferson and his fellow Founders, was the need to save the nation from the contentious religious factions spawned by the Reformation. Like other *philosophes* of the Enlightenment, he sought to prevent a repetition of the sixteenth- and seventeenth-century "wars of religion" that required the state to settle disputes among bloody-minded believers. The only way to stop such internecine battle was to remove conflicting Christian doctrines and practices from the public realm, lest both Europe and the newly born American republic be bathed in religious gore yet again. Tolerance was the chief means for such religious peace, as it came to flower in the Treaty of Westphalia, in Locke's "Letter on Toleration," in Jefferson's *Notes on Virginia*, and the like.

William Cavanaugh maintains that this standard account of the triumph of tolerance is wrongheaded. He demonstrates that the halting of the so-called religious wars was less a political necessity than a political convenience. According to Cavanaugh, Protestants killed Protestants and Catholics killed Catholics in the interest of the new power configurations that developed after the demise of the medieval order. These "wars of religion," far from being internecine ecumenical battles, marked the birth pangs of the sovereign nation-state. It became crucial, therefore, to redescribe both Protestantism and Catholicism. No longer were they understood as particularistic practices of Christianity but rather as subspecies of a putatively more basic thing called "religion."[5] Religion came to be understood, in turn, as "beliefs," as essentially private convictions that one holds quite apart from one's public loyalty to the state. Thus did the emerging nation-states thoroughly centralize political power in order, Cavanaugh argues, to provide "a monopoly on violence within a defined territory." Public discourse was deliberately secularized during the Enlightenment, he notes, in order to protect the state from the real threat posed by the churches: "Christianity produces divisions," writes Cavanaugh, "within the state body precisely because it pretends to be a body which transcends state boundaries."

The First Amendment to the U.S. Constitution obscures this paradoxical marginalizing of the churches. Because Christianity cannot be instituted by law, most Americans remain so accustomed to its cultural authority that legal disestablishment is unnecessary. Yet such Christian hegemony, for all its seemingly public character, remains at once peculiarly privatized and thus subtly coercive. Only when the main activities of the churches are safely confined to the private sphere are they to be benignly "tolerated" by the state. Cavanaugh points out the terribly ironic consequence of this new birth of tolerance—namely, the hegemonic power of the state intolerantly to disbar all publicly ordered religions and all historically nourished traditions. The ideal of tolerance comes, in fact, to exclude the political and communal body of the church, says Cavanaugh, "as a rival to the state body by redefining religion as a purely internal matter, an affair of the soul and not of the body."[6] "The creation of religion, and thus the privatization of the Church," Cavanaugh concludes, "is correlative to the rise of the state."

It follows that the state alone, not the church, can establish a true commonwealth, for religion now pertains chiefly to the newly constructed individual.[7] "The care of each mans soul . . . is left entirely to every mans self," wrote Locke in "A Letter Concerning Toleration."[8] "The legitimate powers of government," added Jefferson, "extend to such acts only as are injurious to others. But it does me no injury for my neighbour to say there are twenty gods, or no god. It neither picks my pocket nor breaks my leg."[9] From such sentiments there emerges a triumphant individualism centered upon a new definition of freedom. In negative terms, liberty means doing no harm to others; in positive terms, it entails the construction of life as one wills. No longer is freedom construed as obedience to a *telos* radically transcending ourselves and thus delivering us from bondage to mere self-interest. Rather is liberty to be found in a life lived according to one's own construal of reality.[10] At its extreme, such individualism holds that one can make up one's identity entirely out of whole cloth and that one can strip away all bothersome particularities that locate one within concrete narrative traditions, so that one is free only as one rids oneself of those troublous commitments and obligations that one has not chosen entirely for oneself. In sum, one is called to be an autonomous self immunized against all moral and social obligations except those that one has independently elected. One's religious "preference" thus becomes the ultimate private choice.[11]

The Piety of Pluralism

Let our intent be clear: we are not denying that acculturated Christianity is still a form of Christianity. Without it, we confess, many of us would not be Christians at all. Even so, we insist that it is a terribly truncated form of the Faith and that our major American writers have had good cause for not making it the animating center of their work. Moralistic liberalism and individualistic pietism are the mirror evils, we also contend, that have made the church understood as the distinctive Body of Christ virtually invisible in America. Concerning our pandemic moralism, R. W. B. Lewis argued a generation ago, in *The American Adam*, that Melville and James joined Hawthorne's protest against the dangerous complacency endemic to moralistic American innocence.[12] It leads to a reformist understanding of human nature as being so malleable to reform that it can be reshaped into a veritable mechanism of righteousness. So did Lionel Trilling, himself a venerable liberal, lament already in the late 1940s, that America has had no other cultural tradition than liberalism: "In the United States at this time liberalism is not only the dominant but even the sole intellectual tradition. For it is a plain fact that nowadays there are no conservative or reactionary ideas in general circulation." Trilling offered his magisterial judgment, not boastfully but regretfully. He complained that, in its prosaic desire to enlarge human freedom through the rational organization of life, liberalism neglects the poetic "imagination of variousness and possibility, which implies the awareness of complexity and difficulty." Liberals often forget, Trilling warned, that "the world is a complex and unexpected and terrible place which is not always to be understood by the mind as we use it in our everyday tasks."[13] Like Lewis, Trilling feared that our moralistic optimism about human nature and destiny had robbed many Americans, including many American writers, of any radical capacity for self-criticism. So did Robert Penn Warren come to berate this same Yankee confidence in the "Treasury of Virtue," as he labeled it, this fund of moral righteousness that Northerners credited to themselves for having put a stop to slavery.[14] The Civil War gave the victors such a shining sense of millennial destiny for the American republic that, in revulsion against it, the defeated Southerners retreated into what Walker Percy called "the great literary secession": the rejection of Northern moral and religious triumphalism in reactionary defense of Southern culture and institutions.[15]

The nineteenth- and twentieth-century pietism that produced such moralism and caused our major American writers to turn away in scorn, if not wrath, is but a distant kinsman of its seventeenth- and eighteenth-century predecessor. In both Europe and the United States, the original pietists were both antihegemonic and politically engaged Christians, offering a powerful corrective to a nominal and accommodationist kind of Christianity that was reduced to mere formal reception of the sacraments, mere verbal assent to creeds, and mere outward adherence to liturgical worship. These early pietists sought to recover the original vitality of the Reformers: in their deeply personal and experiential faith, in their prophetic preaching for the sake of conversion and sanctification, in their confidence that the indwelling Spirit could commend the truth of Scripture to the hearts and lives of the unlearned, in their vigorous opposition to slavery, in their courageous promotion of prison reform, in their evangelistic and missionary zeal, in their creation of Sunday

Schools and Bible societies and colleges, in their advocacy of the freedom of conscience, in their emphasis on the centrality of the laity for the life of the church, and so on. Yet the pietism that began as a minority countermovement in the seventeenth and eighteenth centuries triumphed in the nineteenth century as our quasi-official form of national Christianity.

Timothy Smith, Joel Carpenter, Nathan Hatch, and others have all hailed religious voluntarism as the genius of American Christianity. That citizens are legally free rather than required to join any or no particular church is surely a great good. Not only has it freed the church to carry out the Great Commission in evangelizing non-Christians, but it has also enabled the converted to enact serious social reforms. Yet such pluralism has often been purchased at an enormous and usually unrecognized price. It places such a drastic emphasis on individual conversion and private piety that the church often becomes an afterthought, the place where one seeks merely to confirm what really counts: the vitality of one's private and spiritual relation to God. William Portier points out that such evangelicalism also assumes a Lockean view of the church as a voluntary association of individuals and a metaphysics that gives ontological priority to human will over the created order. The unintended consequence of such religious pluralism is that the churches that embrace it become both individualistic and anti-institutional:

> Pluralism encourages voluntary churches but puts them in the incongruous position of having to develop theories to explain how they can be "public." The correlative of *public* is of course *private*. This means that the seemingly unprecedented field for evangelization [that] pluralism offers is always simultaneously undermined by its corresponding notion that voluntary churches occupy "private" space.
>
> Even as modern political conditions encourage evangelical forms, they tend to deform Christianity insofar as it is ecclesial and incarnate in a culture. Modern notions of tolerance tend to domesticate both the gospel that is being preached and the form of life it entails by treating them simply as one among many private "religions." Soon religious pluralism transforms from a providential fact into a theoretical good, a natural state of things best left undisturbed. If pluralism is a natural state, missionaries are imperialists. Evangelists who take Matthew 28:19 seriously [are said] to impose their private beliefs on others. St. Paul's "Woe is me if I do not preach the gospel" (1 Cor 9:16) turns him into an oppressor.[16]

Emily Dickinson and the Limits of Cultural Christianity

Emily Dickinson was the legatee of such a self-contradictory evangelicalism well before the Civil War and the frontier revivals had established it as the nation's unofficial religion. It left her unable to embrace Christian faith, not, we believe, because she had encountered its authentic expression and found it wanting but rather because she spurned its triumphalist moralism and pietist individualism. That she rejected such moralism may have caused her to take refuge in a religious individualism, retreating into a reclusive life in order to avoid being enlisted for an allegedly Christian cause that she knew to be dubious at best, spurious at worst. During her single year of college life at the Mount Holyoke Female Seminary, the seventeen-year-old Dickinson was tutored by the school's founder, the redoubtable Mary Lyon. Like other Whig evangelicals of her day, Lyon envisioned Christianity as forming a powerful tandem with science and education for bringing about a moral revolution of the entire planet. The kingdom of heaven was soon to come on earth, if not in the nineteenth then surely in the twentieth century, which would so certainly be the *Christian Century* that a still-existing journal was thus named. In an 1842 address setting forth this confident evangelicalism, Lyon envisioned a time rapidly approaching when all people would "act according to the principles of reason and religion" and when "all that now goes into the war channel, will then be consecrated to the service of knowledge and benevolence."[17]

The key to such moral transformation lay in the punctiliar act of becoming a Christian by way of a sudden and emotional conversion experience. Such a dramatic rebirth was public proof that one had personally appropriated the gift of divine grace. A miraculous conversion was the spiritual equivalent of the physical violations of nature that were said to be miraculous evidences of God's existence. "In working toward the conversion of her students at Mount Holyoke," Roger Lundin writes, "Lyon divided them each year into three groups." The "Christians" were those who could testify to the certainty of their salvation experience. The "Hopers" believed themselves on the verge of conversion. The "No-Hopers," by contrast, could not attest to any drastic emotional reversal that proved their faith in Christ. What had begun in the seventeenth century with the Puritan practice of the examined conscience, whereby one sought outward objective evidence of divine election, thus led in the nineteenth century to a radical spiritual subjectivism. Salvation was located not in the church's public and communal enactment of the Gospel by living out the Story of God's presence in the gathered community's practices and doctrines, rather it was radically relocated in the solitary self, in a traumatic individual conversion experience that alone could attest to the efficacy of Christ's work.[18]

Emily Dickinson was numbered on the short list of souls called the No-Hopers. They were the special targets of fervent evangelical attention at Mount Holyoke and Amherst alike. Dickinson remained one of the few holdouts. "How lonely this world is growing," she wrote in the spring of 1850. "Christ is calling everyone here, . . . and I am standing alone in rebellion, and growing very careless." To her friend Abiah Root, Dickinson had confessed several years earlier, "I have not yet made my peace with God. . . . I feel that the world holds a predominant place in my affections. I do not feel that I could give up all for Christ, were I called to die." That Dickinson declined to make a public profession of faith does not mean, as Lundin makes clear, that she was an atheist scoffer at all things Christian. On the contrary, Dickinson admitted "that I shall never be happy without I love Christ." Yet if the love of Christ were signified by an overwhelmingly subjective conversion, Dickinson knew that she lacked it. And if the world's wonder were understood as something to be repudiated, Dickinson could not spurn it. Yet the Jesus of the gospels who remained so dear to Dickinson demanded no such emotional upheaval, no such denials of the good creation. The outward claims of Christian faith were not her chief worry. What vexed Dickinson were her own uncontrollable and delusory emotions. To her friend Root, she thus explained her refusal to attend the Amherst revival meetings of 1850: "I felt that I was so easily excited that I might again be deceived and I dared not trust myself."[19]

A culturally established Christianity seeking to force Emily Dickinson's conversion could not possibly win her permanent esteem. Nor could an establishmentarian kind of Christianity countenance the enormous intellectual difficulties and theological qualms that also prompted Dickinson's refusal to be converted. It contained little room for that recalcitrant doubt that, from Job forward, has always signaled a radical desire for faith. Lundin contends, therefore, that the same Protestant individualism that failed to convert Dickinson prompted her to conceive of her poetic integrity as something she would have to surrender if she became a professed Christian. Why should she have thought otherwise? Given such an awful and heretical dichotomy, Dickinson was surely *right* to refuse such a heroic act of autonomous will, such a gnostic denial of the good creation, and such subjective enthusiasm requiring ever-new infusions of emotion. Dickinson is to be commended rather than condemned for daring not to trust herself to inward upheavals. In rejecting the idol of nineteenth-century Protestant piety, she did not minimize her soul's experience so much as she expanded it. Indeed, Dickinson became our most important poet of the spiritual life, not another one of the many dreary and virtually unreadable Victorian pietists.

A poem at once sprightly and memorable, precisely because it is at once troubling and edifying, is Number 373. Here, we believe, Dickinson sets forth an arrestingly perceptive understanding of the relation between faith and doubt:

> This World is not conclusion.
> A Species stands beyond—
> Invisible, as Music—
> But positive, as Sound—
> It beckons, and it baffles—
> Philosophy, dont know—
> And through a Riddle, at the last—
> Sagacity, must go—
> To guess it, puzzles scholars—
> To gain it, Men have borne
> Contempt of Generations
> And Crucifixion, shown —
> Faith slips—and laughs, and rallies—
> Blushes, if any see—
> Plucks at a twig of Evidence—
> And asks a Vane, the way—
> Much Gesture, from the Pulpit—
> Strong Hallelujahs roll—
> Narcotics cannot still the Tooth
> That nibbles at the soul—[20]

The pseudodeity of triumphalist pietism who can be known within worldly categories also offers his disciples the blessings of finite faith and the comforts of mundane assurance. The true God, by contrast, dwells within the world while standing beyond it, a Reality as unseen as music yet as real as sound. This unknown God who alone can make himself known both attracts and repels, both frightens and captivates. His call to take up the cross and follow him to death is truly terrifying, and yet in such obedient service is the only freedom. Philosophy, with its knowledge of things visible and intelligible, can fathom nearly everything under the sun but this most important thing: the mystery of who is the real God. Eluding all confining human categories, he prompts an agnostic "don't know." The world's wisdom, even at best, is but a set of riddles and conundrums. Airy academics, with their dry distinctions, can only speculate about this species who belongs to no genus. Those who actually gain reality must lose their lives in grappling with the unobvious

God, either dying to themselves in daily martyrdom or else suffering the contempt of both the cultured and uncultured despisers of doubt-filled faith.

Such faith always entails radical risk. It is never something as clear and certain as a proposition. It is an affair of slipping and advancing, of losing and rallying, of weeping and rejoicing. So shy of self-confidence is true faith that it blushes when asked to expound its own piety. John Calvin himself would say no more than that he had come to evangelical faith *subita conversione*—that is, by means of a sudden reversal of his life's path. Knowing that God's own self-identification in Israel and Christ is the only basis for their existence, Christians put no more weight on their experiential evidence than a twig might bear, and as sinners constituting the tattered Bride of Christ, they receive dubious direction than from the wind-blown cock atop Puritan churches. It is meant to announce the Resurrection, of course, but it blows with every wind of doctrine, even as it sometimes crows with uncontrolled erotic energy. Despite the flailing of perfervid preachers and the praise-songs of easy believers, true faith is never free from the toothache of doubt. The feel-good pharmacists of the No-God offer vain narcotics to ease the pain sent by the true God.[21] The real Lord will not anesthetize shallow souls with worldly finalities, even of the most "spiritual" sort. Instead, He implants the molar of doubt no less than the tusk of truth, and they both nibble at the soul like a mouse at cheese. This God is not Blake's Old Nobodaddy, not Hemingway's Our Nada Who Art in Nada, not the Big Guy in the Sky whose death we ought, instead, to celebrate. This, instead, is the God whose Son was himself wracked by doubt as he mounted the bloody tree from which he would rule the world by reconciliation rather than coercion.[22]

"Spoiling the Egyptians": The Life of Faith in a Faithless Time

It will be evident that we are following St. Augustine's injunction to his fellow Christians that they "take the spoils of the Egyptians," making Christian use of the many excellent accomplishments of the Greco-Roman world.[23] Whatever enables Christians to live more faithfully as a storied community over against all unstoried autonomy, and thus against the domination and coercion that such storyless autonomy produces, we must claim unabashedly as our own. Christian interpreters of American literature should follow the example of John Howard Yoder, we believe, in his insistence that "the humanity of Jesus was a cultural reality." Far from transcending history, he was a first-century Jewish rabbi who made disciples precisely within his and their own culture. Just as Jesus retained almost all of his own Judaism, rejecting

Dymess

Hauerwas/ Wood methodology

only those Jews who sought a messiah who would replace Roman force with Jewish force, so must Jesus's contemporary followers exercise a similar discernment concerning American literature, repenting of our hegemonic misdeeds, embracing authors and texts that are congruent with the faith, refusing those that are not, transforming and giving new motivation to previously undiscovered riches, and so on.[24]

Yet the first Augustinian act that Christians in America must perform is not retrieval but repentance, that is, repentance for the sins of hegemonic Christianity. Yoder is blunt about the evils we must confess: "We were wrong. The picture of Jesus [we] have been given by the Empire, by the Crusades, by struggles over holy sites, and by wars in the name of the 'Christian West' is not only something to forget but something to forgive." Such pardon cannot remain mere remorse for past wrongs; it also requires radical *metanoia*, especially as our major American writers remind us of our egregious failures. As we have noted, Christians owe an unpayable debt to the magisterial figures of the nineteenth-century American Renaissance for teaching us the lessons that Christian triumphalism had forgotten: the incurable quality of evil and the utter persistence of tragedy. Yet the call to repentance comes not only from the salutary witness of such "outsiders" as Melville and Hawthorne but also from the church's own Gospel, as Yoder makes clear: "the continuing pertinence of the historical memory of Jesus, via the New Testament, as a lever for continuing critique, is part of the [gospel] message itself. The capacity for, in fact the demand for, self-critique is part of what must be shared with people of other faiths and ideologies."[25]

Yet where in our national literature do we encounter a work of art that gives imaginative life to the church as the one transformative community that, by overcoming the triumphalist allure, is able to reconcile enemies and thus to empower their mutual resistance against the coercions of state and culture alike, whether social or psychological, whether economic or military? Through this baptismal and Eucharistic people, through the presence and power of their Messiah-Redeemer alive and at work in their midst, the triune God is fashioning an alternative history for all people, indeed, for his whole creation. "The church thus exhibits to the present order of things," writes Barry Harvey, "the contours and content of God's providential care for the world: the new humanity and the age to come."[26] Again we ask, where in American literature is the world confronted with anything akin to the "contours and content" of this new creation? We acknowledge the danger of such an imperative query. Nothing could be worse than for Christian faith to be turned into an aesthetic object fit for mere interesting contemplation or escapist enjoyment.[27] As the quintessential bourgeois art form, focused increasingly on the questing individual, the novel is perhaps the aesthetic medium most adaptable to a religious triumphalism that makes the church unnecessary and thus invisible. It poses a danger, therefore, both to the writer who falls prey to its self-indulgence and to the reader who loses himself in the solitude it encourages.[28]

Flannery O'Connor and the Possibilities of God

In our view, Flannery O'Connor is an exemplary Christian writer of the kind whose tribe we hope will increase. While agreeing with the New Critical desire to spring literature free from the prison of subjective self-expression, she nonetheless lamented the soporific self-satisfaction often induced by "the bland Victorian novel of manners." She likened her own work, instead, to Hawthorne's "romances," a strange kind of quasi-allegorical fiction whose grotesqueries are meant to shock and disrupt rather than to comfort and assuage. Her point is that a distinctively Christian fiction will make the reality of the triune God unavoidable, while doing so in nonpropagandistic, noncoercive terms, which is to say, in sacramental terms. Just as baptism resembles nothing so much as drowning and Eucharist appears as a kind of cannibalism, while both events are the very means of life temporal and everlasting, so will Christian fiction be characterized by a necessary alterity, since the central Christian premise is that the world made and redeemed by God is constantly interrupted and transfigured by revelation. *Flannery method*

As the Archbishop of Canterbury declares in an important lecture on O'Connor, her fiction pushes "toward the limits of what is thinkable and 'acceptable,' let alone edifying. She is always taking for granted that God is possible—thinkable or accessible or even manifest—in the most grotesque and empty or cruel situations." Her aim, he insists, is to make the natural supernatural, to create "a recognisable world that is also utterly unexpected," a fictional milieu at once familiar and alien. Thus does she create "agents in fiction who embody excess of meaning, and whose relations with each other and with the usually hidden otherness of God are not limited by the visible, though inconceivable without the visible. . . . The infinite cannot be directly apprehended, so we must take appearance seriously . . . enough to read its concealments and stratagems."[29] *GKC*

Sacramental fiction, it follows, is not didactic.[30] It does not teach or illustrate the truth, as if it the story's meaning could be apprehended apart from its telling and hearing. "Any abstractly expressed compassion or piety or

The infinite cannot be directly apprehended, so we must take appearance seriously."

[handwritten top left: This is Chardin not Maritain.]

[handwritten top right: Truth creates the form — there is no form w/out content, in other words. The form is the frame of the content.]

morality in a piece of fiction is only a statement added to it," no matter where it is inserted. Hence O'Connor's deep conviction that "you don't dream up a receptive form and put the truth in it. The truth creates its own form. Form is necessity in the work of art. You know what you mean but you ain't got the right words for it."[31] The heart of a story or novel must lie, O'Connor learned from Maritain, in "some action, some gesture of a character that is unlike any other in the story, one which indicates where the real heart of the story lies . . . both totally right and totally unexpected . . . both in character and beyond character; it would have to suggest both time and eternity."[32] For Christians, the ultimately unutterable event—at once horribly ordinary and yet transcendently redemptive in and through its horror—is also the true form for fiction. As the instrument for shameful death that thus has been transfigured into the true pattern of life, the cross discloses the disturbing character of God himself. "A God who fails to generate desperate hunger and confused and uncompromising passion," writes Rowan Williams, "is no God at all." O'Connor's grotesque characters are who they are, he adds, because "God is as God is, not an agent within the universe, not a source of specialised religious consolation. If God is real, the person in touch with God is in danger, at any number of levels." To create such hunger and passion, Williams concludes, "is to risk creating in people a longing too painful to bear or a longing that will lead them to take such risks that it seems nakedly cruel to expose them to that hunger in the first place."[33]

[handwritten left margin: Terrible Beauty]

Knowing well that this God-generated hunger and passion are most dreadfully distorted in the curse that lies on both her region and nation—slavery and its legacy in lynchings and segregation and the many other injustices committed against black people—O'Connor also knew that she could write about this most explosive of subjects only at great risk to the integrity of her own art. She was steadfastly opposed to thesis-driven fiction of the kind that Eudora Welty produced in "Where Is the Voice Coming From?," a short story written for the *New Yorker* in protest against the slaying of Medgar Evers, the Jackson, Mississippi dentist and civil rights leader. Fiction dedicated to an idea, no matter how noble, reduces art to propaganda and sentimentality. In "The Artificial Nigger," therefore, O'Connor sought to deal with this most salient and dangerous of subjects in sacramental rather than moral terms alone.[34]

[handwritten left margin: Dryness's work is almost like sentimental propaganda.]

It is a story that would seem at first to constitute an obvious lesson in black-white relations, as we are shown how a youth named Nelson learns to hate blacks through the duplicitous agency of his racist grandfather named Head. Though neither of them is shown to have any relation to the church, it

[handwritten bottom: vs Heart   > connect this w/ Booth   sacramental vs. morals]

like Two rams locked horns

is nonetheless evident that racial hatred is the atmospheric condition that they unconsciously inhabit, a milieu no doubt formed by the culturally established religion of their Southern region. Yet in a setting that would seem to encourage a moralistic response—"Be kind to blacks, since they have done you no harm, despite the great harm you have done to them"—O'Connor reveals a ruthless Nietzschean contest of wills at work in what seems to be an almost Rousseauian scene. Two souls who ought to be joined in the deepest mutuality, a grandfather and a grandson living in remote northeast Georgia, find themselves locked, instead, in a ruthless struggle for domination. What was meant to be their natural desire for God, and thus the right ordering of their loves, has become their unnatural will-to-power. At every opportunity for their potential reconciliation, therefore, they become ever more fixed in their alienation, until finally they come to a total impasse. They seem as unlikely candidates for reconciliation, whether with God, blacks, or each other, as can be imagined. So tightly have Nelson and Mr. Head entangled themselves in the knot of recrimination and justification that they seem beyond saving. The circle of demonically self-perpetuating sin, O'Connor reveals, can be broken only by divine goodness. *—as in "full nelson"*

the weightiness of Bill's program

Much of the story's power derives from the potential instruments of their redemption: a genteel black man walking the length of the train, a motherly black woman standing at a neighborhood door.[35] It is thus altogether appropriate that Nelson and Mr. Head should encounter one final offer of redemption sacramentally mediated by a black man. It is granted when, hopelessly lost, bewildered, and estranged, the grandfather and grandson wander into a white suburb of Atlanta. There they discover a cast cement Negro statue in front of an elegant house. This degrading lawn jockey is neither carrying a lantern nor grasping a horse's reins—two of the more benign statuary images of black servitude—but rather holding a piece of watermelon, as if blacks were capable of nothing more than the cheap gratification of their appetites. He is supposed to be a smiling and carefree "darky," but he has a chipped eye, he lurches forward at an awkward angle, and the watermelon he is supposedly eating has turned brown. "It was not possible," declares the narrator, "to tell if the artificial Negro were meant to be young or old; he looked too miserable to be either." It is doubtful that Nelson and Mr. Head have ever seen a crucifix, but they would surely know the gospel song called "The Old Rugged Cross." Able at last to recognize this third black sign of their redemption, they are both transfixed and transformed by this "emblem of suffering and shame": "They stood gazing at the artificial Negro as if they were faced with some great mystery, some monument to another's victory that brought them together in

they are changed by symbol of culture used by the tts to Transform

"It doesn't possess any thing.
The tts uses it as her canvas.

Symbol/icon?

174   STANLEY HAUERWAS AND RALPH C. WOOD

their common defeat. They could both feel it dissolving their differences like an action of mercy."

Though meant to signal the proud triumph of whites over blacks, the scornful effigy becomes a sacrament of reconciliation to these mutually sinful kinsmen. The crimes they have committed against each other begin to melt away in the presence of this inhabited cross. It possesses transcendent reconciling power because its wretchedness attests not only to the anguish of human injustice but also to the mercy of divine suffering. There is nothing saccharine about the scene. Nelson and Mr. Head do not fall to their knees in tearful embrace. The narrator reminds the reader, on the contrary, that the boulder of the grandfather's pride is far from crushed: "Mr. Head had never known before what mercy felt like because he had been too good to deserve any." Even while feeling forgiven for the first time, he still wants to remind Nelson of his superiority, hence his wisecrack about white folks having so few real Negroes under their command that they now need artificial ones. He also refuses Nelson's imploring eyes that call for him "to explain once and for all the mystery of existence." Neither can the boy long hold on to the revelation they have both received. He lapses, instead, into platitudes about the city being a place he is glad to have seen once but will never visit again.

Not for a moment does O'Connor suggest that Nelson and Mr. Head have suddenly much less permanently overcome their sinfulness that they have adopted a proper regard for blacks or that they will never again engage in a vicious contest of wills. A long road of renewal and redemption lies before them. Yet they have both been permanently altered by their encounter with the bent and harrowed emblem of the Suffering Servant. Neither of them will be able fully to exorcise this Negro reminder of the grace that dissolves all personal and racial pride. Nelson speaks more truly than he knows when he cries out, "Let's go home before we get ourselves lost again." No longer are they lost in the religious sense, and they are returning home in more than the physical sense. As they arrive at their remote station, O'Connor's narrator reminds us that Luciferian evil has been routed: "The train glided past them and disappeared like a frightened serpent into the woods." Yet only Mr. Head fully comprehends the good that has been born never again to die:

> Mr. Head stood very still and felt the action of mercy touch him again but this time he knew that there were no words in the world that could name it. He understood that it grew out of agony, which is not denied to any man and which is given in strange ways to children. He understood it was all a man could carry into death to give his Maker and he suddenly burned with shame that he had so little of it to take with him. He stood appalled, judging himself with the thoroughness of God, while the action of mercy

There is more truth in a single line from O'Connor
Than in entire books by other authors.

The Xtn. story, if it isn't true, is nonetheless a story that should be true. It's that beautiful.

covered his pride like a flame and consumed it. He had never thought himself a great sinner before but he saw now that his true depravity had been hidden from him lest it cause him despair. He realized that he was forgiven for sins from the beginning of time, when he had conceived in his own heart the sin of Adam, until the present, when he had denied poor Nelson. He saw that no sin was too monstrous for him to claim as his own, and since God loved in proportion as He forgave, he felt ready at that instant to enter Paradise.[36]

This is one of the most controverted passages in the whole of O'Connor's work; it has met both secular and literary opposition. Critics who value "showing" over "telling" complain that O'Connor has condescended to *explain* what the action of mercy means, when she should have simply *dramatized* it. Unsympathetic readers protest the use of overt theological language in a story that, up to this point, has shown no overt religious concern. Both objections are misplaced. While the passage is laden with religious language, O'Connor has made clear from the beginning that Nelson and Mr. Head are engaged in a struggle whose proportions are absolute, and that their lostness at the end is metaphysical rather than geographical. Mr. Head has called out, in fact, "Oh Gawd I'm lost! Oh hep me Gawd I'm lost!" When Nelson continues to scorn his grandfather despite this pleading confession, Mr. Head "felt he knew what time would be like without seasons and what heat would be like without light and what man would be like without salvation."[37] *contentless frame —*

I wonder if these same critics fault J. London or S. Crane too harsh for their "Telling" of nature's indifference.

For O'Connor at last to make explicit the theological concerns that were heretofore largely implicit is not for her to indulge in literary heavy-handedness but to provide sacramental illumination. The author is not required to disappear entirely from her text, standing aloof from it in pure aesthetic neutrality, paring her fingernails. As Wayne Booth demonstrated decades ago, the supposedly impersonal and objective author always remains present in her fiction—whenever she moves inside a character's mind, whenever she gives speech to a reliable character, whenever she resorts to literary allusion or mythic pattern or symbolic reference, whenever she orders the narration of events that have previously occurred, whenever she chooses to recount one incident rather than another, and in many other ways.[38] The question is not whether the author will show *or* tell, therefore, but how she will do *both*, and here O'Connor is unapologetic in her telling.

We suspect that critics who complain about the narrative directness of this passage are secretly offended by its theological radicality. The black novelist Alice Walker is a happy exception to the sad rule, famously declaring that O'Connor's work is not about race but grace: "*Essential* O'Connor is not about race at all, which is why it is so refreshing, coming, as it does, out of such a *racial* culture. If it can be said to be 'about' anything, then it is 'about' prophets and prophecy, 'about' revelation, and 'about' the impact of supernatural grace on human beings who don't have a chance of spiritual growth without it."[39] Mr. Head's discovery of this grace is scandalous, because he fathoms the mystery of the gospel in ways that are offensive especially to Christians who want to rule the nation. He is shown the mercy that is beyond adequate naming, because, in ways unknown to Nietzsche it is beyond good and evil, utterly transcending conventional piety and morality. Here is a mercy that cannot be earned by prior acts of ethical excellence or even by sufficiently pious repentance. Mr. Head sees that mercy is the only gift that he can return to God in his future life, because it is the only gift that can prevent his sinful presumption in this present life. The pattern of forgiveness as preceding and enabling repentance is the pattern everywhere present in Scripture, from Hosea's refusal to divorce his prostitute wife to Christ's words from the cross. Jesus asks God to forgive those who are crucifying him, not because they have begged his pardon but because he wants to break the chain of anger and vengeance that has entrapped them. To have given the crowds their due, cursing them in judgment, would have been to seal them in the vicious and unbreakable circle of sin.

Far from being an example of what Dietrich Bonhoeffer called "cheap grace"—that is, a false reliance on God's forgiveness as an excuse for a self-indulgent and untransformed life—Mr. Head sees that, precisely to the extent that he has been forgiven, he is also judged and found terribly wanting. He discerns, moreover, that his sin consists not chiefly in the cruel acts he has committed against either blacks or Nelson. The roots of his transgression are buried deep in the Adamic condition of utter alienation from God. Having inherited this aboriginally sinful state, he has made it guiltily his own in betraying Nelson and despising blacks. And since every single sin partakes of systemic universal evil, Mr. Head knows that he is also responsible for the most monstrous of sins, even the crucifixion of Jesus. Yet God has hidden this worst of all truths from Mr. Head, lest it crush him in damning judgment. Rather than negating divine justice, therefore, divine mercy intensifies it. So fully is he cleansed by such confession-prompting grace that he felt "ready at that instant to enter Paradise."

In "The Artificial Nigger," Flannery O'Connor sounds the fathomless depths of the love of the triune God. It was her favorite story, because it is the work that gives the fullest fictional embodiment to her firmest convictions about both race and religion. Here she instructs herself and her readers in the

Teville
Beauty

An iconic image is always an
ironic one, b/c it is a reflection of
the infinite in & through the finite.

and ironic

HOW THE CHURCH BECAME INVISIBLE   177

meaning of the Gospel, as she turns a broken racist lawn jockey into an ironic testament to the mystery of Charity, a mystery that, though often hidden and always scandalous, remains deeper by far than the mystery of iniquity. Her "artificial nigger" thus becomes the ultimate antiracist emblem. It reveals something profounder than the evident evils of slavery and discrimination. It discloses the subtle kind of grace that inheres in a suffering that can be redemptively borne because God in Christ has borne it himself.

Yet O'Connor remained unable to depict a faithful community wherein such drastic divine grace might be socially embodied and ethically sustained. Perhaps because her own Catholicism was complicit in the racial crimes of her region, she could not draw on the witness of her own communion. Priests figure significantly in such stories as "The Enduring Chill" and "The Displaced Person," but they function as solitary representatives of the church, not as pastors of any particular flock of believers. It is also noteworthy that her most convincing fictional depiction of the transforming power of the Gospel, "Parker's Back," leaves the protagonist in sad solitude, totally bereft of any Christian community to undergird his newfound faith. Even so, O'Connor succeeds, more than any other American writer, in vivifying the Christ who calls his people to live against the lure of coercion and oppression and thus in accord with the divine Charity: the true grain of the universe.[40]

Death Comes for the Archbishop

It is exceedingly ironic that the one authentic portrayal of the church in American literature is located not in the center but, at least from the complacent perspective of Europe and New England, on the negligible periphery of the Continent, and not in the Protestant but in the Catholic community. In Willa Cather's *Death Comes for the Archbishop*, the church is brought forth from the shadows of its paradoxical invisibility. That Cather accomplished this recovery of the church's public and countercultural role is exceedingly odd, given the general propensity of her work. Like Lionel Trilling, she lamented the spiritual and aesthetic thinness of the progressivism of her era, the liberalism that expended itself almost entirely on worthy social causes, largely to the neglect of religious complexity and artistic depth. The churches having offered her but little alternative, Cather, like Dickinson, drew her artistic inspiration largely from a romantic idealism that centered upon individual sympathy and noble striving. "The world is little, people are little, human life is little," declares Thea Kronberg in *The Song of the Lark*. "There is only one big thing," she adds, "desire."[41] "Desire," declares a teacher in *The Professor's*

House, "is creation, is the magical element in that process. If there were an instrument by which to measure desire, one could foretell achievement."[42] Those imbued with desire make new worlds for themselves, however illusory, while those who lack it sink into the deadness of the various conformities. Hence Cather's ardent attention to pioneers of both the land and the spirit, those who discover the infinite resources available to them in both nature and art. "A pioneer should have imagination," the narrator announces in *O Pioneers!*, "should be able to enjoy the idea of things more than the things themselves."[43] Against the gross materialism of her time, therefore, Cather was increasingly drawn to the definition of human happiness that she first articulated in *My Ántonia*, a motto that is also inscribed on her gravestone in New Hampshire: happiness is "to become a part of something entire, whether it is sun and air, goodness and knowledge . . . to be dissolved into something complete and great."

At its worst, Cather's work is imbued with an aestheticism that prompts a character to declare, in *The Professor's House*, that "Art and religion (they are the same thing in the end, of course) have given man the only happiness he has ever had."[44] "Religion," Myra Henshaw contends in *My Mortal Enemy*, "is different from everything else; *because in religion seeking is finding.* . . . She seemed to say [the narrator explains] that in other searchings it might be the object of the quest that brought satisfaction, or it might be something incidental that one got on the way; but in religion, desire [is] fulfillment, it [is] the seeking itself" that offers the reward.[45] Though fictional declarations can never be identified with the author's own sentiments, Cather's essay on Carlyle makes clear that she worshipped at the shrine of *poesis*: "Art of every kind is an exacting master, more so even than Jehovah. He says only, 'Thou shalt have no other God before me.' Art, science and letters cry, 'Thou shalt have no other Gods at all.' They accept only human sacrifices."[46]

Death Comes for the Archbishop is not entirely free of such aestheticism, but it remains the most convincing fictional depiction of the church in American fiction. Not only did Cather admit that the writing of this novel gave her more joy than all the others and that abandoning Fathers Latour and Vaillant at the end was like a painful parting with old friends, but she also made it her most experimental work. As if to confess that in depicting the faithful lives of an archbishop and his vicar in the New World she was entering territory not entirely reducible to art, she abandoned almost all of the conventional fictional devices—plot, suspense, foreshadowing, flashbacks, and the like. Knowing well that evil seems intrinsically more interesting than good, and that goodness is enormously difficult to make artistically convincing, she dared nonetheless to let these two winsome priests hold the reader's interest. Cather admitted that the hagiographies recorded in *The Golden Legend* impressed her, yet not because the fantastic miracles that the saints allegedly performed are portrayed so dramatically, but because the martyrdoms that they actually suffered are narrated so casually, as ordinary occurrences. The deaths of the saints, Cather learned, are but the culmination and summation of their lives. Hence Cather's decision not to proceed chronologically but episodically, not to call her work a novel but a narrative, not to withhold the story's final outcome but to announce it in the title itself. For art and faith fully to be integrated, something revolutionary was required.

This is not to say that the work lacks artistic structure. On the contrary, the prologue in Rome is mirrored with a final remembrance of the France that the archbishop and his vicar had left forty years earlier. There is also a miracle recounted near the beginning and again near the end. The saintliness of Latour and Vaillant is also set in sharp relief by the corruption of the various other cardinals and priests. Cather also creates a clear opposition between the Indians and the Americans, much to the detriment of the newcomers. The bishop and his vicar themselves form a fine complementary pair: Latour the keen-minded man, handsome and artistic; Vaillant the practical man, homely and indifferent to beauty. Yet such parallels and balances are not artificial devices so much as signs that, while the grotesque may serve as a means of drastic discovery, as in Flannery O'Connor, the Christian life itself requires an art form far less dramatic, something steadier and more ordinary, namely, the fortitude marked by daily religious discipline within the church.

The church in the New World, Cather knew, would need to set itself in right relation to a natural and human order unlike anything it had encountered in Europe or Asia: great desert spaces and magnificent open skies and native peoples having a way of life almost unfathomable to the allegedly civilized West. Several of Archbishop Latour's meditations get at this strange new world, as he remarks on the cloud and rock formations of New Mexico, especially the mesas. They seem like the church itself in its antiquity and incompleteness; they are akin to vast Gothic cathedrals waiting to be finished, yet having their own integrity of sky and stone,

> as if, with all the materials for world-making assembled, the Creator had desisted, gone away and left everything on the point of being brought together, on the eve of being arranged into mountain, plain, plateau. The country was still waiting to be made into a landscape.

. . . The great tables of granite set down in an empty plain were inconceivable without their attendant clouds, which were part of them, as the
smoke is part of the censer, or the foam of the wave.[47]

Latour's thoroughly baptized imagination discerns analogues of the holy
everywhere in the natural order. Yet he is not eager to find easy Christian
correspondences, as if this barren landscape were not also hard and cruel. He
notices, for example, that almost all of the American pioneers are motivated by
a consuming desire for material gain. Against them Cather sets the attitudes
and practices of the archbishop's Indian traveling companion, Eusabio:

When they left the rock or tree or sand dune that sheltered them for the
night, the Navajo was careful to obliterate every trace of their temporary
occupation. He buried the embers of the fire and the remnants of food,
unpiled any stones he had piled together, filled up the holes he had scooped
in the sand. . . . Father Latour judged that, just as it was the white man's
way to assert himself in any landscape, to change it, make it over a little (at
least to leave some mark of memorial of his sojourn), it was the Indian's way
to pass through a country without disturbing anything; to pass and leave no
trace, like fish through water, or birds through air.

It was the Indian manner to vanish into the landscape, not to stand
out against it. . . . Moreover, these Indians disliked novelty and change.
They came and went by the old paths worn into the rock by the feet of
their fathers, used the old natural stairway of stone to climb to their mesa
towns, carried water from the old springs, even after the white men had
dug wells.

. . . They seemed to have none of the European's desire to "master"
nature, to arrange and re-create. They spent their ingenuity in the other
direction; in accommodating themselves to the scene in which they found
themselves. This was not so much from indolence, the Bishop thought,
as from an inherited caution and respect. It was if the great country were
asleep, and they wished to carry on their lives without awakening it; or as
if the spirits of earth and air and water were things not to antagonize and
arouse. . . . The land and all that it bore they treated with consideration; not
attempting to improve it, they never desecrated it.[48]

In her critique of the Western and Cartesian urge to subdue nature for human
use, Cather would seem to be an early environmentalist. Yet she makes Latour
thoroughly Christian in his conviction that man is not meant to live in animal
identity with nature. The priest avidly cultivates his own garden and orchard,
adding cherries and apricots, apples and quinces, and the "peerless pears of
France" to the starchy Indian diet limited largely to corn. After enjoying an
especially flavorful meal prepared by Father Vaillant, Father Latour observes

that "soup like this is not the work of one man. It is the result of a constantly refined tradition. There are nearly a thousand years of history in this soup." The products of the enclosed garden, whether flowers or fruits, prove indispensable not only to the senses but also to the soul. The bishop even quotes Pascal's remark that "man was lost and saved in a garden." Humanity is not meant for nature alone, Cather suggests, even if civilized existence entails a tragic spoliation of nature's pristine glory:

> Beautiful surroundings, the society of learned men, the charm of noble women, the graces of art, could not make up to [Latour] for the loss of those light-hearted mornings of the desert, for that wind that made one a boy again. He had noticed that this peculiar quality in the air of new countries vanished after they were tamed by man and made to bear harvests. . . . The moisture of plowed land, the heaviness of labour and growth and grain-bearing utterly destroyed it; one could breathe that [air] only on the bright edges of the world, on the great plains and the sage-brush desert.[49]

Lacking this tragic sense that many good things require the sacrifice and loss of many other good things, the reverential world of Native Americans remains strangely self-enclosed. The Indians dwelling on their nearly impregnable mesa at Ácoma have become spiritually obdurate, hardened not only against Christian culture but also, as Father Latour observes, against transformation of any kind at all: "through all the centuries that his own [European] part of the world had been changing like the sky at daybreak, this people had been fixed, increasing neither in numbers nor desires, rock-turtles on their rock. Something reptilian he felt here, something that had endured by immobility, a kind of life out of reach, like the crustaceans in their armour."[50]

There is also something reptilian about the Indian conflation of the holy and the demonic in their in their worship of a giant mythological snake. One of the narrative's most disturbing scenes occurs when Father Latour and his Hopi guide named Jacinto take refuge from a fierce snowstorm in a cave that had once been the secret site of Indian snake-worship. Though the towering cavern reminds him of a Gothic chapel, the archbishop feels an instant repugnance for the place, perhaps because blood sacrifice had apparently been performed there. He is troubled not only by the fusty odor permeating the frigid air but also by the cave's "extraordinary vibration," a noise humming "like a hive of bees, like a heavy roll of distant drums." The droning sound causes Latour's head to swirl in dizzying confusion. Jacinto also invites the bishop to put his ear to a secret fissure in the floor of the cave, so that he too may hear the deep underground roar of a primordial, snakelike river:

The water was far, far below, perhaps as deep as the foot of the mountain, a flood moving in utter blackness under ribs of antediluvian rock. It was not a rushing noise, but the sound of a great flood moving with majesty and power.

"It is terrible," he said at last, as he rose.

"*Sí, padre.*" Jacinto began spitting on the clay he had gouged out of the seam, and plastered it up again.[51]

Rebecca West remarks that a writer such as D. H. Lawrence would have attempted to penetrate the crack in the floor and to pursue both the snake and the river, offering the reader a direct encounter with chthonic terror and might. Instead, Cather narrates the portentous scene wholly from Latour's perspective.[52] In so doing, she enables the reader to share his discernment that the primal forces of the cosmos, whether natural or spiritual, are not to be toyed with, much less worshipped. Nietzsche acknowledged that, if one stares too long at the Abyss, it will stare back. Though the cave had perhaps saved his life, Father Latour always remembers it "with horror," so terrible is his revulsion at a religion that reveres evil as well as good, turning them into contraries that are not opposed so much as coinciding. No wonder that, during his single night in the cave, the archbishop makes sure to "read his breviary long by the light of the fire." Nor does he later contest the candid judgment of an American trader: "no white man knows anything about Indian religion, Padre."[53]

Far more admirable than either the Americans who live in contempt for nature or the Indians who worship it uncritically are the Mexicans who have embraced Christianity without abandoning their deep regard for the rhythms of the world. A good deal of paganism remains alive in these simple Christians, Father Latour admits, especially in their fondness for the trinkets and trumpery of conventional religious practice, such as the amulets that seem magically to guarantee the fruitfulness of the fields. Latour patiently accommodates their wooden Virgins dressed as poor and sorrowful Mexican mothers, their St. Josephs attired as Mexican *rancheros*; they express the authentic piety of the people, not the imported spirituality of refined Europeans such as himself and Vaillant. The bishop is utterly untroubled, therefore, that the nursery-like Madonnas serve the Mexican believers as both "their doll and their queen, something to fondle and something to adore, as Mary's Son must have been to Her": "These poor Mexicans, [Latour] reflected, were not the first to pour out their love in this simple fashion. Raphael and Titian had made costumes for Her in their time, and the great masters had made music for Her, and the great architects had made cathedrals for Her. Long before Her years on earth, in the long twilight between the Fall and the Redemption, the pagan sculptors were always trying to achieve the image of a goddess who should yet be a woman."[54] The sacraments of the church, Latour and Vaillant remained convinced, prevent such popular devotional practices from degenerating into magical paganism. The Mexicans long for baptism and marriage, because they have learned, if only in an inchoate way, that their lives are given ultimate direction and hope only as they receive what they cannot give themselves: the grace that puts them in right relation to God and thus to each other. Yet never does Cather depict the archbishop or his vicar as anything other than ordinary parish priests doing their work. Even when, having been dispatched by Latour to administer the sacrament to dying Indians during an outbreak of black measles at Las Vegas, Vaillant contracts the illness himself, Cather reports his heroic action as a mere matter of fact, not with hagiographic hyperbole. Vaillant is also as shrewd as he is holy. He wheedles a Mexican who is overjoyed that the priest has made his house "right with Heaven" into giving him not one but both of his prized pearl-white mules, Contento and Angelica, so that the archbishop might also have a proper mount. Though the inveigled Señor Lujon "felt he had been worried out of his mules, . . . yet he bore no resentment. He did not doubt Father Joseph's devotedness, nor his singleness of purpose. After all, a Bishop was a Bishop, and a Vicar was a Vicar, and it was not to their discredit that they worked like a pair of common parish priests."[55]

Common parish priests, like exalted bishops and vicars, are not immune from doubts and worries about the worthiness of their endeavors. After more than two decades in New Mexico, and with only minimal success to show for his efforts, Latour faces his dark night of the soul, his massive sense of spiritual emptiness and vocational failure, on a snowy December evening: "His work seemed superficial, a house built upon the sands. His great diocese was still a heathen country. The Indians travelled their old road of fear and darkness, battling with evil omens and ancient shadows. The Mexicans were children who played with their religion." Latour recovers from his bout of *acedia* not in solitary wrestling with God but in a communal encounter with an old Mexican woman named Sada. Though enslaved to a family of viciously anti-Catholic Protestants for nineteen years, she has courageously fled at last to the sacristy of the church to seek solace. Leading the weeping woman into the Lady Chapel, the priest kneels and prays with her, knowing that her tears spring from ecstasy far more than sorrow. For the archbishop to have comforted this solitary sufferer who remains utterly negligible by the world's measure is for him to have recovered far more than his own personal faith; Father Latour has also rediscovered the absolute indispensability of the church and its sacraments, its prayers and vigils, its saints and martyrs, for human existence to remain human:

> Never, as he afterward told Father Vaillant, had it been permitted him to behold such deep experience of the holy joy of religion as on that pale December night. He was able to feel, kneeling beside her, the preciousness of the things of the altar to her who was without possessions; the tapers, the image of the Virgin, the figures of the saints, the Cross that took away indignity from suffering and made pain and poverty a means of fellowship with Christ. Kneeling beside the much enduring bond-woman, he experienced those holy mysteries as he had done in his young manhood. . . .
>
> Not often, indeed, had Jean-Marie Latour come so near to the Fountain of all Pity as in the Lady Chapel that night; the pity that no man born of woman could ever utterly cut himself off from; [the pity] that was for the murderer on the scaffold, as it was for the dying soldier or the martyr on the rack.[56]

This is the same "Pity" that we encounter at the climax of Flannery O'Connor's "The Artificial Nigger." Perhaps because she wrote as an anti-Puritan, high-church Episcopalian, Cather gives this pity an unapologetically Marian and Catholic quality. It is not enough, therefore, that Archbishop Latour promises to "remember [Sada] in my silent supplications before the altar as I do my own sisters and nieces"; he must also offer the Blessed Sacrifice of the Mass, as he calls it, in a church whose very edifice makes proper tribute to the Son and Mother of God. Though the cathedral at Santa Fe need (indeed, it must) not be a replica of European models, neither can it exist in utter disregard for the achievements of Christendom. And so Latour yearns for a properly Romanesque church, not a fancy Gothic structure of the kind being constructed in Victorian England but a sanctuary that would link the church of the New World more directly with the Roman world from which the ancient church first emerged. When he at last discovers the native rock from which the cathedral stones can be quarried, the archbishop experiences a veritable epiphany: "Every time I come here, I like this stone better. I could have hardly hoped that God would gratify my personal taste, my vanity, if you will, in this way. I tell you, *Blanchet* [his nickname for Vaillant], I would rather have found this hill of yellow rock than have come into a fortune to spend in charity. The Cathedral is near my heart, for many reasons. I hope you do not think me very worldly.[57]" The practical uselessness of this lavish sanctuary, its princely cost having been better used to succor the poor, its utter irrelevance for the present moment, its taking many decades, perhaps even centuries, to become thoroughly at one with the place, all of these objections are nothing to the point. Like the European cookery and gardens and orchards that Latour and Vaillant value so highly, the cathedral is not a gargantuan ornament but an essential embodiment of the Gospel. The church, Cather insists, offers not a gnostic deliverance of naked souls but rather a salvation meant for bodies that require *things*: the blessings of eye and palate, of the auditory and olfactory senses, of the heart and the will no less than the stomach and the genitals. Hence the need for an appropriate architectural witness that will point permanently to the God who has tabernacled in the world through his Son and his Church and its sacramental story.

It is altogether fitting that Latour should not die at the rural retreat where he had retired but in the shadow of his cathedral, not amidst the still silence of the natural world but within the reverent stir of the church. As he takes leave of the past, the aged priest thinks less and less of his beloved Clermont in France, recognizing instead that to be Christian is to dwell in perpetual exile, to live as a resident alien having no permanent citizenship in any other city than one not made with hands. Neither is the dying priest vexed by worries over the future, confident that God will preserve the Indians in their inseparable connection to the land. Everything temporal has begun to merge into a single moment of memory and vision: "He was soon to have done with calendared time, and it had already ceased to count for him. He sat in the middle of his own consciousness; none of his former states of mind were lost or outgrown. They were all within reach of his hand, and all comprehensible."[58]

Father Latour makes surely the most blessed death in all of American literature, not so much because he dies in peaceful gratitude for the fulfillment of his mission but because his whole life has been a preparation for death. Such advanced training in dying is not, for Christians, the same thing that Socrates calls for in Plato's *Apology*. It is a matter of the priest's having rightly ordered his loves through his vocation in the church and thus having brought his life to its true completion.[59] As Latour himself observes, he departs this life, not from having contracted a cold but from "having lived," from having lived so fully that he "accomplished an historic period," as the narrator says. The fullness of his life accomplishes not his salvation alone but also that of his community. Latour has been formed by the church and for the sake of the church. Cather's narrator is right to observe, therefore, that it was not only the Mexicans of Santa Fe who fell on their knees at the tolling of Jean-Marie

Latour's death bell but "all American Catholics as well."[60] She might well have said "all American Christians as well," since *Death Comes for the Archbishop* remains the one important work of American literature wherein the church, though nearly everywhere else occluded from our imaginative vision, clearly and redemptively emerges.

12

"The Play of the Lord"

On the Limits of Critique

Roger Lundin

Stanley Hauerwas and Ralph Wood have written a trenchant critique of American culture. Their thesis is clear, vivid, and pointed. It is that Christians in America have come to equate American opportunity with the human good and "have made American opportunity virtually coterminous with Christian freedom." From this, it follows that Christianity in America has what they call a distinctly "Constantinian" form, and "American churches have enjoyed a cultural establishment that, for being so subtle, may be far more pernicious than the old-style conflation of realms."

For Hauerwas and Wood, this indictment of American culture and the Christian churches in it connects with American literature by way of the tacit question to which their chapter serves as an extended answer. Why has America "produced so few writers who are Christian in any substantive sense of the word?" Why have "nearly all of our eminent writers [been] heterodox at best, atheist or even nihilist at worst?" Their answer focuses upon three authors—Emily Dickinson, Flannery O'Connor, and Willa Cather—and seeks to account for the heterodoxy of the first (Dickinson) by placing the blame squarely on the Constantinian cooptation of the church, which "has become virtually invisible in America. It has so fully identified itself with the American project that our artists have had little cause to heed any unique and distinctively Christian witness in the churches."

This is a large argument that makes broad and forceful claims on a number of fronts, and by the nature of the sociological, ecclesiological, and theological vision that informs it, it does not lend itself well to being quibbled with here or qualified there. It has the undeniable virtue of providing a sheltering, comprehensive perspective upon our modern theological confusion and political conflict. But at the same time, that very comprehensiveness may make one feel that there are only two options available in regard to this argument, that is, either accept the invitation to clamber aboard the Anabaptist ark or face the whelming flood alone.

Whether or not that is the case, to shift to a more intimate and manageable, landlocked frame of reference, like the speaker in Robert Frost's "Birches," "I should prefer," in this case, to believe it possible to differ with Hauerwas and Wood on certain details even as I resonate with their larger argument about the oblique relationship of Christianity to many of America's finest writers. With its impressively tight fusion of Anabaptist ethics and Barthian theology, the thesis put forward by Hauerwas and Wood may be as indivisible as the "Truth" and "all her matter-of-fact about the ice storm" in Frost's poem. Nevertheless, I would prefer to play like the boy on the branches in that poem, climbing their argument, so to speak, "*Toward* heaven," bending it in places, but never seeking to break it.

I begin by pressing against the argument with a two-part questioning of the category of the Constantinian. To be certain, Hauerwas and Wood raise important questions about the "complacency endemic to moralistic American innocence"; they tellingly criticize the nineteenth-century rise of a bland pietism that sets no challenges for the established order; and in a critique of voluntarism that draws upon the work of Timothy Smith, Nathan Hatch, and others, they have their finger on the pulse of the American practice of preferential self-construction.

Hauerwas and Wood are right: this situation represents a farrago of cultural compromises and personal excesses. But does it constitute a Constantinian state of affairs? The extended justification for the use of this term comes at the close of the first section of their account. Drawing on the work of William Cavanaugh, the argument here is concise, tight, and coherent—perhaps too coherent. This compressed yet intricate rereading of the history of tolerance and democratic liberties tacitly relies so strongly upon the categories of the *latent* and the *hidden* that accepting it might require a quasi-gnostic acquisition of key insights, before the uninitiated can begin to see how modern democracy is "far more pernicious than the old-style conflation" that originally marked Constantinianism.

On this point, I am inclined to regret the idea of an either-or choice, vis-à-vis the question of Christendom and the Church, and to agree instead with Charles Taylor's suggestion as to how Christians might avoid falling "into one of two untenable positions": either "we pick certain fruits of modernity," such as human rights, even as we reject and condemn the modern "breakout" from

Christianity that underlies these developments, *or* in reaction, we side with the "exclusive humanism" of the radical Enlightenment and jettison all vestiges of Christian belief and commitment. Instead, Taylor urges us gradually to "find our voice from within the achievements of modernity, [and] measure the humbling degree to which some of the most impressive extensions of a gospel ethic depended upon a breakaway from Christendom, and from within these gains try to make clearer to ourselves and others the tremendous dangers that arise in them."[1]

On another level, the Constantinian claim does not need to be challenged so much as supplemented. *or supplanted* To say that Emily Dickinson, William Faulkner, and other great writers "have little substantive regard for Christianity because our churches have made it virtually impossible for them to do so" may minimize the real intellectual struggles and willful difficulties they encountered in their entanglements with faith.

Dickinson, for example, resisted anything resembling a conventional view of sin, for she considered epistemological categories more pertinent to her quarrel with God than volitional ones. "Of God we ask one favor," she wrote near the end of her life,

> that we may be forgiven—
> For what, he is presumed to know—
> The Crime, from us, is hidden—[2]

In like manner, on matters of belief, Faulkner was a yearning observer gazing upon an experience of wholeness he could admire but not share. In *The Sound and the Fury*, Dilsey may sit "bolt upright beside [Benjy], crying rigidly and quietly in the annealment and the blood of the remembered Lamb," but Faulkner could not imagine that blood as having been shed for him.[3] For Dickinson and Faulkner, there were moral and willful barriers to belief that were not created by any lack of non-Constantinian communities in their midst.

Perhaps even more important than the volitional obstacles were the genuine intellectual struggles these two and others had with belief and the practice of the Christian faith. The sudden collapse of the argument from design in the mid-nineteenth century left Dickinson with a palpable sense of loss. Charles Darwin vexed her, and the higher criticism made her skeptical about the Bible's veracity and uncertain of her own destiny. An astute student of cultural history, Dickinson sensed the gravity of the changes being wrought by the intellectual forces at play in the nineteenth century:

> Those—dying then,
> Knew where they went—

They went to God's Right Hand—
That Hand is amputated now
And God cannot be found—

The abdication of Belief
Makes the Behavior small—
Better an ignis fatuus
Than no illume at all—[4]

It is true, as Wood and Hauerwas argue, that Dickinson took offense at the "triumphalist moralism and pietist individualism" of her evangelical milieu, yet that is but part of the story. For her, as for Melville, Twain, Wharton, Frost, and others, the barriers to belief involved serious questions of epistemology, historical consciousness, and scientific materialism. By the time of the Civil War, Andrew Delbanco has argued, the Christian narratives of divine providence "were disintegrating. After the war it seemed clear that an entirely new kind of story would be needed for the narration of human lives and that the new stories would not be about God's supervision. They would be about blind luck."[5] The nineteenth-century crisis of providence called for a sustained theological engagement with substantial intellectual concerns. Christian thought in the second half of the nineteenth century, however, proved largely inadequate to that task, as, in Mark Noll's words, "the religious habits of mind that had built a Protestant Christian America divided and eventually petered out after the war."[6] The failure of the Christian response to this loss may have included elements covered in the Constantinian critique, but it also encompassed intellectual difficulties that the communal example of a noncoercive Christianity could not in itself resolve.

There is another crucial point at which I wish to press against the argument of Hauerwas and Wood. It has to do with what I would call the question of irony and agency, and perhaps I can best get at this by turning to the opening of their illuminating discussion of Flannery O'Connor. I agree that she "is an exemplary Christian writer," whose fiction seeks to "make the reality of the triune God unavoidable." But the last clause in this sentence really caught my attention. O'Connor presses the triune case, they explain, "in nonpropagandistic, noncoercive terms." And these, they say, are "sacramental terms," which means they are not didactic but suggestive, not persuasive in a rhetorical sense but attractive in a poetic way. "Sacramental fiction," they conclude, "is not didactic."

About O'Connor's stories, these may be accurate judgments about the relationship of the story to the reader, but do they also apply to the actions that unfold within the stories themselves or to the dramas that play themselves out in the world and the church itself? Are the characters who drive people to God noncoercive? Does God not intend for suffering, including the suffering that we inflict on others and which we endure from them, to teach us and to teach them something? In O'Connor's fiction, that is, there is a great deal of violence, propaganda, and coercion, and these forces play an integral part in the drama of grace and redemption. In O'Connor's stories alone, women and men are brought before God through the prospect of imminent execution, as a result of being gored by a bull, as a result of a son's having to witness the humiliation and death of the mother he despises, when a father discovers his neglected son hanging at the end of a rope, through a disabled young woman having her artificial leg stolen, by means of a book hurled into the face of an obtuse woman, and through a bloody beating that a man sustains on his tattooed back.

At the conclusion of "A Good Man is Hard to Find," the Misfit says of the Grandmother he has just shot, "she would of been a good woman, if it had been somebody there to shoot her every minute of her life."[7] What are we to make of all these misfits in O'Connor's stories—from the criminal who assists in sanctifying a woman with the threat of death, to Manley Pointer who steals Hulga's leg, to the Wellesley girl who smacks Mrs. Turpin in the eye with a copy of *Human Development*? How do their violent acts and coercive behaviors fit into the divine scheme of things? In O'Connor's Catholic theology, they would no doubt represent that portion of nature sufficient to serve the preliminary purposes of grace. But in the anti-Constantinian view, where might these acts belong?

The difficulty here relates to issues raised by Hauerwas and Wood's deep appreciation for Willa Cather's *Death Comes for the Archbishop*. "Father Latour," they write, "makes surely the most blessed death in all of American literature." Formed by the church for the sake of the church, Latour offers in life and death a heroic example of authentic Christian life, and *Death Comes for the Archbishop* is "the one important work of American literature" in which the church emerges fully and redemptively, they argue.

It is possible to question this latter claim without gainsaying the power of Cather's novel. One can think of any number of works of American fiction in which the church, or some significant facet of it, is portrayed with admiration or even reverence. Father Mapple's sermon is a beacon in the otherwise darkened world of *Moby Dick*; in *The Marble Faun*, Nathaniel Hawthorne agonizingly admires the confessional practices of the Roman Church; and in Dilsey's section in *The Sound and the Fury*, William Faulkner offers in Reverend Shegog's sermon one of the most evocative treatments of the crucifixion and resurrection we are likely to encounter anywhere, whether in the pages of a novel or from the pulpit of a church.

Such treatments of Christianity and the church may not be as robust as the one put forward in *Death Comes for the Archbishop*, but they point to a persistent pattern in the fiction of the United States. Like Cather with Father Latour, Melville with Father Mapple, and Faulkner with Reverend Shegog, we in the modern world often find ourselves admiring what we can neither believe nor enact. Now to be sure, in the case of Hauerwas and Wood, the matter of belief is not in question but that of enactment is. How are we to reconcile their desire to overcome "the triumphalist allure" and to resist "the coercions of state and culture alike" with the manner in which such triumphalism and coercion often work, in fiction as well as life, toward redemptive ends?

In his remarkable study of the fiction of Isak Dinesen (Karen Blixen), Robert Langbaum notes that she was intrigued by characters who had been somehow called to play tragic parts in the larger comedy of life. "Barabbas, Judas, Pilate, Caiaphas," explains Langbaum, "fascinate Isak Dinesen as the tragic figures in the divine comedy of the Passion. They were tragically sacrificed, their suffering is endless, in order to make possible Jesus's comic sacrifice, the happy outcome of which was never in doubt."[8] Or, as one of Dinesen's characters makes a similar point in "The Deluge at Norderney":

> "Nothing sanctifies, nothing, indeed, is sanctified, except by the play of the Lord, which is alone divine. You speak like a person who would pronounce half of the notes of the scale—say, *do, re* and *mi*—to be sacred, but *fa, sol, la*, and *si* to be only profane, while, Madame, no one of the notes is sacred in itself, and it is the music, which can be made out of them, which is alone divine. . . . The lion lies in wait for the antelope at the ford, and the antelope is sanctified by the lion, as is the lion by the antelope, for the play of the Lord is divine."[9]

To be sure, this vision of life could be taken to be fatalistic, and if pushed to the extreme, it could be used to justify anything, even crime, as a necessity. But it need not be pushed to that extreme, and in its modest guise, it provides a most useful model for understanding the ironies and ambiguities of human historicity and the particular interplay of Christian belief and American culture.

For example, such a view enables us to take a somewhat different approach to the American past than that put forward in "How the Church Became Invisible." At the beginning of the chapter, Hauerwas and Wood declare: "Let our intent be clear: we are not denying that acculturated Christianity is still Christianity. Without it, we confess, many of us would not be Christians at all. Even so, we insist that it is a terribly truncated form of the Faith." There follows, a few pages later, a stringent critique of the "enormous and usually unrecognized price" to be paid for the freedom of affiliation at the heart of American Constantinian Christianity. The paragraph in question begins by saying that it is "surely a great good" that "citizens are legally free rather than required to join any or no particular church" in America, yet it concludes with the claim that such an emphasis upon freedom creates churches that are "both individualistic and anti-institutional." And thus American religious pluralism ends up producing a barren form of Christianity "that gives ontological priority to human will over the created order."

But how are we to unpack these ironies? How can we untangle the skein, so that a "nonpropagandistic, noncoercive" church may stand as a pure countercultural example free of corrupting and entangling alliances? My sense is that there is no real way to unweave this historical web. Works as different as Edmund Morgan's *Visible Saints*, W. H. Auden's "Greatness Finding Itself," and Nathan Hatch's *The Democratization of American Christianity* have argued convincingly that the voluntaristic excesses we understandably deplore are in many cases the unintended consequences of the same reforming impulse that many among us—Anabaptists, Lutherans, Methodist, and Anglicans alike—treasure and admire. And, I might add, I have learned similar lessons from the American writers I most highly respect, such as Frederick Douglass, Ralph Waldo Emerson, Emily Dickinson, Herman Melville, Nathaniel Hawthorne, and Henry James.

Dietrich Bonhoeffer spoke to this matter when he wrote to his parents from his Berlin prison cell in late 1943. "Today is Reformation Day," he wrote, and "one wonders why Luther's action had to be followed by consequences that were the exact opposite of what he intended." He wanted a unity of the church and the West, "and the consequence was the disintegration of the church and of Europe"; he promoted freedom, and "the consequence was indifference and licentiousness"; he envisioned a genuine secular social order free of clerical coercion, and the "result was . . . the gradual dissolution of all real cohesion and order in society." From his student days, Bonhoeffer recalled a disagreement between Karl Holl and Adolf von Harnack "as to whether the great historical intellectual and spiritual movements made headway through their primary or their secondary motives." At the time he thought Holl was right to argue the former case. "Now I think he was wrong. As long as a hundred years ago Kierkegaard said that today Luther would say the opposite of what he said then. I think he was right—with some reservations." Or to put it another way, Bonhoeffer is saying that were Luther to return, he would play the lion to the antelope he once was.

At Christmas of 1942, Bonhoeffer wrote in secret to a handful of his fellow conspirators in the fight against Hitler. In opposition to his own pacifist principles, Bonhoeffer had signed on to the plot to overthrow the Nazi regime. Now, at the darkest hour of their dangerous effort, he wrote to remind his fellow conspirators: "We will not and must not be either outraged critics or opportunists, but must take our share of responsibility for the moulding of history in every situation and at every moment, whether we are the victors or the vanquished." Within the ironic complexities of history, he assures them, "free and responsible action" depends upon "a God who demands responsible action in a bold venture of faith, and who promises forgiveness and consolation to the man who becomes a sinner in that venture."[10]

At the close of O'Connor's "Revelation," Mrs. Turpin has a vision of souls "rumbling toward heaven." There are black souls and white trash, freaks and lunatics at the front of the line, and at its end there "was a tribe of people whom [Mrs. Turpin] recognized at once as those who, like herself and Claud, had always had a little of everything and the God-given wit to use it right."[11] If there is a place for the poor, the dispossessed, and even the virtuous on the rumbling lope to heaven, and if the antelope and the lion may both take their place upon the ark, is it too much to hope that in these places and processions, there might be room even for some Constantinians, an Amherst recluse or two, and even a few branch-climbing Calvinists?

Notes

Introduction

1. Jonathan Edwards, *A Jonathan Edwards Reader*, ed. John E. Smith, Harry S. Stout, and Kenneth P. Minkema (New Haven, CT: Yale University Press, 1995), 281. Elisa New discusses this passage in a significantly different context in Chapter 3.

2. Jenny Franchot, "Invisible Domain: Religion and American Literary Studies," *American Literature* 67 (1995): 839–40, 842.

3. Although the current debate over the nature of American Studies is not a primary focus of this book, several essays, particularly those by Buell at the beginning and Hauerwas and Wood at the end, address some of its most important concerns. For the contours of the present argument over this topic, see Donald E. Pease and Robyn Wiegman, eds., *The Futures of American Studies* (Durham, NC: Duke University Press, 2002); Alan Wolfe, "Anti-American Studies: The Difference Between Criticism and Hatred," *The New Republic*, February 10, 2003, pp. 25–32; Michael Bérubé, "The Loyalties of American Studies," *American Quarterly* 56 (2004): 223–33; Leo Marx, "On Recovering the 'Ur' Theory of American Studies," *American Literary History* 17 (2005): 118–34; and Wai Chee Dimock and Lawrence Buell, eds., *Shades of the Planet: American Literature as World Literature* (Princeton, NJ: Princeton University Press, 2007), esp. 1–16.

4. Kenneth Burke, *The Philosophy of Literary Form*, 3rd ed. (1941; repr., Berkeley: University of California Press, 1973), 109.

5. Burke, *Philosophy*, 110.

6. Burke, *Philosophy*, 110–11.

7. Burke, *Philosophy*, 111–12.

8. Walter Benjamin, *Illuminations: Essays and Reflections*, ed. Hannah Arendt, trans. Harry Zohn (1968; repr., New York: Schocken, 1969), 256.

Chapter 1

1. Friedrich Nietzsche, *The Genealogy of Morals*, ed. Oscar Levy, trans. Horace Samuel (1914; repr., New York: Gordon, 1974), 111; emphasis in original.

2. Jacques Derrida, *The Gift of Death*, trans. David Wills (Chicago: University of Chicago Press, 1995), 49.

3. Geoffrey Hill, *Style and Faith: Essays* (New York: Counterpoint, 2003), 20.

4. Tim O'Brien, *The Things They Carried* (New York: Penguin, 1991), 86.

5. Heather McHugh, "What He Thought," in *Hinge & Sign: Poems, 1968–1993* (Middletown, CT: Wesleyan University Press, 1994), 4.

6. Hill, *Style and Faith*, 123.

7. Walter Pater, *The Renaissance: Studies in Art and Poetry*, ed. Donald L. Hill (Berkeley: University of California Press, 1980), 106.

8. Ralph Waldo Emerson, *Essays and Lectures*, ed. Joel Porte (New York: Library of America, 1983), 20.

9. John Milton, *Paradise Lost: An Authoritative Text, Backgrounds and Sources, Criticism*, ed. Scott Elledge (New York: Norton, 1975), 61, 118.

10. Emerson, *Essays and Lectures*, 28.

11. Cynthia Ozick, *Art & Ardor: Essays* (1983; repr., New York: Dutton, 1984), 193.

12. M. H. Abrams, *Natural Supernaturalism: Tradition and Revolution in Romantic Literature* (New York: Norton, 1971), 12.

13. Richard Rorty, *Contingency, Irony, and Solidarity* (Cambridge: Cambridge University Press, 1989), 6.

14. Kenneth Burke, *The Rhetoric of Religion* (Boston: Beacon, 1961), 1.

15. Wallace Stevens, *Collected Poems* (New York: Knopf, 1954), 524.

16. Derrida, *Gift of Death*, 103.

17. George Santayana, *Interpretations of Poetry and Religion* (New York: Scribner, 1900), 26, 105.

18. Allen Tate, *Essays of Four Decades*, 3rd ed. (1968; repr., Wilmington, DE: ISI, 1999), 570, 575.

19. W. B. Yeats, *The Variorum Edition of the Poems of W. B. Yeats*, ed. Peter Allt and Russell K. Alspach (New York: Macmillan, 1957), 631.

20. Northrop Frye, *Anatomy of Criticism: Four Essays* (Princeton, NJ: Princeton University Press, 1957), 125.

21. Samuel Taylor Coleridge, *Biographia Literaria*, ed. James Engell and W. Jackson Bate (Princeton, NJ: Princeton University Press, 1983), 1:304; emphasis in original.

22. Andre Dubus, *Selected Stories* (1988; repr., New York: Vintage, 1996), 458, 461, 462, 471, 475–76.

23. Flannery O'Connor, quoted in William S. Doxey, "A Dissenting Opinion of Flannery O'Connor's 'A Good Man is Hard to Find,'" in *A Good Man Is Hard to Find*, ed. Frederick Asals (New Brunswick, NJ: Rutgers University Press, 1993), 100.

24. Alfred Kazin, *God and the American Writer* (New York: Vintage, 1997), 13.

25. Harley Granville-Barker, *Three Plays* (New York: Brentano's, 1909), 269.

26. György Lukács, *The Theory of the Novel: A Historico-Philosophical Essay on the Forms of Great Epic Literature*, trans. Anna Bostock (Cambridge, MA: MIT Press, 1971), 88.

27. Nathaniel Hawthorne, *Tales and Sketches*, ed. Roy Harvey Pearce (New York: Library of America, 1982), 360.

28. Nathaniel Hawthorne, *The Scarlet Letter: An Authoritative Text, Backgrounds and Sources, Criticism*, 2nd ed., ed. Sculley Bradley, et al. (New York: Norton, 1978), 145–46.

29. Herman Melville, *Pierre; or, The Ambiguities*, ed. Harrison Hayford, Hershel Parker, and G. Thomas Tanselle (Evanston, IL: Northwestern University Press, 1971), 177–78.

30. Henry James, *Literary Criticism*, ed. Leon Edel (New York: Library of America, 1984), 363, 396.

31. Herman Melville, "Hawthorne and His Mosses," in *Moby-Dick*, 2nd ed., ed. Hershel Parker and Harrison Hayford (New York: Norton, 2002), 521.

32. Lionel Trilling, *Beyond Culture: Essays on Literature and Learning* (New York: Viking, 1965), 197–98, 204.

33. Cleanth Brooks, *William Faulkner: The Yoknapatawpha Country* (New Haven, CT: Yale University Press, 1963), 262.

34. Emile Durkheim, *The Elementary Forms of the Religious Life*, trans. Joseph Ward Swain (New York: Free Press, 1965), 244–45.

35. Roberto Calasso, *Literature and the Gods*, trans. Tim Parks (2001; repr., New York: Vintage, 2002), 173.

36. Roberto Calasso, *K*, trans. Geoffrey Brock (New York: Knopf, 2005), 22.

37. Herman Melville, *Moby-Dick*, ed. Harrison Hayford, Herschel Parker, and G. Thomas Tanselle (Evanston and Chicago: Northwestern University Press and The Newberry Library, 1988), 347.

38. David S. Reynolds, *Faith in Fiction: The Emergence of Religious Literature in America* (Cambridge, MA: Harvard University Press, 1981), 100, 121.

39. Lawrance Thompson, *Melville's Quarrel with God* (Princeton, NJ: Princeton University Press, 1952), 239.

40. R. P. Blackmur, *Selected Essays*, ed. Denis Donoghue (New York: Ecco, 1986), 294, 178, 195, 179.

41. Tate, *Essays of Four Decades*, 285.

42. Emerson, *Essays and Lectures*, 488–89.

43. Tate, *Essays of Four Decades*, 284.

44. R. P. Blackmur, *Outsider at the Heart of Things: Essays*, ed. James T. Jones (Urbana: University of Illinois Press, 1989), 272.

45. Tate, *Essays of Four Decades*, 287.

46. Emily Dickinson, *The Poems of Emily Dickinson*, ed. R. W. Franklin (Cambridge, MA: Belknap Press of Harvard University Press, 1998), 582. This poem is #1581 in the Franklin numbering scheme.

47. Henry James, *The Art of the Novel: Critical Prefaces* (New York: Scribner, 1962), 262.

48. Henry Adams, *Mont-Saint-Michel and Chartres* (1904; repr., Boston: Houghton, 1936), 197.

49. Henry Adams, *Esther*, ed. Lisa MacFarlane (New York: Penguin, 1999), 159.

50. F. Scott Fitzgerald, *The Great Gatsby* (1925; repr., New York: Collier, 1992), 104.

51. Northrop Frye, *Northrop Frye on Modern Culture*, ed. Jan Gorak (Toronto: University of Toronto Press, 2003), 255–56.

52. Theodore Dreiser, *An American Tragedy* (1925; repr., New York: Liveright, 1929), 356.

53. R. P. Blackmur, *Henry Adams*, ed. Veronica A. Makowsky (New York: Harcourt, 1980), 202.

54. Harold Bloom, *The American Religion: The Emergence of the Post-Christian Nation* (New York: Simon, 1992), 15, 257, 259, 264.

Chapter 2

1. For disparate diagnoses of American religious diversity, see Diana L. Eck, *A New Religious America: How a "Christian Country" Has Now Become the World's Most Religiously Diverse Nation* (San Francisco: Harper, 2001); and David W. Wills, *Christianity in the United States: A Historical Survey and Interpretation* (Notre Dame: University of Notre Dame Press, 2005).

2. For two significant and symptomatic arguments, see Walter Benn Michaels and Donald E. Pease, eds., *The American Renaissance Reconsidered* (Baltimore: Johns Hopkins University Press, 1985); and especially John Carlos Rowe, *At Emerson's Tomb: The Politics of Classic American Literature* (New York: Columbia University Press, 1997). See Russ Castronovo, *Necro Citizenship: Death, Eroticism, and the Public Sphere in the Nineteenth Century United States* (Durham, NC: Duke University Press, 2001), for an exemplary work of contemporary antebellum literary scholarship that accords significant attention to Emerson in the context of having internalized a more capaciously multicultural perspective from which standpoint Emerson no longer figures as *the* centrally seminal presence that he did in F. O. Matthiessen's field-inaugurating *American Renaissance: Art and Expression in the Age of Emerson and Whitman* (New York: Oxford University Press, 1941), and for the quarter-century thereafter.

3. Angus Fletcher, *Allegory: The Theory of a Symbolic Mode* (Ithaca, NY: Cornell University Press, 1964).

4. Herman Melville, "Hawthorne and His Mosses," in *Moby-Dick*, 2nd ed., ed. Hershel Parker and Harrison Hayford (New York: Norton, 2002), 521.

5. In passing, I would also take issue with Donoghue's Lawrance Thompsonian reading of Melville as a God-defier. This is a part, but only part, of Melville's career-long meditations on the mystery of iniquity.

6. "The Unpardonable Sin," Hawthorne writes, "might consist in a want of love and reverence for the Human Soul; in consequence of which, the investigator pried into its dark depths, not with a hope or purpose of making it better, but from a cold philosophical curiosity,—content that it should be wicked in whatever kind or degree, and only desiring to study it out." *The American Notebooks*, ed. Claude M. Simpson (Columbus: Ohio State University Press, 1972), 251.

7. Denis Foster, "The Embroidered Sin: Confessional Evasion in *The Scarlet Letter*," *Criticism* 25 (1983): 141–63.

8. Sydney E. Ahlstrom, *A Religious History of the American People* (New Haven, CT: Yale University Press, 1972), 1079.

9. See especially Robert Wuthnow, *After Heaven: Spirituality in America Since the 1950s* (Berkeley: University of California Press, 1998).

Chapter 3

1. Emily Dickinson, *The Poems of Emily Dickinson*, ed. R. W. Franklin (Cambridge, MA: Belknap Press of Harvard University Press, 1998), 114, 190. These poems are #255 and #413 in the Franklin numbering scheme; all further references to Dickinson's poetry will give the Franklin number and will be cited within the text.

2. Kenneth B. Murdock, *Literature and Theology in Colonial New England* (Cambridge, MA: Harvard University Press, 1949), 58.

3. See Perry Miller, *The New England Mind: The Seventeenth Century* (Cambridge, MA: Harvard University Press, 1954), 331–62. Miller's insistence on Ramus as the key to the plain style has not been persuasive to other critics. As Theodore Dwight Bozeman puts it, the "Scripture was approached . . . not as a logical structure, but as dramatic event . . . the 'first work' of the preacher thus was to engage the imagination with 'lively representations.'" *To Live Ancient Lives: The Primitivist Dimension in Puritanism* (Chapel Hill: University of North Carolina Press, 1988), 37. Critics have followed Kenneth Murdock in seeing in Puritan preaching an "attachment to dialectics rather than rhetoric too deep rooted to be attributed to the influence of one man." "The Puritan Literary Attitude," in *Puritanism in Early America*, ed. George Waller (Boston: Heath, 1950), 97. For analysis of Cotton's plain style as it fuses discrete moments in Christian history, see Bozeman's *To Live Ancient Lives*. For the dialectical relationship with Scripture, see especially Rosamond Rosenmeier, *Anne Bradstreet Revisited* (Boston: Twayne, 1991); Mason Lowance, *The Language of Canaan: Metaphor and Symbol in New England from the Puritans to the Transcendentalists* (Cambridge, MA: Harvard University Press, 1980), 41–54; and Lisa M. Gordis, *Opening Scripture:*

Bible Reading and Interpretive Authority in Puritan New England (Chicago: University of Chicago Press, 2003).

4. Harry S. Stout, *The New England Soul: Preaching and Religious Culture in Colonial New England* (New York: Oxford University Press, 1986), 43. The student of plain style will want to study the indispensable work by Stout, as well as such introductions to New England preaching as can be found in Larzer Ziff, *Puritanism in America: New Culture in a New World* (New York: Viking, 1973); Andrew Delbanco, *The Puritan Ordeal* (Cambridge, MA: Harvard University Press, 1989); Janice Knight *Orthodoxies in Massachusetts: Rereading American Puritanism* (Cambridge, MA: Harvard University Press, 1994); Peter White and Harrison Meserole, *Puritan Poetry and Poetics: Seventeenth-Century American Poetry in Theory and Practice* (University Park: Pennsylvania State University Press, 1985); Robert Daly, *God's Altar: The World and the Flesh in Puritan Poetry* (Berkeley: University of California Press, 1978); and the excellent introduction and relevant headnotes in Alan Heimert and Andrew Delbanco, *The Puritans in America: A Narrative Anthology* (Cambridge, MA: Harvard University Press, 1985). All of these works serve to remind the reader that "plainness" was not a denial of the aesthetic but a criterion for the aesthetic's necessarily experiential and affective character. Plainness is a description of directness of impact, of the capacity of imagery to enter and move the believer. As Murdock quotes Thomas Shepard, "the word is an exact picture, it looks every man in the face that looks on it, if God speaks in it." Quoted in Murdock, *Literature and Theology*, 58.

5. Delbanco, *The Puritan Ordeal*, 129. Delbanco's description of "sermon-drunk" Puritans, hanging their hopes of a new, better social order on homiletics, offers an extraordinary portrait of a culture given over to literary experience.

6. John Cotton, *Christ, the Fountaine of Life* (1651; repr., New York: Arno, 1972), 125.

7. This "internal difference" is precisely what homiletic plain stylists like Cotton sought to achieve in the breast of the believer: the "heavenly hurt" of a purely internal movement toward faith. On the subject of the plain style's affective dimensions and its dialectical power to "move" the believer, I have learned much from Knight and especially from Teresa Toulouse, on whose description of the nonrational, experiential, and affective tradition from Cotton through Emerson this chapter builds. See also Ivy Schweitzer's fascinating chapter on John Fiske's elegy on John Cotton, a chapter that explores Cotton's penchant for such "dense internal complication." In Fiske's elegy, Cotton's plainness is what allows the believer to experience, or even to connect, and thus to understand: "The knott sometimes seems a deformity / It's a mistake, tho such be light set by / The knott it is the Joynt, the strength of parts / The bodies-beauty, so this knott out-starts / What others in that place, they ought to bee . . . / When knotty theames and paynes some meet with then / As knotty and uncouth their tongue and pen / So 'twas not heere, he caus'd us understand / And tast the sweetnes of the knott in hand. / When knotty querks and quiddities broacht were / By witt of man he

sweetely Breathed there." Schweitzer explicates this text interestingly, showing how the knot stands both for spiritual difficulty and the ministerial rhetoric that plainly presents that difficulty's sweetness. The "knot is a point of connection that permits articulation: movement, cohesion, and 'the bodyies-beauty.'" Ivy Schweitzer, *The Work of Self-Representation: Lyric Poetry in Colonial New England* (Chapel Hill: University of North Carolina Press, 1991), 59. (The quotation from John Fiske is on page 75.)

8. Bozeman is especially effective in describing how temporal layerings of this kind are paradoxically characteristic of Puritan "primitivism." This concern to preserve the coincidence of temporalities in one, the deepest time within the most contemporary, is fundamental to Dickinson's and later poets of New England.

9. Myra Jehlen, *American Incarnation: The Individual, the Nation, and the Continent* (Cambridge, MA: Harvard University Press, 1986). Jehlen's argument is that self and continent, subject and nation, invariably reinforce each other.

10. Jonathan Edwards, *A Jonathan Edwards Reader*, ed. John E. Smith, Harry S. Stout, and Kenneth P. Minkema (New Haven, CT: Yale University Press, 1995), 281.

11. Edwards, *Reader*, 27, 13.

12. Teresa Toulouse, *The Art of Prophesying: New England Sermons and the Shaping of Belief* (Athens: University of Georgia Press, 1987), 174. This essay builds extensively on Toulouse's description of the nonrational, experiential, and affective tradition from Cotton through Emerson.

13. Knight describes Cotton's peculiarly persuasive theology as, in effect, oozing grace just where the edges of a figure soften and tenderize each other.

14. Cotton, *Christ, the Fountaine*, 121.

15. Cotton, *Christ, the Fountaine*, 114. Cotton's fondness for climatic, fluent, and evanescent metaphors is one way in which he protects his sermons from deadness. As Larzer Ziff explains, for Cotton, the sermon is an event in time, an essentially transitory "act" rather than a product, which succeeds insofar as it "affects" but fails when it relies on merely mechanical, that is, rhetorical stimulations. Such images and figures as the sermon deploys should, ideally, be as self-consuming as weather, lest liveliness go moribund in rhetorical effects. Theresa Toulouse goes further to suggest that Cotton's own method is essentially "lyric," and she draws on Sharon Cameron's work on Dickinson to claim that "particular means of presenting religious truth" dramatize the "heart of an experience rather than its outward form."

Chapter 4

1. Ralph Waldo Emerson, *Essays and Lectures*, ed. Joel Porte (New York: Library of America, 1983), 59, 58.

2. Ralph Waldo Emerson, *The Complete Works of Ralph Waldo Emerson*, vol. 8 (Boston: Houghton, 1904), 17.

3. Henry David Thoreau, *A Week on the Concord and Merrimack Rivers; Walden, or, Life in the Woods; The Maine Woods; Cape Cod*, ed. Robert F. Sayre (New York: Library of America, 1985), 580.

4. Walt Whitman, *Complete Poetry and Collected Prose*, ed. Justin Kaplan (New York: Library of America, 1982), 247.

5. Emerson, *Essays and Lectures*, 23.

6. Emerson, *Complete Works*, vol. 8: 72, 17, 15.

7. Emerson, *Essays and Lectures*, 80.

Chapter 5

1. Sondra A. O'Neale, *Jupiter Hammon and the Biblical Beginnings of African-American Literature* (Metuchen, NJ: Scarecrow, 1993), 59.

2. In this chapter, I am conscious of only limping along a path that has been expertly charted by a number of others, including James Weldon Johnson, *The Book of American Negro Poetry* (New York: Harcourt, Brace, 1922); Eugene D. Genovese, *Roll, Jordan, Roll: The World the Slaves Made* (1972; repr., New York: Vintage, 1976), 213–54; Dena J. Epstein, *Sinful Tunes and Spirituals: Black Folk Music to the Civil War* (Urbana: University of Illinois Press, 1977), 217–37; Albert J. Raboteau, *Slave Religion: The "Invisible Institution" in the Antebellum South* (New York: Oxford University Press, 1978); Theophus Smith, *Conjuring Culture: Biblical Formations of Black America* (New York: Oxford University Press, 1994); Raboteau, "Exodus, Ethiopia, and Racial Messianism: Texts and Contexts of African-American Consciousness," in *Many Are Chosen: Divine Election and Western Nationalism*, ed. William R. Hutchison and Hartmut Lehmann (Minneapolis: Fortress, 1994), 175–96; Vincent L. Wimbush, ed., *African Americans and the Bible: Sacred Texts and Social Textures* (New York: Continuum, 2000); Eddie S. Glaude, Jr., *Exodus! Religion, Race, and Nation in Early Nineteenth-Century Black America* (Chicago: University of Chicago Press, 2000).

3. David Brion Davis, "Reconsidering the Colonization Movement: Leonard Bacon and the Problem of Evil," *Intellectual History Newsletter* 14 (1992): 4.

4. Among the growing number of authors who have written perceptively on the general subject, I have been especially helped by David Brion Davis, *The Problem of Slavery in the Age of Revolution, 1770–1823* (Ithaca, NY: Cornell University Press, 1975), 523–56; Robert Bruce Mullin, "Biblical Critics and the Battle over Slavery," *Journal of Presbyterian History* 61 (1983): 210–26; Larry Tise, *Proslavery: A History of the Defense of Slavery in America, 1701–1840* (Athens: University of Georgia Press, 1987); John R. McKivigan and Mitchell Snay, eds., *Religion and the Antebellum Debate Over Slavery* (Athens: University of Georgia Press, 1998); Albert Harrill, "The Use of the New Testament in the American Slave Controversy: A Case History in the Hermeneutical Tension between Biblical Criticism and Christian Moral Debate," *Religion and American Culture* 10

(2000): 149–86; Stephen R. Haynes, *Noah's Curse: The Biblical Justification of American Slavery* (New York: Oxford University Press, 2002); and Elizabeth Fox-Genovese and Eugene D. Genovese, *The Mind of the Master Class: History and Faith in the Southern Slaveholders' Worldview* (New York: Cambridge University Press, 2005). My own efforts to deal with the history of these debates are found in *America's God: From Jonathan Edwards to Abraham Lincoln* (New York: Oxford University Press, 2002), 367–438.

5. Henry Van Dyke, "The Character and Influence of Abolitionism," in *Fast Day Sermons: or the Pulpit on the State of the Country* (New York, 1861), 137.

6. Morris J. Raphall, "Bible View of Slavery" in *Fast Day Sermons*, 235–36.

7. Morris J. Raphall, "The Present Crisis" and "Doctrinal Basis of Christianity," *Christian Recorder* (April 13, 1861), 54.

8. I have not treated poetry in this chapter, mostly because of limitations in what I know about the subject, though much help is now available for that genre from the black authors anthologized along with whites in James G. Basker, ed., *Amazing Grace: An Anthology of Poems about Slavery, 1660–1810* (New Haven, CT: Yale University Press, 2002).

9. Olaudah Equiano, *The Interesting Narrative of the Life of Olaudah Equiano, or Gustavus Vassa, the African. Written by Himself*, in *The Classic Slave Narratives*, ed. Henry Louis Gates, Jr. (1987; repr., New York: New American Library, 2002), 192, 239.

10. Frederick Douglass, *Narrative of the Life of Frederick Douglass, an American Slave*, in *Autobiographies*, ed. Henry Louis Gates, Jr. (New York: Library of America, 1994), 97, 299.

11. Quobna Ottobah Cugoano, *Thoughts and Sentiments on the Evil of Slavery*, ed. Vincent Carretta (New York: Penguin, 1999), 45.

12. David Ruggles, *The Abrogation of the Seventh Commandment by the American Churches*, in *Early Negro Writing, 1760–1837*, ed. Dorothy Porter (Boston: Beacon, 1971), 479–80, 481, 487.

13. Henry Highland Garnet, *The Past and the Present Condition, and the Destiny, of the Colored Race: A Discourse Delivered at the Fifteenth Anniversary of the Female Benevolent Society of Troy, N.Y, Feb. 14, 1848* (Miami: Mnemosyne, 1969), 11, 18.

14. The series ran in each weekly issue of the *Christian Recorder* from February 23, 1861, into the summer.

15. "Chapters on Ethnology," *Christian Recorder* (February 23, 1861; March 2, 1861), chapters 26, 30.

16. Lemuel Haynes, *Black Preacher to White America: The Collected Writings of Lemuel Haynes, 1774–1833*, ed. Richard Newman (Brooklyn: Carlson, 1990), 167, 151–52, 154–55, 157.

17. Samuel Hopkins, *A Dialogue Concerning the Slavery of the Africans* (Norwich, 1776).

18. Haynes, *Black Preacher*, 19, 21, 25.

19. David Walker, *Appeal, in Four Articles; Together with a Preamble, to the Coloured Citizens of the World, But in Particular, and Very Expressly, to Those of the United States of America*, ed. Charles M. Wiltse (1829; repr., New York: Hill & Wang, 1965), 14, 66, 59, 43, 75, 42.

20. Frederick Douglass, "The Pro-Slavery Mob and the Pro-Slavery Ministry," *Douglass' Monthly* (March 1861), 417–18.

21. Daniel Coker, *A Dialogue Between a Virginian and an African Minister . . . Humbly Dedicated to the People of Colour in the United States of America* (1810), in *Negro Protest Pamphlets*, ed. Dorothy Porter (New York: Arno, 1969), 25, 34.

22. Coker, *Dialogue*, 19–21, 27–35, 22.

Chapter 6

1. Thandeka, *Learning To Be White: Money, Race, and God in America* (New York: Continuum, 1999).

2. Olaudah Equiano, *The Interesting Narrative of the Life of Olaudah Equiano, or Gustavus Vassa, the African. Written by Himself*, in *The Classic Slave Narratives*, ed. Henry Louis Gates, Jr. (1987; repr., New York: New American Library, 2002), 62, 59, 200–201, 201–2.

3. Frederick Douglass, *Narrative of the Life of Frederick Douglass, an American Slave*, in *Autobiographies*, ed. Henry Louis Gates, Jr. (New York: Library of America, 1994), 18.

4. Douglass, *Narrative*, 24.

5. Douglass, *Narrative*, 42.

6. Douglass, *Narrative*, 44.

7. W. E. B. DuBois, *The Souls of Black Folk*, ed. Henry Louis Gates, Jr. and Terri Hume Oliver (New York: Norton, 1999), 10.

8. DuBois, *Souls*, 10–11.

9. DuBois, *Souls*, 11.

10. DuBois, *Souls*, 162–63.

11. DuBois, *Souls*, 133–34; emphasis added.

12. DuBois, *Souls*, 74, 129.

13. James Baldwin, *Go Tell It on the Mountain* (1952; repr., New York: Dell, 1985), 200–201; emphasis added.

14. Baldwin, *Go Tell It*, 202–4.

15. Baldwin, *Go Tell It*, 204–5.

16. James Baldwin, *The Fire Next Time* (1962; repr., New York, Vintage, 1993), 105.

17. Melba Beals, *Warriors Don't Cry: A Searing Memoir of the Battle to Integrate Little Rock's Central High* (New York: Pocket, 1994), 246, 310.

18. James McBride, *The Color of Water: A Black Man's Tribute To His White Mother* (New York: Riverhead, 1996), 90–91, 228–29.

Chapter 7

1. Terry Eagleton, *After Theory* (New York: Basic, 2003), 40.
2. Barbara Christian, "The Race For Theory," in *The Nature and Context of Minority Discourse*, ed. Abdul R. JanMohamed and David Lloyd (Oxford: Oxford University Press, 1990), 38, 39, 41; emphasis in original.
3. Bruce Ellis Benson, "Traces of God: The Faith of Jacques Derrida," *The Australian Financial Review* (January 25–28, 2001): 8; emphasis in original.
4. Alister E. McGrath, *Luther's Theology of the Cross: Martin Luther's Theological Breakthrough* (Oxford: Blackwell, 1985), 149, 150.
5. John Nunes, "The African American Experience and the Theology of the Cross" in *The Theology of the Cross for the 21st Century: Signposts for a Multicultural Witness*, ed. Alberto L. Garcia and A. R. Victor Raj (St. Louis: Concordia, 2002), 220, 221.
6. Joel B. Green and Mark D. Baker, *Recovering the Scandal of the Cross: Atonement in New Testament and Contemporary Contexts* (Downers Grove, IL: InterVarsity, 2000), 19, 24.
7. Wilson Jeremiah Moses, *Black Messiahs and Uncle Toms: Social and Literary Manipulations of a Religious Myth* (University Park: Pennsylvania State University Press, 1982), 8, 9, 1–4, 226.
8. Kelly Brown Douglas, *The Black Christ* (Maryknoll, NY: Orbis, 1994), 10, 4.
9. Moses, *Black Messiahs*, 1.
10. Phillis Wheatley, *Complete Writings*, ed. Vincent Carretta (New York: Penguin, 2001), 12.
11. Wheatley, *Complete Writings*, 16.
12. Moses, *Black Messiahs*, 64.
13. Frederick Douglass, *Narrative of the Life of Frederick Douglass, an American Slave*, in *Autobiographies*, ed. Henry Louis Gates, Jr. (New York: Library of America, 1994), 65.
14. Harriet Jacobs, *Incidents in the Life of a Slave Girl* in *Slave Narratives*, ed. William L. Andrews and Henry Louis Gates, Jr. (New York: Library of America, 2000), 762–73.
15. James Weldon Johnson, *Complete Poems*, ed. Sondra Kathryn Wilson (New York: Penguin, 2000), 31–34.
16. Michael Thurston, *Making Something Happen: American Political Poetry Between the World Wars* (Chapel Hill: University of North Carolina Press, 2001), 35.
17. Green and Baker, *Recovering the Scandal*, 24, 25.
18. Richard Wright, *Native Son* (1940; repr., New York: Harper, 2005), 273, 282–83, 284–85.
19. Wright, *Native Son*, 286–87.
20. Wright, *Native Son*, 311.
21. Wright, *Native Son*, 337.
22. Wright, *Native Son*, 338.
23. Wright, *Native Son*, 339, 338.

24. Wright, *Native Son*, 287.
25. Wright, *Native Son*, 288, 295–96, 422.
26. Toni Morrison, *Paradise* (1998; repr., New York: Plume, 1999), 12, 7.
27. Morrison, *Paradise*, 143, 145.
28. Morrison, *Paradise*, 146.
29. Morrison, *Paradise*, 147; emphasis in original.
30. Morrison, *Paradise*, 143, 147, 154.
31. Eugene McCarraher, "*After Theory*, Theology?," *Books and Culture* (May/June 2004): 5.

Chapter 8

1. David Brion Davis, *The Problem of Slavery in the Age of Revolution, 1770–1823* (Ithaca, NY: Cornell University Press, 1975), 263.
2. James Madison, quoted in *Early American Views on Negro Slavery: From the Letters and Papers of the Founders of the Republic*, ed. Matthew T. Mellon (Boston: Meador, 1934), 158.
3. David Brion Davis, *Challenging the Boundaries of Slavery* (Cambridge, MA: Harvard University Press, 2003), 33.
4. Richard Newman, Patrick Rael, and Phillip Lapsansky, eds., *Pamphlets of Protest: An Anthology of Early African-American Protest Literature, 1790–1860* (New York: Routledge, 2001), 42.
5. Absalom Jones, "Petition of Absalom Jones and Seventy-Three Others" in *Early Negro Writing, 1760–1837*, ed. Dorothy Porter (Boston: Beacon, 1971), 330–32, 331.
6. Newman, *Pamphlets of Protest*, 47, 67.
7. Another factor that helps explain black abolitionists' optimism in the Revolutionary and post–Revolutionary eras was that race relations had not deteriorated and hardened. By the 1840s most whites believed that blacks were innately inferior to blacks and incapable of self-government, whereas many Revolutionary-era whites, especially in the North, attributed black inferiority to environmental factors—specifically bondage and oppression.
8. See David Brion Davis, *The Problem of Slavery in Western Culture* (Ithaca, NY: Cornell University Press, 1966); Davis, *Slavery and Human Progress* (New York: Oxford University Press, 1984), 5–8; and Eugene D. Genovese, *From Rebellion to Revolution: Afro-American Slave Revolts in the Making of the Modern World* (Baton Rouge: Louisiana State University Press, 1979). During the Spartacus Revolt of 73 BCE, Spartacus and his soldiers enslaved many of their former masters. The Zanj rebels of 869 CE, the largest servile war before the Haitian Revolution, held numerous slaves. And most maroon slave communities exploited people as slaves.
9. David Brion Davis, *Problem of Slavery in Western Culture*, part III; Davis, *Problem of Slavery in the Age of Revolution*, 113–63, 184–96; C. L. R. James, *The*

Black Jacobins: Toussaint L'Ouverture and the San Domingo Revolution, new ed. (1980; repr., New York: Penguin, 2001); and Laurent Dubois, *Avengers of the New World: The Story of the Haitian Revolution* (Cambridge, MA: Belknap Press of Harvard University Press, 2004). Jack P. Greene recently uncovered an example of antislavery ideology in a 1709 speech made by a black from Guadeloupe. Although this early use of natural rights theory was not coupled with rebellion, it is an important document, for it shows how blacks and slaves revised the emerging language and ideology of whites for their own ends. See Jack P. Greene, "'A plain and Natural Right to Life and Liberty': An Early natural Rights Attack on the Excesses of the Slave System in Colonial British America," *William and Mary Quarterly*, 57 (2000): 793–808. One might conclude that Vermont's 1777 constitution, the first constitution in history to prohibit slavery outright, was an example of immediatism. But Vermont's antislavery constitution was possible only because there were few blacks in the state. The first instance of gradual abolition is usually seen as the famous 1688 Germantown Friends antislavery petition. Another eighty-six years would elapse before the Philadelphia Yearly Meeting of the Society of Friends, in 1774, adopted rules forbidding Quakers to buy or sell slaves. St. Domingue's constitution of 1801, which prohibited slavery forever, is especially remarkable given that ten years earlier, when rebellion began, most of the island's occupants were slaves.

10. David Brion Davis, "The Emergence of Immediatism in British and American Antislavery Thought," in *From Homicide to Slavery: Studies in American Culture* (New York: Oxford University Press, 1986), 238–57.

11. There are examples of lower-class whites and blacks commingling and fraternizing in the colonial period, but there is very little evidence to analyze whether they befriended one another as equals and embraced the ideal of equality, in the way that abolitionists later did. In this earlier period, blacks and whites at the bottom of the social ladder formed alliances based on shared conditions and common purposes, but the degree of egalitarian beliefs is largely unknown. They may have come together simply as part of a shared quest for survival, for when whites rose in rank, they abandoned their former alliances. Over time, plebeian whites increasingly used "whiteness" to preserve their self-respect and distance themselves from blacks.

12. James Oliver Horton and Lois E. Horton, *In Hope of Liberty: Culture, Community and Protest Among Northern Free Blacks, 1776–1860* (New York: Oxford University Press, 1997), 177–236; and James Brewer Stewart, "Modernizing 'Difference': The Political Meanings of Color in the Free States, 1776–1840," *Journal of the Early Republic* 19 (1999): 691–712.

13. Paul Goodman, *Of One Blood: Abolitionism and the Origins of Racial Equality* (Berkeley: University Of California Press, 1998), 23–44; and John Stauffer, *The Blacks Hearts of Men: Radical Abolitionists and the Transformation of Race* (Cambridge, MA: Harvard University Press, 2002), 1–44.

14. Abraham Lincoln, *The Collected Works of Abraham Lincoln*, vol. 7, ed. Roy P. Basler (New Brunswick, NJ: Rutgers University Press, 1953), 281.

15. Abraham Lincoln, *Selected Speeches and Writings* (New York: Vintage, 1992), 450.

16. Frederick Douglass, *Life and Times of Frederick Douglass* (1892; repr., New York: Collier, 1962), 366.

17. Alexander Crummell, *The Future of Africa: Being Addresses, Sermons, etc., etc., Delivered in the Republic of Liberia* (1862; repr., New York: Negro Universities Press, 1969), 327–28.

18. David Brion Davis, *Inhuman Bondage: The Rise and Fall of Slavery in the New World* (New York: Oxford University Press, 2006), esp. chap. 3. While some scholars argue that the curse on Ham gradually lost popularity during the antebellum era, owing to the rise of ethnological justifications of slavery, there is rich evidence suggesting that the curse remained an enormous burden for blacks. See for example Mia Bay, *The White Image in the Black Mind: African-American Ideas about White People, 1830–1925* (New York: Oxford University Press, 2000), 26–30, 121–22; Albert J. Raboteau, *A Fire in the Bones: Reflections on African-American Religious History* (Boston: Beacon, 1995), 54–55; and Patrick Rael, *Black Identity and Black Protest in the Antebellum North* (Chapel Hill: University of North Carolina Press, 2002), 254.

19. Frederick Douglass, "Claims of the Negro Ethnologically Considered" in *The Frederick Douglass Papers*, vol. 2, ed. John W. Blassingame (New Haven, CT: Yale University Press, 1982), 519–20, 522.

20. See for example Edmund Morgan, "The Great American Crime," *New York Review of Books*, December 3, 1998: 16, and Joanne Pope Melish, *Disowning Slavery: Gradual Emancipation and "Race" in New England, 1780–1860* (Ithaca, NY: Cornell University Press, 1998).

21. Olaudah Equiano, *The Interesting Narrative of the Life of Olaudah Equiano, or Gustavus Vassa, the African. Written by Himself,* in *The Classic Slave Narratives*, ed. Henry Louis Gates, Jr. (1987; repr., New York: New American Library, 2002), 200.

22. Frederick Douglass, *My Bondage and My Freedom*, ed. John Stauffer (New York: Modern Library, 2003), 156.

23. David Paul Nord, "Newspapers and American Nationhood, 1776–1826," *Proceedings of the American Antiquarian Society* 100 (1991): 391.

24. Douglass, *Life and Times*, 479, 480.

25. Whitefield believed that the North American colonies could not succeed without the labor of black slaves. See Davis, *Problem of Slavery in Western Culture*, 148, 385.

26. Douglass, *My Bondage*, 64–65. Douglass emphasizes violent resistance throughout this work, from his dedication to Gerrit Smith, where he ranks "slavery with piracy and murder," which needs to be dealt with as such, to his advice to slaves: "if he kills his master, he imitates only the heroes of the revolution. Slaveholders

I hold to be individually and collectively responsible for all the evils which grow out of the horrid relation." *My Bondage*, xxxv, 104–5.

27. Raboteau, *A Fire in the Bones*, 117–40.

Chapter 9

1. C. Wright Mills, *The Power Elite*, afterword by Alan Wolfe (New York: Oxford University Press, 2000).

2. C. Wright Mills, *White Collar: The American Middle Classes* (New York: Oxford University Press, 1951).

3. Morris Dickstein, *Gates of Eden: American Culture in the Sixties* (New York: Basic, 1977), 59.

4. It would be published as C. Wright Mills, *Sociology and Pragmatism: The Higher Learning in America* (New York: Oxford University Press, 1966).

5. Erik Erikson, *Young Man Luther: A Study in Psychoanalysis and History* (New York: Norton, 1962).

6. David Riesman in collaboration with Reuel Denney and Nathan Glazer, *The Lonely Crowd: A Study of the Changing American Character* (New Haven, CT: Yale University Press, 1950), 149–70, 247, 334–36, 352.

7. Betty Friedan, *The Feminine Mystique* (1963; repr., New York: Dell, 1983), 163, 180, 284, 334.

8. Daniel Horowitz, *Betty Friedan and the Making of the Feminine Mystique: The American Left, the Cold War, and Modern Feminism* (Amherst: University of Massachusetts Press, 1998), 171.

9. Friedan, *Feminine Mystique*, 188, 351–53.

10. Arthur Schlesinger, Jr., *The Vital Center: The Politics of Freedom* (Boston: Houghton, 1949), 170.

11. Reinhold Niebuhr, *The Irony of American History* (New York: Scribner, 1952), 88, 155.

12. Benjamin DeMott, "Rediscovering Complexity," *Atlantic Monthly*, September 1988, 74.

13. Robert K. Merton, "The Unanticipated Consequences of Purposive Social Action," *American Sociological Review* 1 (1936): 894–904.

14. Richard Hofstadter, *The Age of Reform: From Bryan to F.D.R.* (New York: Knopf, 1955), 40.

15. Richard Hofstadter, "Pseudo-Conservatism Revisited (1962)," in *The Radical Right: The New American Right*, exp. ed., ed. Daniel Bell (Garden City, NY: Doubleday, 1964), 99.

16. Richard Hofstadter, *The Paranoid Style in American Politics, and Other Essays* (New York: Knopf, 1965), 3–40.

17. Paul Boyer, *When Time Shall Be No More: Prophecy Belief in Modern American Culture* (Cambridge, MA: Belknap Press of Harvard University Press, 1992).

18. Daniel Bell, "The Dispossessed," in *Radical Right*, 1–45.

19. Will Herberg, *Protestant, Catholic, Jew: An Essay in American Religious Sociology* (1955; repr., Chicago: University of Chicago Press, 1983), 59.

20. H. Richard Niebuhr, *The Kingdom of God in America* (1937; repr., New York: Harper, 1959), 193.

21. Herberg, *Protestant, Catholic, Jew*, 260.

22. Henry Fielding, *Tom Jones*, ed. John Bender and Simon Stern (Oxford: Oxford University Press, 1998), 109.

23. Alan Wolfe, *The Transformation of American Religion: How We Actually Live Our Faith* (New York: Free Press, 2003).

24. Herberg, *Protestant, Catholic, Jew*, 86.

25. Herberg, *Protestant, Catholic, Jew*, 83.

26. Herberg, *Protestant, Catholic, Jew*, 120.

27. Herberg, *Protestant, Catholic, Jew*, 265.

28. Peter L. Berger, *The Sacred Canopy: Elements of a Sociological Theory of Religion* (Garden City, NY: Doubleday, 1967).

29. Herberg, *Protestant, Catholic, Jew*, 3.

Chapter 10

1. David Riesman, "Preface" to *The Lonely Crowd*, xli.

2. Nathaniel Parker Willis, *Poems, Sacred, Passionate, and Humorous* (New York: 1849), 249.

3. Saul Bellow, *The Adventures of Augie March* (1953; repr., New York: Penguin, 1999), 10.

4. Richard Crossman, ed., *The God that Failed* (New York: Harper, 1950).

5. Thomas Jefferson, "Notes on the State of Virginia," in *Writings*, ed. Merrill D. Peterson (New York: Library of America, 1984), 285; Eisenhower, quoted in Sydney Ahlstrom, *A Religious History of the American People*, 2nd ed. (New Haven, CT: Yale University Press, 2004), 954.

6. Robert N. Bellah, "Civil Religion in America," *Daedalus*, 96 (1967): 1–21.

7. Walt Whitman, *Complete Poetry and Collected Prose*, ed. Justin Kaplan (New York: Library of America, 1982), 949.

8. Alexis de Tocqueville, *Democracy in America*, ed. J. P. Mayer, trans. George Lawrence (Garden City, NY: Doubleday, 1969), 297.

Chapter 11

1. We express our gratitude to the participants in the Pew Symposium for their thoughtful critique of an earlier version of this chapter, especially to Mark Noll for his warning against our simplistic use of the category called Constantinianism. We are also grateful to Kurt Berends for his suggestion that we focus our argument on the ironic invisibility—indeed, the unnecessity—of the church in American literature. Nor would we fail to thank John Stauffer for suggesting that

we consider Willa Cather's *Death Comes for the Archbishop* as a crucial exception to the rule.

2. Manfred Vogel, in an unpublished lecture given at Wake Forest University in 1974.

3. "The cup of blessing which we bless, is it not a participation in the blood of Christ? The bread which we break, is it not a participation in the body of Christ? Because there is one bread, we who are many are one body, for we all partake of the one bread" (I Cor. 10:16–17).

4. John Howard Yoder, "The Disavowal of Constantine: An Alternative Perspective on Interfaith Dialogue," in *The Royal Priesthood: Essays Ecclesiological and Ecumenical,* ed. Michael Cartwright (Grand Rapids, MI: Eerdmans, 1994), 242–61.

5. To accept the category "religion" is also to accept the Enlightenment definition of it—namely, as a human phenomenon called "religiousness," an empirically observable and quantifiable genus of anthropological behavior that expresses itself in several particular species, so that the totality of the religions can be viewed and evaluated from some timeless and placeless perspective outside them all. This is the old modern chimera in which we have little interest, not only because it is at once mistaken and boring but also because it does violence to our own central convictions as Christians. We work on the contrary assumption, believing it to be fully congruent with God's own self-definition in the Jews and Jesus and his Church, that human life is historical through and through, that it is communal all the way up and down. There is no such thing as untraditioned truth and unlensed seeing, no standing outside time and space to view things, as Kierkegaard wittily put it, "sub specie aeternitatis." God alone might enjoy such a perspective—though precisely the opposite turns out to be the case. The God of Israel and Christ, of the synagogue and the church, refuses to live and move and have his being as a timeless and placeless deity, choosing instead to have his triune communal life only in relation to his cosmos and his people.

6. William T. Cavanaugh, "The City: Beyond Secular Parodies," in *Radical Orthodoxy,* ed. John Milbank, Catherine Pickstock, and Graham Ward (New York: Routledge, 1999), 189, 192.

7. The invention of this word to mean "existing as a separate indivisible entity" is an entirely modern occurrence deriving from the seventeenth century. The word "person," by contrast, is ancient. For the Greeks, it meant mask or character, office or capacity; for Christians in the Middle Ages, it signified a human being. The Greeks found the notion of a private person or individual self to be so subhuman that they called it literally 'ιδιοτης. Not to be a communal person is not to be a person at all, since we are human only insofar as we derive our existence from life together in the polis. The medievals, in turn, employed the word idiot in a similar fashion—namely, to signify a blockhead or a fool, a clown or a jester incapable of rational conduct. For a critique of the entire idea of selfhood as something separate from the body political and physical, see Stanley

Hauerwas, "The Sanctified Body: Why Perfection Does Not Require a 'Self,'" in *Sanctify Them in the Truth: Holiness Exemplified* (Nashville: Abingdon, 1998), 77–91.

8. John Locke, *A Letter Concerning Toleration*, trans. James Tully (Indianapolis: Hackett, 1983), 48.

9. Thomas Jefferson, "Notes on the State of Virginia," in *Writings*, ed. Merrill D. Peterson (New York: Library of America, 1984), 285.

10. Justice Anthony Kennedy, in his majority opinion for *Planned Parenthood v. Casey*, the 1992 Supreme Court decision upholding its 1973 ruling on *Roe v. Wade*, clearly articulated the privatism and subjectivism that are the sorriest legacy of the American Enlightenment: "At the very heart of liberty," wrote Justice Kennedy, "is the right to define one's own concept of existence, of meaning, of the universe, of the mystery of human life." As the sovereign secular state leaves the public square vacant of shared moral content and common ethical ends, citizens are required to find their personal identity almost entirely in private associations: families, friends, civic clubs, churches. Once these "voluntary" groups are relegated to the sphere of personal preference, dislodged from their intended status as vital communities and life-sustaining institutions, they soon wither and die—unless they cultivate their own deliberately countercultural existence.

11. The rise of the modern nation-state is premised on the elevation of autonomous creatures defined by their accumulation of privately owned goods. As propertied creatures, modern individuals have relation to other individuals by means of self-protecting contracts. These contracts have only a temporal duration and are contingent upon the agreement of the contracting parties. They can also be dissolved by limiting clauses as well as by mutual consent. No longer is there an unbreakable bond that unites community members, much less the entire body politic, in devotion to common ends. The very basis of such a politics has also disappeared—namely, the indissoluble covenant between God and his people, as this bond is sealed through the sacraments. "It is not surprising," Cavanaugh writes, "that . . . Descartes placed 'among the [antique] excesses all of the promises by which one curtails something of one's freedom,' that Milton wrote a treatise on divorce, or that Kant condemned the covenants that bind one's descendants." "The City," in *Radical Orthodoxy*, 190. The one moral norm, it follows, is the injunction to respect the dignity of others by not denying them the freedom to exercise their own autonomy. Michael J. Sandel notes that procedural liberalism opposes "any view that regards us as obligated to fulfill ends that we have not chosen—ends given by nature or God, for example, or by our identities as members of families, peoples, cultures, or traditions. . . . For the liberal self, what matters above all, what is most essential to our personhood, is not the ends we choose but our capacity to choose them" *Democracy's Discontent: America in Search of a Public Philosophy* (Cambridge, MA: Belknap Press of Harvard University Press, 1996), 12. American civil religion arose as representatives of the major American religious traditions agreed to ignore their confessional

particularities for the sake of the battle against racial injustice, but then declined into a religion of civility centered on bland politeness and invertebrate tolerance. See Ralph C. Wood, *Flannery O'Connor and the Christ-Haunted South* (Grand Rapids, MI: Eerdmans, 2004), 17–22.

12. R. W. B. Lewis, *The American Adam: Innocence, Tragedy, and Tradition in the Nineteenth Century* (Chicago: University of Chicago Press, 1955). So did Flannery O'Connor cite James and Hawthorne no less than Edgar Allan Poe as three nineteenth-century writers who understood endemic evil and tragedy, as most other American writers do not.

13. Lionel Trilling, *The Liberal Imagination: Essays on Literature and Society* (1950; repr., New York: Anchor, 1953), vii, xii.

14. Warren was no less vehement in his denunciation of the South's "Great Alibi," the convenient excuse that defeat and occupation gave to Southerners for doing virtually nothing about their region's chronic poverty and illiteracy, its racism and violence and political corruption. See *The Legacy of the Civil War: Meditations on the Centennial* (New York: Random, 1961).

15. Quoted in Benjamin B. Alexander, "Good Things Out of Nazareth: The Unpublished Letters of Flannery O'Connor and Walker Percy," an unpublished essay.

16. William L. Portier, "Here Come the Evangelical Catholics," *Communio* 31 (2004): 35–66, 42–43; emphasis in original. Portier offers a caveat that we also affirm: "the point of such critique [of modern pluralism] is not to advocate doing away with legal tolerance but to show its limits and to exhort Christians to transcend it."

17. Mary Lyon, quoted in Roger Lundin, *Emily Dickinson and the Art of Belief*, 2nd ed. (Grand Rapids, MI: Eerdmans, 2004), 37.

18. Lundin, *Emily Dickinson*, 40–41.

19. Emily Dickinson, quoted in Lundin, *Emily Dickinson*, 53, 28, 50.

20. Emily Dickinson, *The Poems of Emily Dickinson*, ed. R. W. Franklin (Cambridge, MA: Belknap Press of Harvard University Press, 1998), 171. This poem is #373 in the Franklin numbering scheme.

21. We have in mind Karl Barth's denunciation of what he calls the No-God of a merely civil faith. Barth regards this pseudo-divinity as the most pernicious of all human inventions, because it stanches any radical transformation of either persons or communities. Such a god, says Barth, confirms "the course of the world and of men as it is." Belief in this comforting and consoling deity is ever so difficult to surrender: We suppose that we know what we are saying when we say 'God'. We assign to him the highest place in our world: and in so doing we place Him on fundamentally one line with ourselves and with things. We assume that He needs something: and so we assume that we are able to arrange our relation to Him as we arrange other relationships. We press ourselves into proximity with Him: and so, all unthinking, we make Him nigh unto ourselves. We allow ourselves an ordinary communication with Him, we permit ourselves to reckon with Him as though this were not extraordinary behaviour on our part. We dare to deck

selves out as his companions, patrons, advisers, and commissioners. We con-
nd time with eternity." *The Epistle to the Romans*, 6th ed., trans. Edwyn C.
Hoskyns (New York: Oxford University Press, 1968), 40, 44.

22. With the gradual triumph of civil Christianity in America, the role of the public atheist has virtually vanished. Robert Ingersoll, Clarence Darrow, and H.
L. Mencken seem like figures from the antique past. Once the churches cease
making radical theological witness, atheists are left with nothing to deny. We are
left with nothing more stringent than the flaccid aesthetic atheism of Richard
Rorty.

23. Augustine, *On Christian Doctrine*, trans. D. W. Robertson, Jr. (New York: Bobbs-
Merrill, 1958), 75.

24. Christians are summoned, says Yoder, to "represent within society, through and
in spite of withdrawal from certain of its activities, as well as through and in spite
of involvement with others, a real judgment upon the rebelliousness of culture
and a real possibility of reconciliation for all." Quoted in Fritz Oehlschlaeger,
Love and Good Reasons: Postliberal Approaches to Christian Ethics and Literature
(Durham, NC: Duke University Press, 2003), 276n40.

Dyrness & his ilk

25. Yoder, "Disavowal of Constantine" in *Royal Priesthood*, 250–51. Yoder cites the
Tower of Babel story in Genesis 11 as an argument against hegemonic universal-
ism. Rather than reading the destruction of Babel as angry divine punishment,
he sees it as a benevolent divine corrective against an arrogant attempt to replace
dependence on God with an imperially enforced uniformity. The Babylonians
"were the first foundationalists," Yoder writes, seeking to overcome all historically
developing diversity by recourse to their own cultural power. The "confusion" of
tongues at Babel is thus God's gracious intervention to continue the process of
dispersion and diversification whereby we are meant to learn humility through
respect for the other. It "is not a punishment or tragedy," Yoder concludes, "but
the gift of new beginnings, liberation from a blind alley." *For the Nations: Essays
Public and Evangelical* (Grand Rapids, MI: Eerdmans, 1997), 63.

26. Barry Harvey, *Politics of the Theological: Beyond the Piety and Power of a World
Come of Age* (New York: Lang, 1995), 12.

27. As Wendell Berry is reported to have said, "Not only should we not read the
Bible as literature; we shouldn't even read *literature* as 'literature.'"

28. These dangers may explain the penchant of the New Critics—who were almost
all Christians—for reading novels and poems in curiously amoral terms, as auto-
telic works of art engaged with nothing outside themselves, standing alone as
autonomous artifacts in pure ahistorical timelessness rather than interpreting
them as laden with authorial concerns and commitments and, thus, as embodiments of personal vision and as serious moral attempts to grapple with social
and historical forces. For all that we gratefully learned from such criticism, it
was a notably apolitical enterprise, the fitting academic footnote, perhaps, to the
moral complacency of the Eisenhower era.

29. Rowan Williams, *Grace and Necessity: Reflections on Art and Love* (Harrisburg, PA: Morehouse, 2005), 100–103.

30. For O'Connor, the real opposites to the sacramental imagination are the sentimental and the pornographic. The former undermines faith as the latter destroys art. They are both shortcuts to emotional fulfillment, bypassing the hard moral and spiritual obstacles scattered along the road to truth. Tough-minded charity discerns the worth of human beings through the aperture of God's own costly sacrifice, while soft-core pity sees them through the lens of easy and all-sanctioning feelings.

31. Flannery O'Connor, *The Habit of Being: Letters of Flannery O'Connor*, ed. Sally Fitzgerald (New York: Farrar, 1979), 218.

32. Flannery O'Connor, *Mystery and Manners: Occasional Prose*, sel. and ed. Robert and Sally Fitzgerald (New York: Farrar, 1969), 111.

33. Williams, *Grace and Necessity*, 118.

34. In secular and religiously affiliated colleges and universities alike, the very title of "The Artificial Nigger" has proved so offensive that the story is rarely taught. And since the odious word appears in nearly all of O'Connor's work—always used by characters in ways utterly appropriate to their milieu, never used gratuitously by her narrators—her fiction has been both censured and censored, much to the moral and spiritual impoverishment of students and faculty alike.

35. For full analysis of these scenes, including a treatment of the O'Connor-Welty controversy, see Ralph Wood, *Flannery O'Connor and the Christ-Haunted South*, 143–92.

36. Flannery O'Connor, *Collected Works*, ed. Sally Fitzgerald (New York: Library of America, 1988), 229, 230, 231.

37. O'Connor, *Collected Works*, 228, 229.

38. Wayne C. Booth, *The Rhetoric of Fiction* (Chicago: University of Chicago Press, 1961), 16–20.

39. Alice Walker, *In Search of Our Mother's Gardens* (New York: Harcourt, 1983), 53; emphasis in original.

40. For an extended argument for our case, see Stanley Hauerwas, *With the Grain of the Universe: The Church's Witness and Natural Theology* (Grand Rapids, MI: Brazos, 2001).

41. Willa Cather, *The Song of the Lark*, in *Early Novels & Stories*, ed. Sharon O'Brien (New York: Library of America, 1987), 360.

42. Willa Cather, *The Professor's House*, ed. Frederick M. Link (1925; repr., Lincoln: University of Nebraska Press, 2002), 30.

43. Cather, *O Pioneers!*, in *Early Novels*, 161.

44. Cather, *Professor's House*, 69.

45. Willa Cather, *My Mortal Enemy* (1926; repr., New York: Vintage, 1961), 94; emphasis in original.

46. Willa Cather, *The Kingdom of Art: Willa Cather's First Principles and Critical Statements, 1893–1896*, ed. Bernice Slote (Lincoln: University of Nebraska Press, 1967), 423.

47. Willa Cather, *Death Comes for the Archbishop* (1927; repr., New York: Vintage, 1971), 95.

48. Cather, *Archbishop*, 233–34.

49. Cather, *Archbishop*, 39, 267, 275.

50. Cather, *Archbishop*, 103.

51. Cather, *Archbishop*, 129, 130; emphasis in original.

52. Rebecca West, "The Classic Artist," in *Willa Cather and Her Critics*, ed. James Schroeter (Ithaca, NY: Cornell University Press, 1967), 68. West asks caustically: "Does not such transcendental [Lawrentian] courage, does not such ambition to extend consciousness beyond its present limits and elevate man above himself, entitle his art to be ranked as more important than that of Miss Cather?"

53. Cather, *Archbishop*, 131, 134.

54. Cather, *Archbishop*, 257.

55. Cather, *Archbishop*, 61, 63.

56. Cather, *Archbishop*, 211, 217–18.

57. Cather, *Archbishop*, 217, 245; emphasis in original.

58. Cather, *Archbishop*, 290.

59. "There is plenty of death in Hawthorne and Melville, in Poe and James, in Hemingway and Fitzgerald, but none that anyone prepares for. Death is violent or accidental, sickly or swift, but in any case not anticipated, awaited, prepared for. Nor are the last words of these representative American men and women memorable." Michael Platt, "The Happiness of Willa Cather," in *The Catholic Writer*, ed. Ralph McInerny (San Francisco: Ignatius, 1991), 144.

60. Cather, *Archbishop*, 269, 273, 299.

Chapter 12

1. Charles Taylor, *A Catholic Modernity?: Charles Taylor's Marianist Award Lecture, with responses by William M. Shea, Rosemary Luling Haughton, George Marsden, Jean Bethke Elshtain*, ed. James L. Heft (New York: Oxford University Press, 1999), 36–37.

2. Emily Dickinson, *The Poems of Emily Dickinson*, ed. R. W. Franklin (Cambridge, MA: Belknap Press of Harvard University Press, 1998), 604. This poem is #1675 in the Franklin numbering scheme.

3. William Faulkner, *The Sound and the Fury* (1929; repr. New York: Vintage, 1990), 297.

4. Dickinson, *Poems*, 582; poem #1581.

5. Andrew Delbanco, *The Death of Satan: How Americans Have Lost the Sense of Evil* (New York: Farrar, 1995), 144.

6. Mark A. Noll, *America's God: From Jonathan Edwards to Abraham Lincoln* (New York: Oxford University Press, 2002), 445.

7. Flannery O'Connor, *Collected Works*, ed. Sally Fitzgerald (New York: Library of America, 1988), 153.

8. Robert Langbaum, *Isak Dinesen's Art: The Gayety of Vision* (1964; repr., Chicago: University of Chicago Press, 1975), 66.

9. Isak Dinesen, *Seven Gothic Tales* (1934; repr. New York: Vintage, 1991), 14–15; emphasis in original.

10. Dietrich Bonhoeffer, *Letters and Papers from Prison*, ed. Eberhard Bethge (New York: Macmillan, 1972), 123, 7, 6.

11. O'Connor, *Collected*, 654.

INDEX